THE SIXTH GUN

DUST TO DEATH

ONI PRESS

AN ONI PRESS PUBLICATION

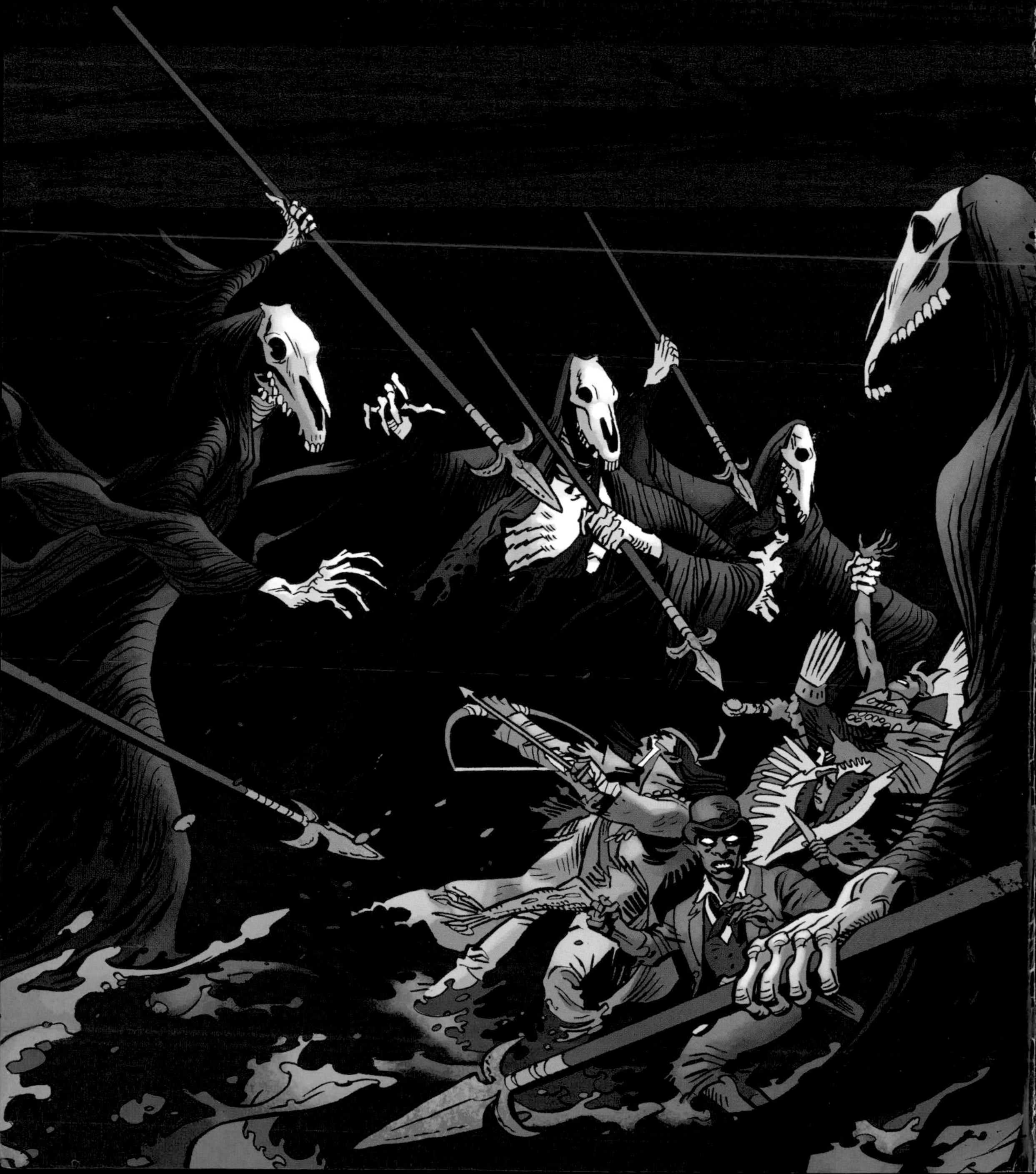

THE SIXTH GUN

Dust to Death

Valley of Death

BRIAN HURTT

A.C. ZAMUDIO

Colored by
RYAN HILL

Dust to Dust

CULLEN BUNN

Illustrated by
TYLER CROOK

Colored by
BILL CRABTREE

CRANK!

CHARLIE CHU

Designed by
KEITH WOOD

THE SIXTH GUN

DUST TO DEATH

PUBLISHED BY ONI PRESS, INC.

JOE NOZEMACK *publisher*

JAMES LUCAS JONES *editor in chief*

FRED RECKLING *director of publicity*

CHEYENNE ALLOTT *director of sales*

CHARLIE CHU *senior editor*

ROBIN HERRERA *editor*

ARI YARWOOD *associate editor*

TROY LOOK *production manager*

HILARY THOMPSON *graphic desinger*

JARED JONES *production assistant*

BRAD ROOKS *inventory coordinator*

JUNG LEE *office assistant*

ONI PRESS, INC.
1305 SE MARTIN LUTHER KING JR. BLVD.
SUITE A
PORTLAND, OR 97214
USA

onipress.com
facebook.com/onipress
twitter.com/onipress
onipress.tumblr.com
instagram.com/onipress

First edition: December 2015

ISBN: 978-1-62010-268-8
eISBN: 978-1-62010-269-5

Library of Congress Control Number: 2015943725

10 9 8 7 6 5 4 3 2 1

Keeper of the Crossroads.

Known and feared by many names, this powerful creature is Lord of the Realm of Death.

A rabbit skull encased in Blood Amber. Bound within is the spirit of the death god, Yum Kimil.

Long before he was the great spiritual leader of the Four Tribes, he was a bold, headstrong warrior who yearned to be legend.

Warrior, mystic, vagabond. A living myth, he wanders the earth in search of the mysteries of creation.

This powerful witch comes out of her self-imposed isolation to share a secret knowledge with the Four Tribes. A warning of an evil that threatens to destroy all of creation.

DUST TO DUST

BILLJOHN O'HENRY — A bounty hunter and adventurer.

SALLY O'HENRY — Billjohn's ailing daughter.

MERCER — A Pinkerton and agent of the Knights of Solomon.

DRAKE SINCLAIR — A rogue and schemer... as well as Billjohn's closest friend.

ABIGAIL REDMARSH — A "procurer of knowledge" who has worked with Billjohn and Drake on occasion.

SILAS "BITTER RIDGE" HOLLISTER — A cruel man who possesses the Fourth Gun, which is said to raise the dead.

CHAPTER
ONE

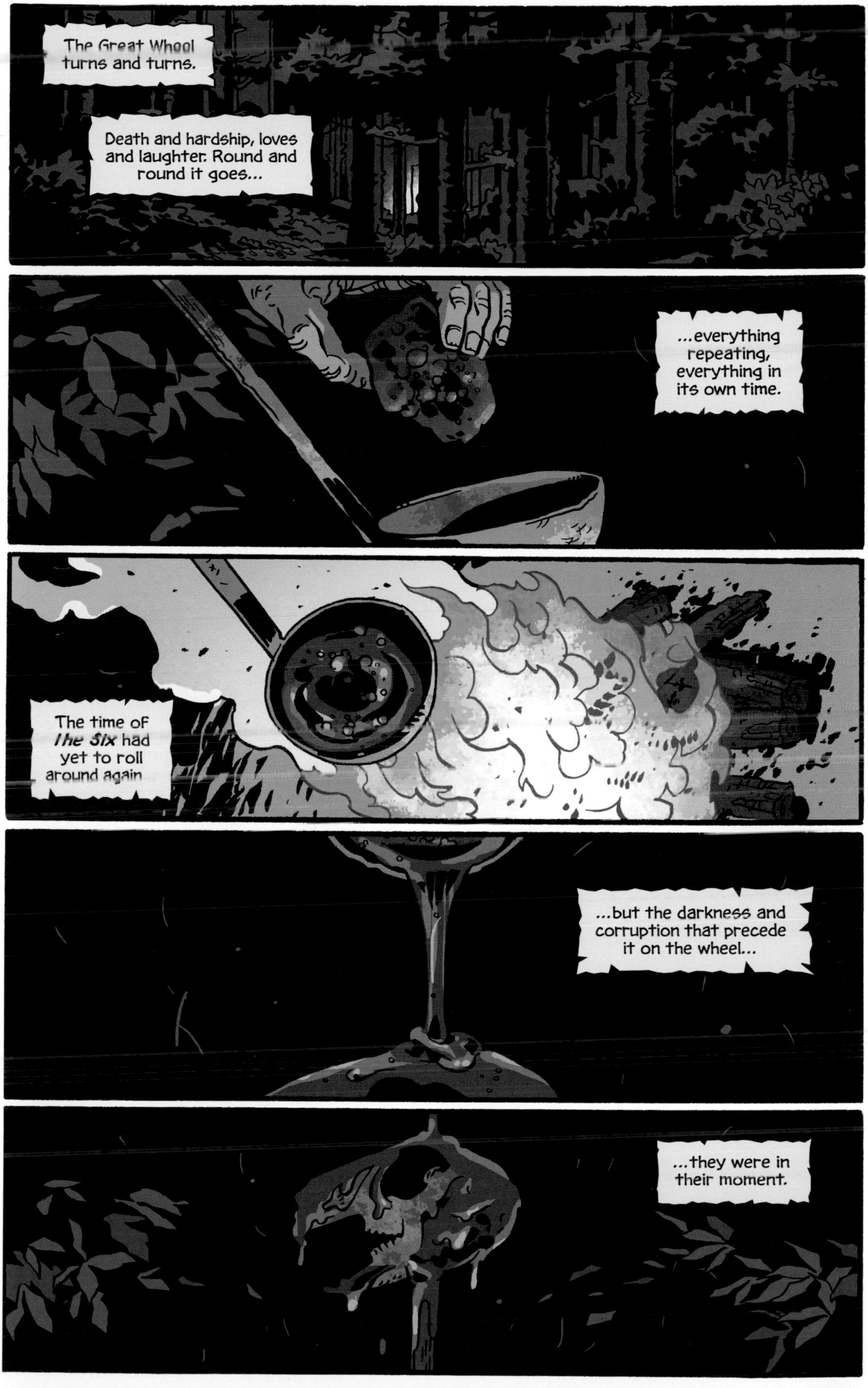

The Great Wheel turns and turns.
Death and hardship, loves and laughter. Round and round it goes...
...everything repeating, everything in its own time.
The time of *The Six* had yet to roll around again
...but the darkness and corruption that precede it on the wheel...
...they were in their moment.

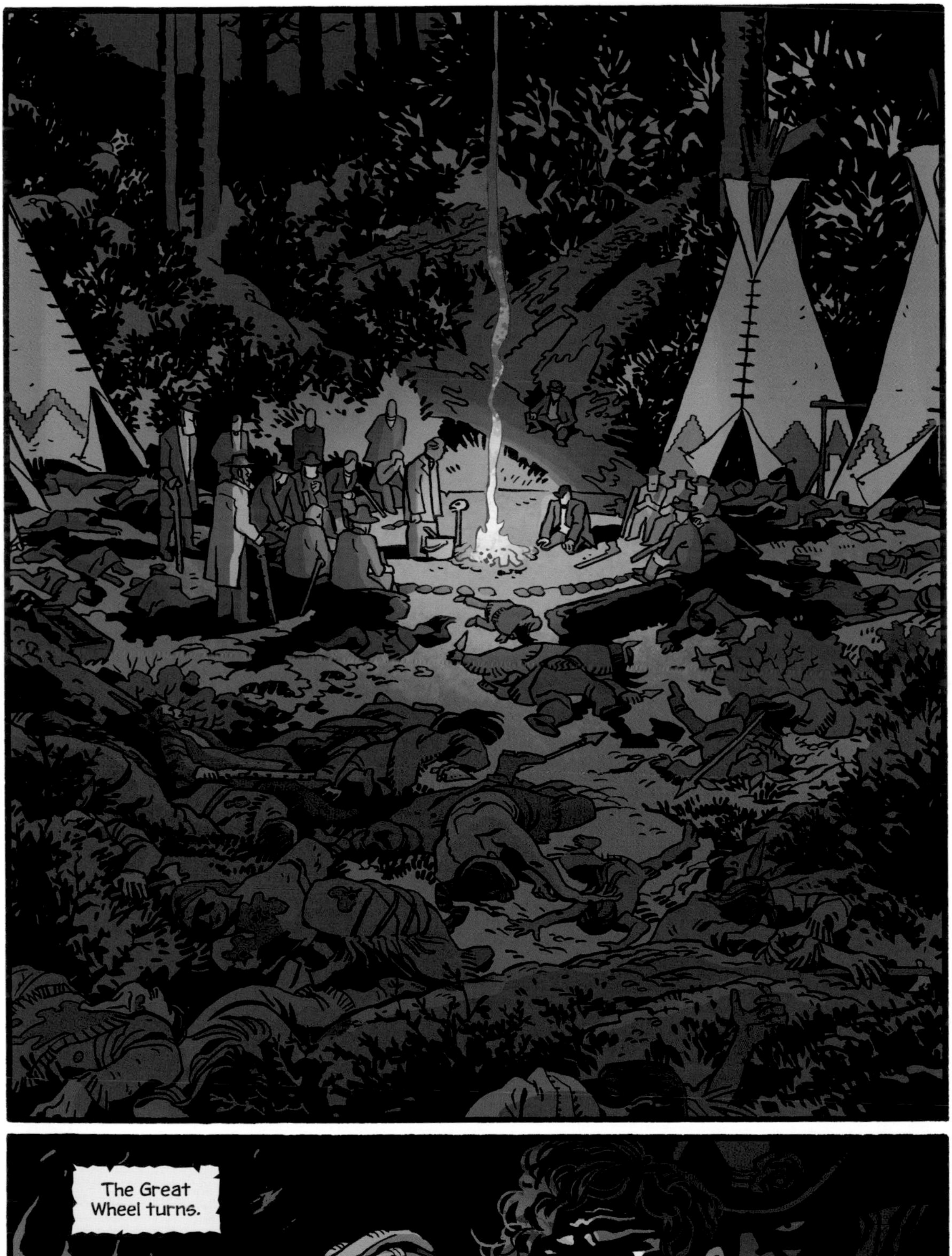

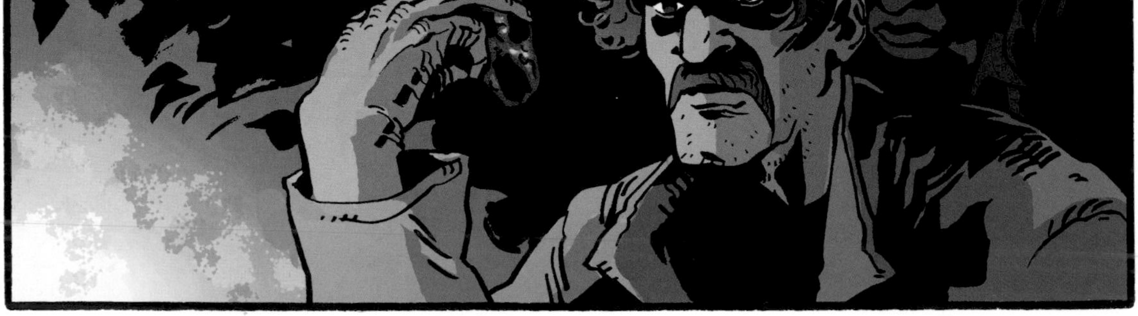
The Great Wheel turns.

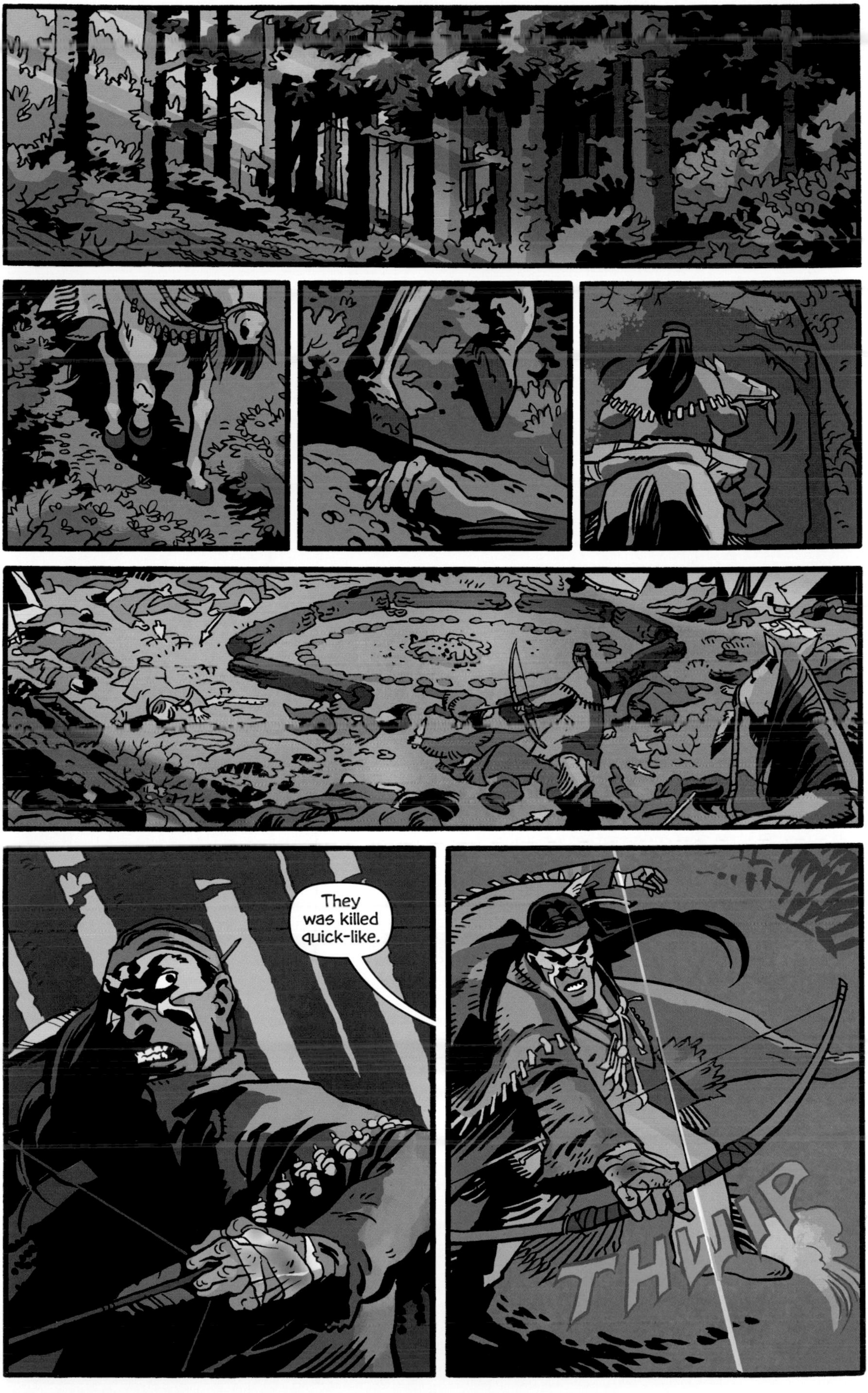
They was killed quick-like.
THWIP

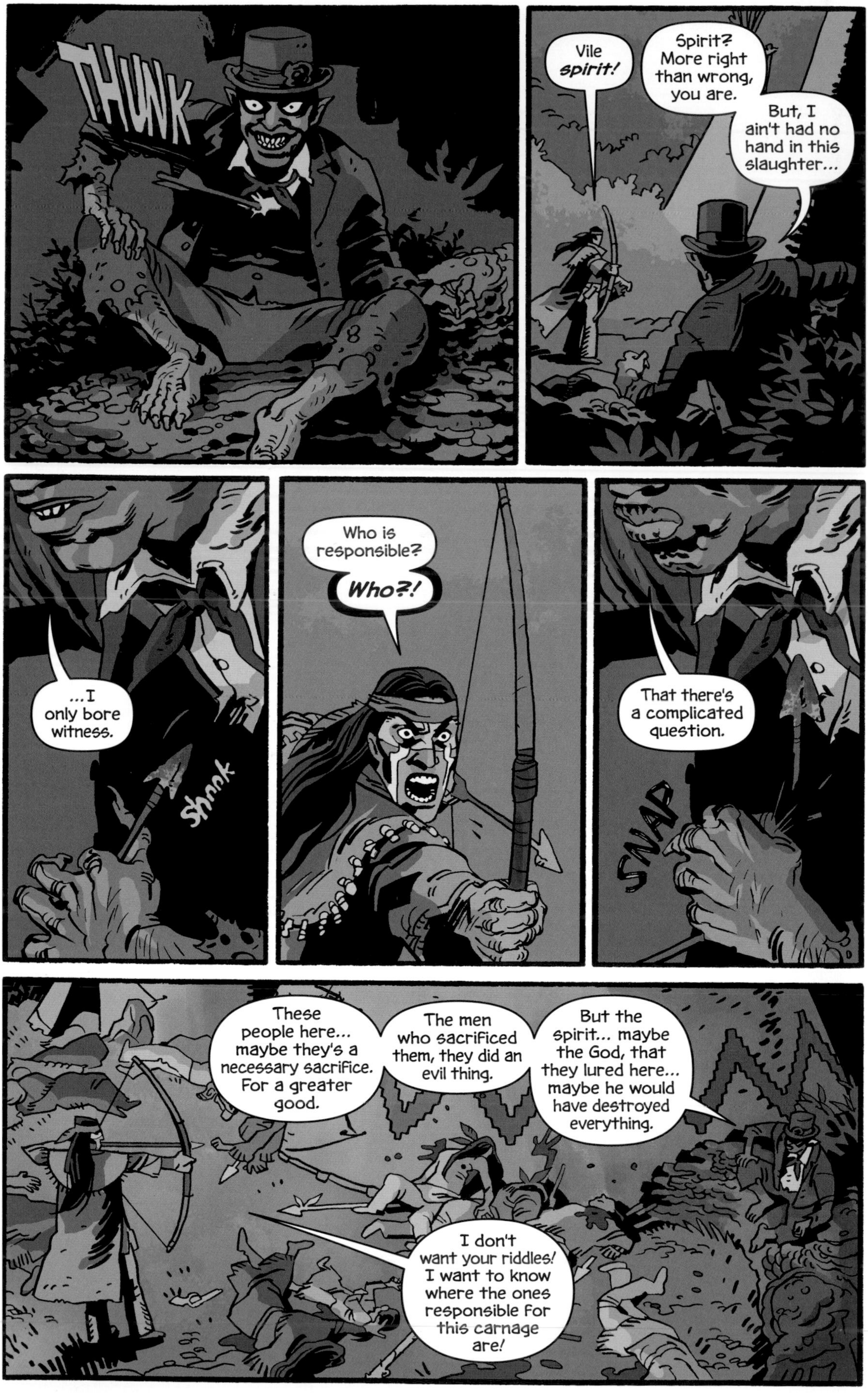
THUNK
Vile spirit!
Spirit? More right than wrong, you are.
But, I ain't had no hand in this slaughter...
...I only bore witness.
shnnk
Who is responsible? Who?!
That there's a complicated question.
SNAP
These people here... maybe they's a necessary sacrifice. For a greater good.
The men who sacrificed them, they did an evil thing.
But the spirit... maybe the God, that they lured here... maybe he would have destroyed everything.
I don't want your riddles! I want to know where the ones responsible for this carnage are!

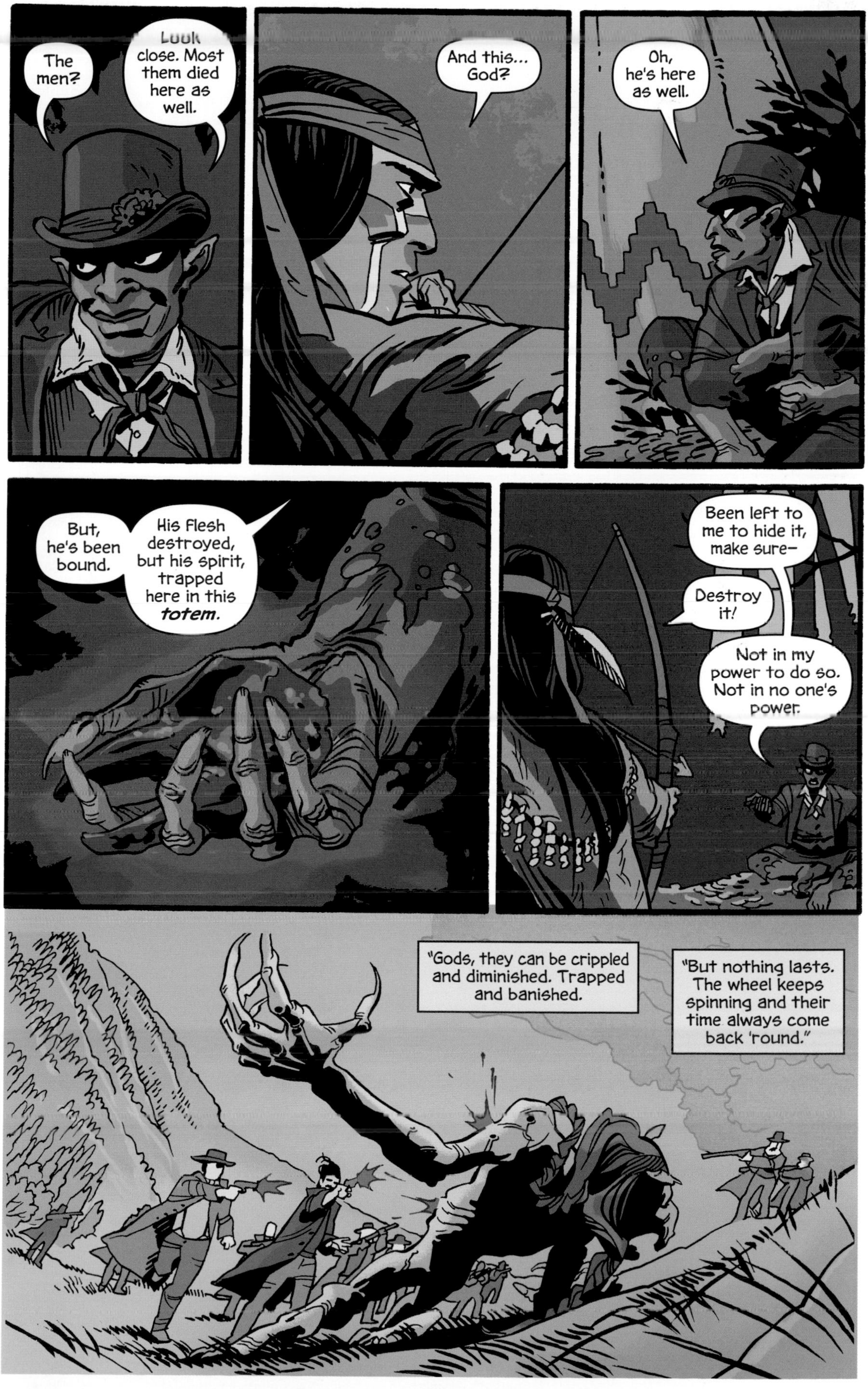
The men?
Look close. Most them died here as well.
And this... God?
Oh, he's here as well.
But, he's been bound.
His flesh destroyed, but his spirit, trapped here in this *totem*.
Been left to me to hide it, make sure—
Destroy it!
Not in my power to do so. Not in no one's power.
"Gods, they can be crippled and diminished. Trapped and banished.
"But nothing lasts. The wheel keeps spinning and their time always come back 'round."

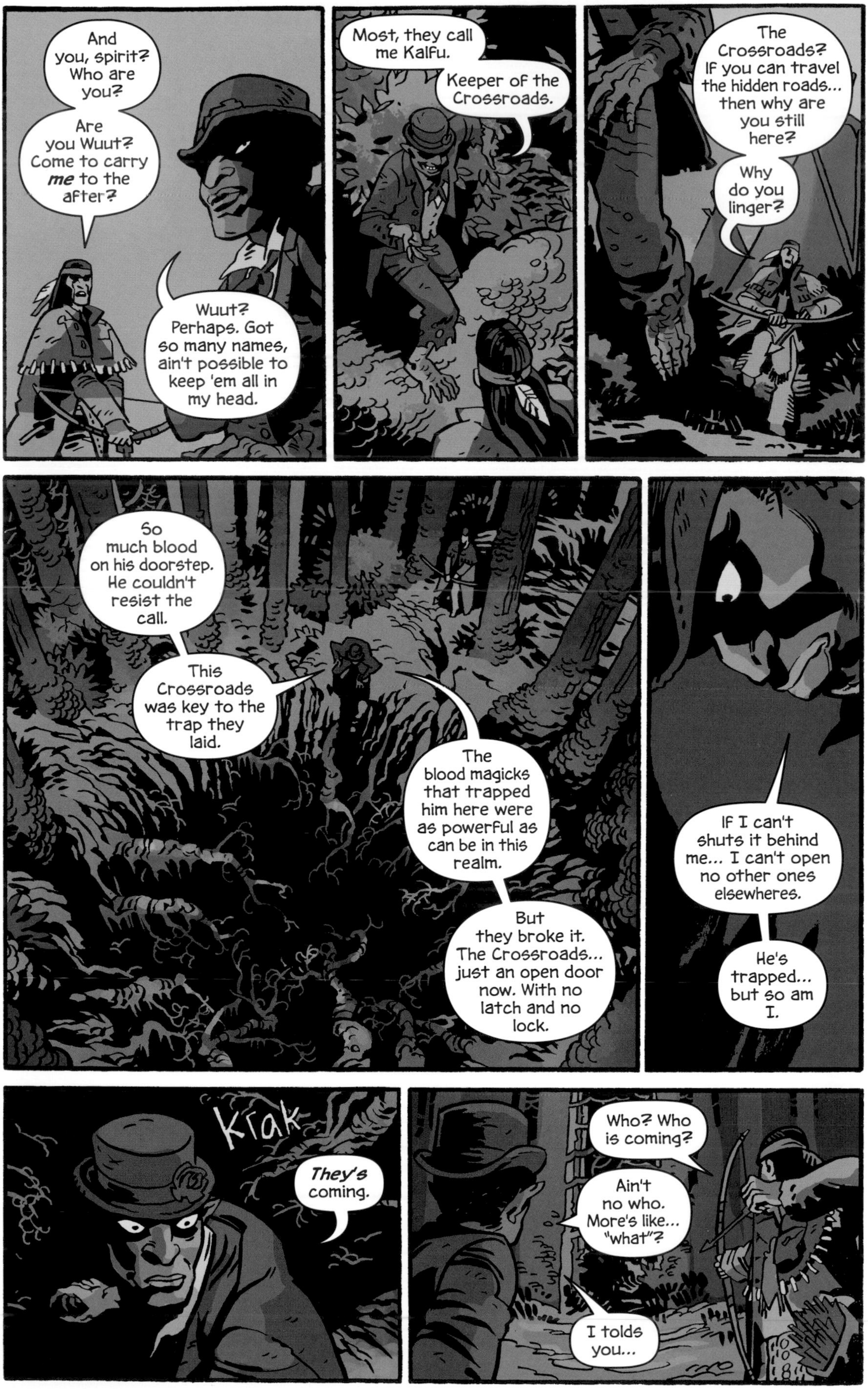
And you, spirit? Who are you?
Are you Wuut? Come to carry *me* to the after?
Wuut? Perhaps. Got so many names, ain't possible to keep 'em all in my head.
Most, they call me Kalfu.
Keeper of the Crossroads.
The Crossroads? If you can travel the hidden roads... then why are you still here?
Why do you linger?
So much blood on his doorstep. He couldn't resist the call.
This Crossroads was key to the trap they laid.
The blood magicks that trapped him here were as powerful as can be in this realm.
But they broke it. The Crossroads... just an open door now. With no latch and no lock.
If I can't shuts it behind me... I can't open no other ones elsewheres.
He's trapped... but so am I.
Krak
They's coming.
Who? Who is coming?
Ain't no who. More's like... "what"?
I tolds you...

"...the door is open."

Gods, spirits, psychopomps, and all manner of Other walk the *Winding Path.*

A path that binds and connects all the Realms.

A path that can lead to truth or can lead one astray.

It exists not in the mortal realm but above it. Beneath it. All around it.

Few of this realm know of its existence.

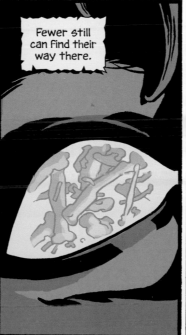

Fewer still can find their way there.

Even then it is only the spirit and not the flesh that walks these hidden paths.

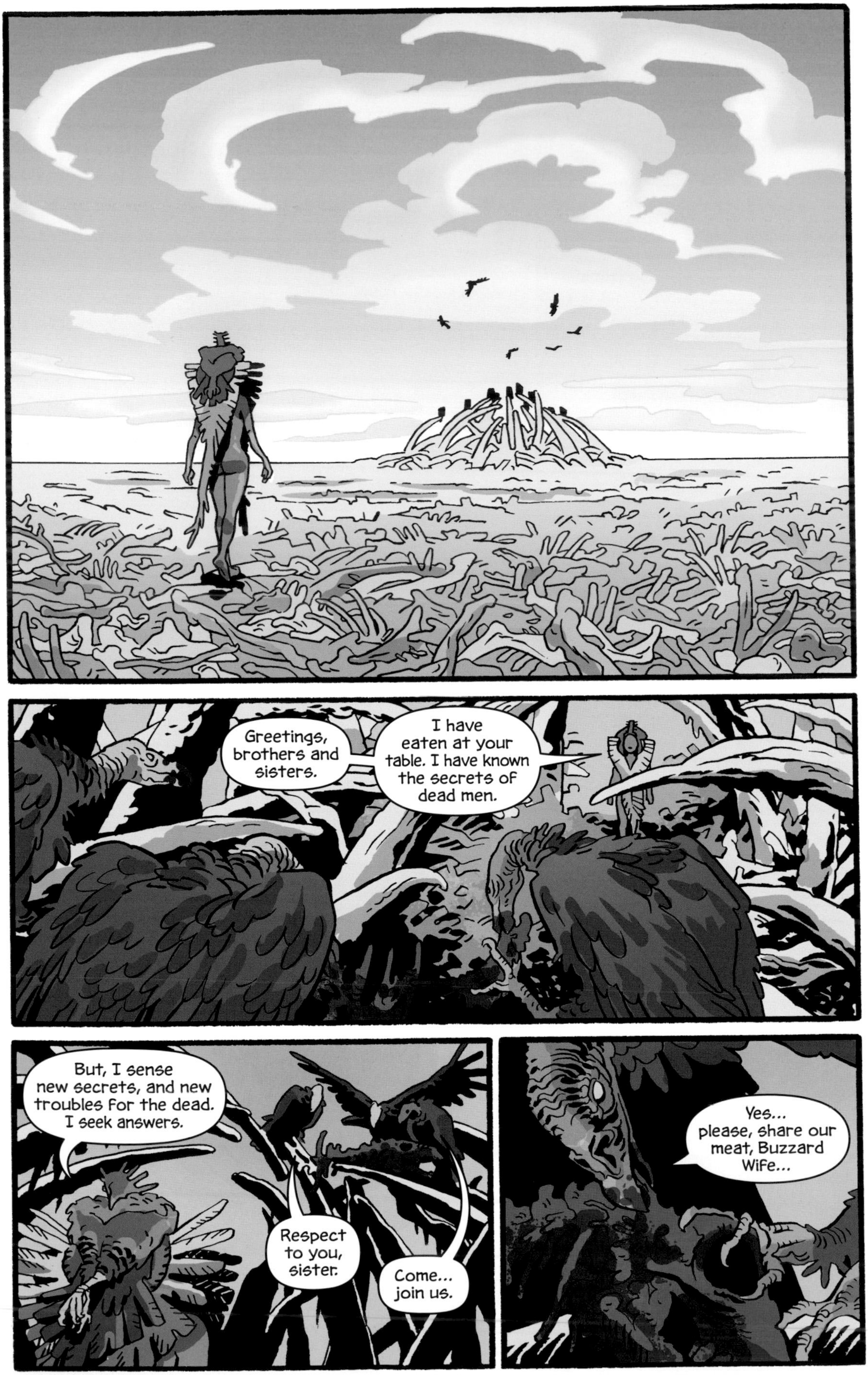
Greetings, brothers and sisters.
I have eaten at your table. I have known the secrets of dead men.
But, I sense new secrets, and new troubles for the dead. I seek answers.
Respect to you, sister.
Come... join us.
Yes... please, share our meat, Buzzard Wife...

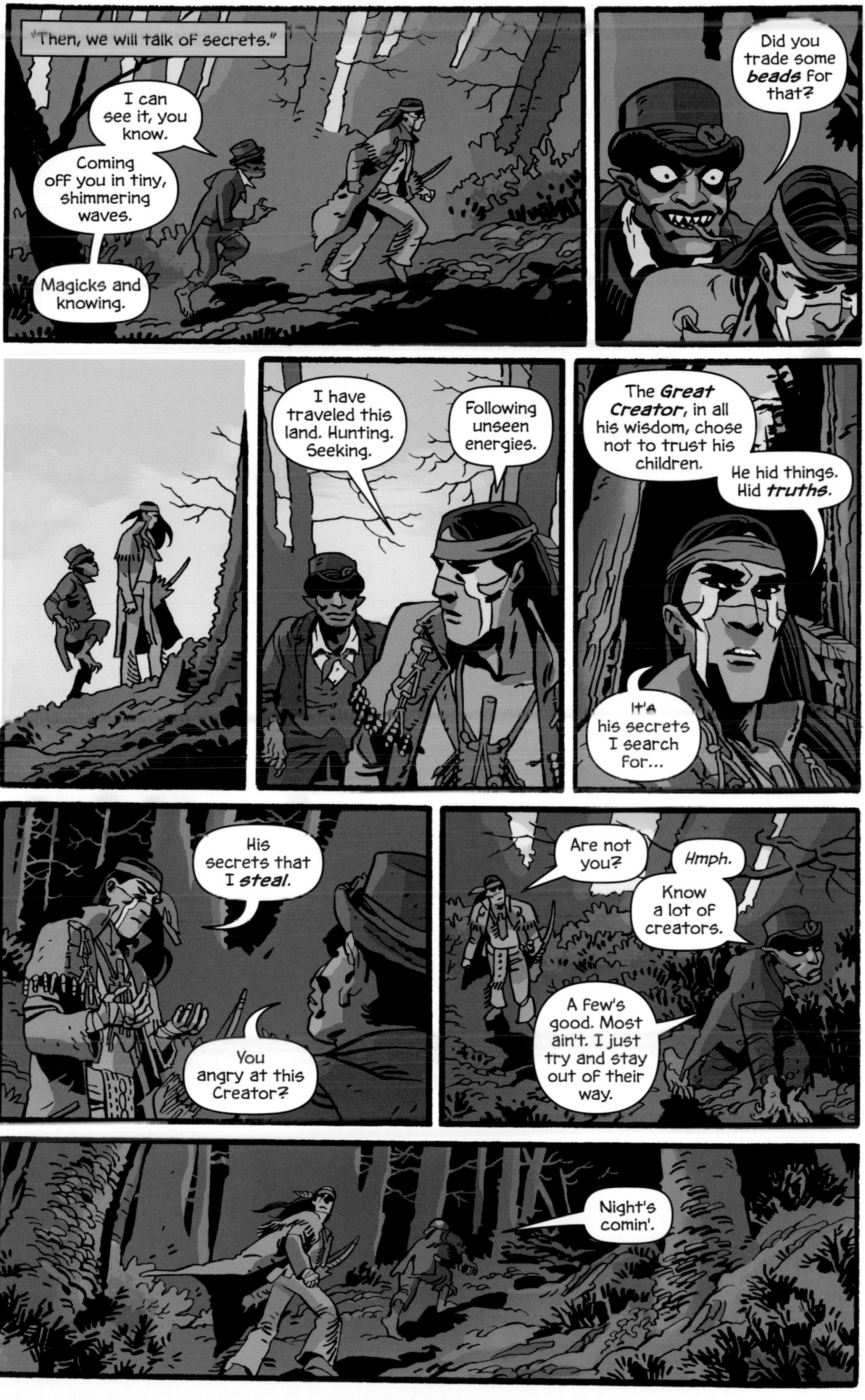
"Then, we will talk of secrets."
I can see it, you know.
Coming off you in tiny, shimmering waves.
Magicks and knowing.
Did you trade some *beads* for that?
I have traveled this land. Hunting. Seeking.
Following unseen energies.
The *Great Creator*, in all his wisdom, chose not to trust his children.
He hid things. Hid *truths*.
It's his secrets I search for...
His secrets that I *steal*.
You angry at this Creator?
Are not you?
Hmph.
Know a lot of creators.
A few's good. Most ain't. I just try and stay out of their way.
Night's comin'.

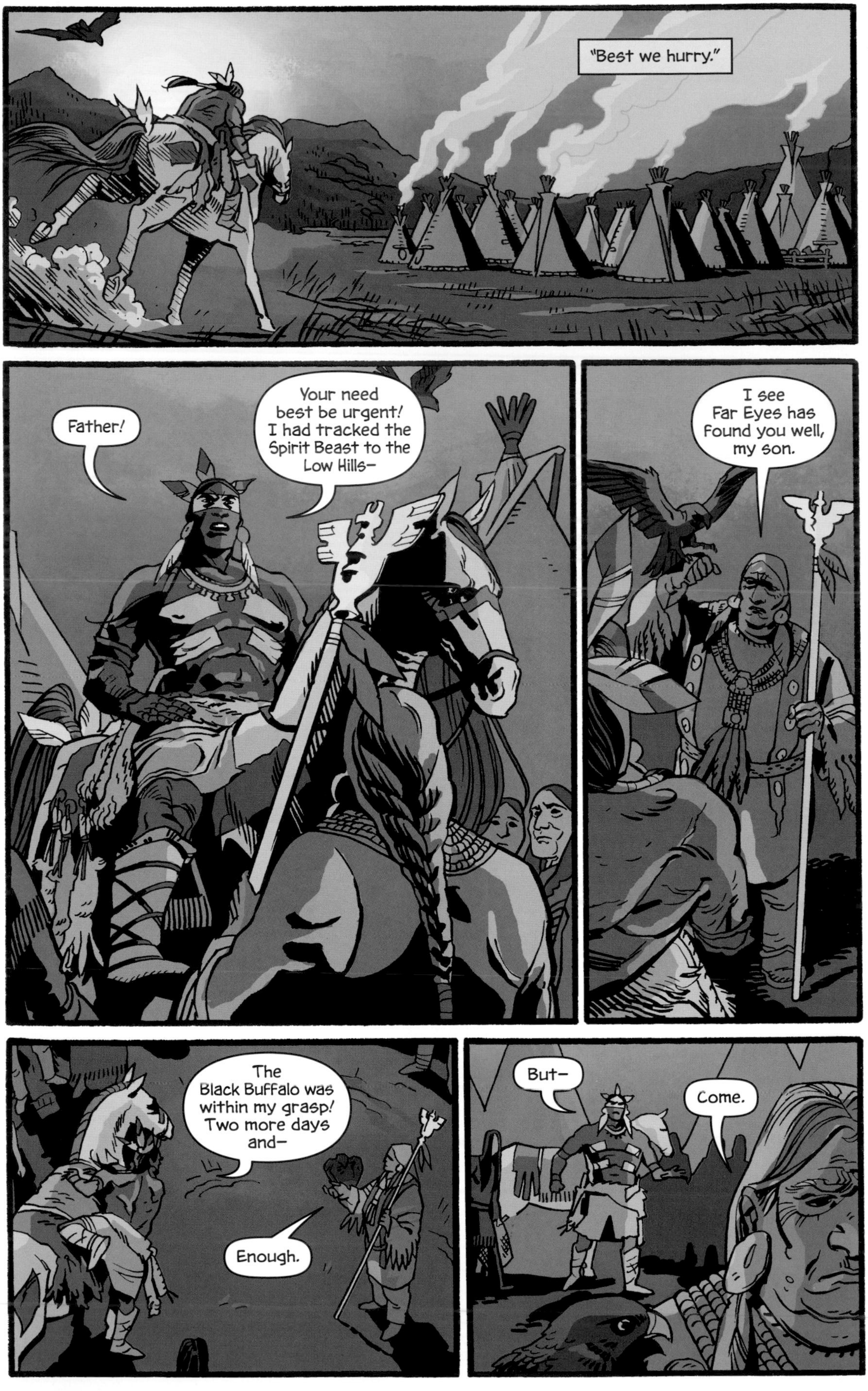
"Best we hurry."
Father!
Your need best be urgent! I had tracked the Spirit Beast to the Low Hills–
I see Far Eyes has found you well, my son.
The Black Buffalo was within my grasp! Two more days and–
Enough.
But–
Come.

Your trophy hunts and fireside tales can wait.

What lies ahead is worthy of a thousand songs.

A thousand songs?

IF you succeed.

IF you do not... there will be no one to write the songs. No one to hear them.

Father, nothing can be as dire as—

Nothing!

Yes.

Just that. Nothingness and death.

Worrying news comes to us.

Further north, in the Valley Beyond the Stones, there is *death*...

...spreading. Crawling. And, at its center... *nothing.*

An absence. A *hole* in the Supreme Being's creation.

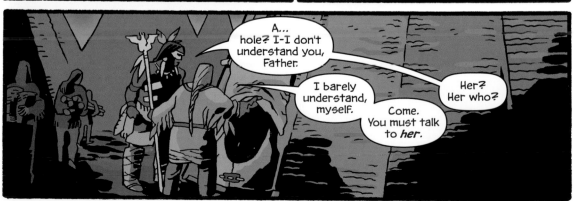

A... hole? I-I don't understand you, Father.

I barely understand, myself.

Come. You must talk to *her.*

Her? Her who?

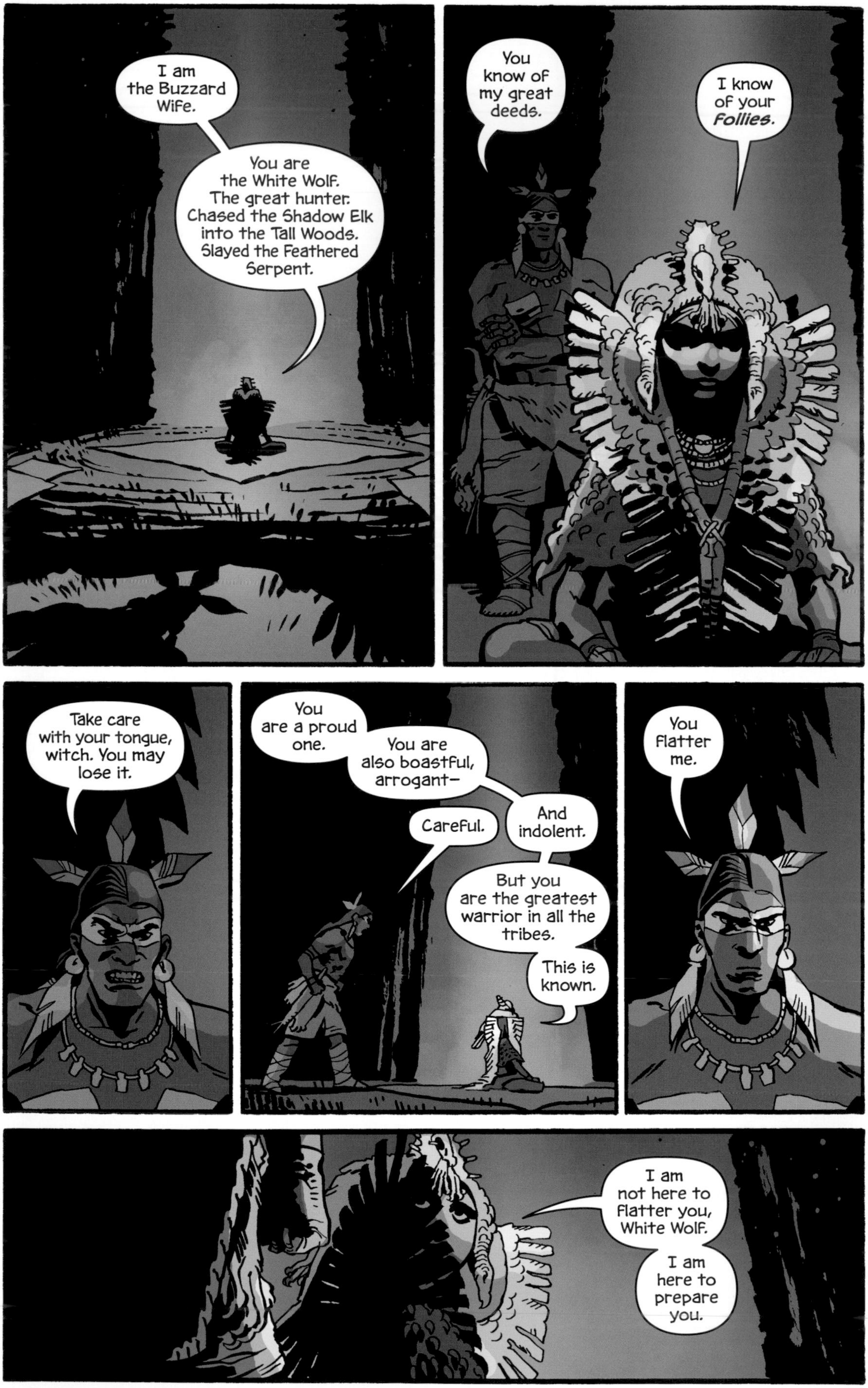
I am the Buzzard Wife.
You are the White Wolf. The great hunter. Chased the Shadow Elk into the Tall Woods. Slayed the Feathered Serpent.
You know of my great deeds.
I know of your *Follies*.
Take care with your tongue, witch. You may lose it.
You are a proud one.
You are also boastful, arrogant–
Careful.
And indolent.
But you are the greatest warrior in all the tribes.
This is known.
You flatter me.
I am not here to flatter you, White Wolf.
I am here to prepare you.

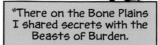

Ill omens in the scattered bones. Visions in waking hours.

Our lands, ashes. Our waters, blood.

I sought answers. So, I ventured to the Realm of the Dead.

"There on the Bone Plains I shared secrets with the Beasts of Burden.

"And they with me."

The stone is rolled away.

There now hangs but a veil between our *here* and theirs.

Death *bleeds* into your realm through the open door.

And death... it is decay.

It is consumption.

It is *inevitable.*

I do not believe in the inevitable.

And that is why you have been chosen.

You will join me in leading a party north.

Live or die, our one task must be accomplished...

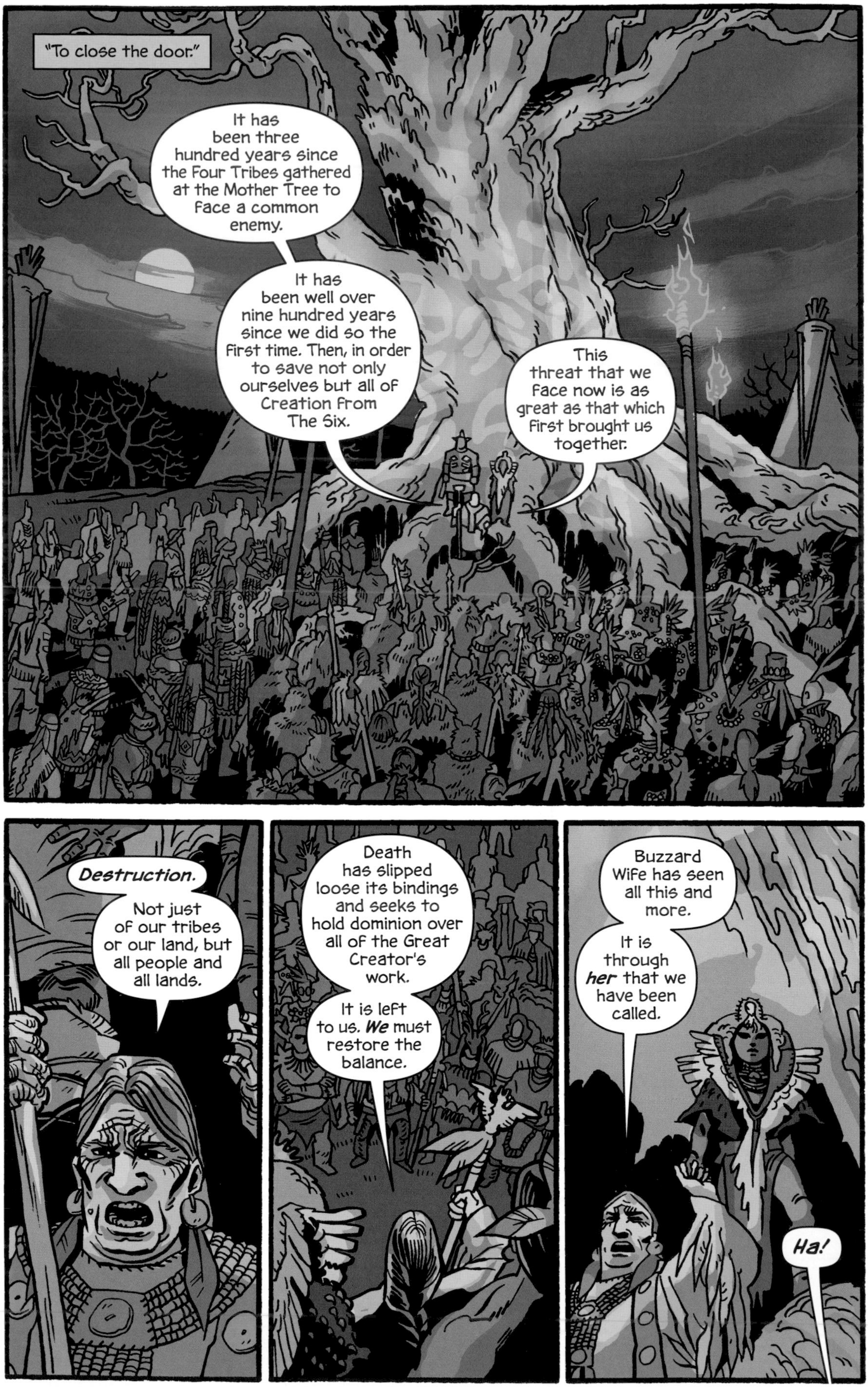
"To close the door."
It has been three hundred years since the Four Tribes gathered at the Mother Tree to face a common enemy.
It has been well over nine hundred years since we did so the first time. Then, in order to save not only ourselves but all of Creation from The Six.
This threat that we face now is as great as that which first brought us together.
Destruction.
Not just of our tribes or our land, but all people and all lands.
Death has slipped loose its bindings and seeks to hold dominion over all of the Great Creator's work.
It is left to us. *We* must restore the balance.
Buzzard Wife has seen all this and more.
It is through *her* that we have been called.
Ha!

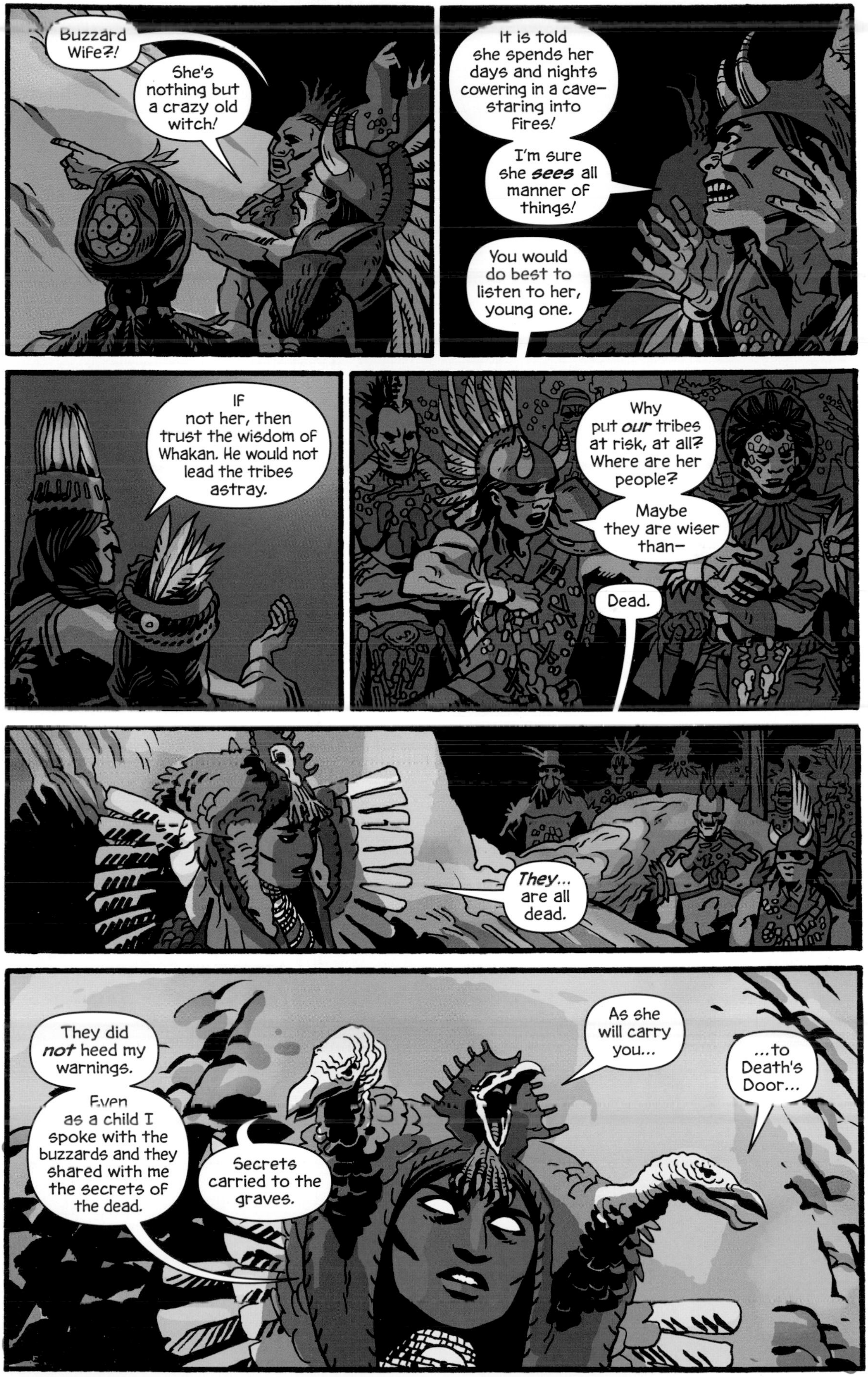
Buzzard Wife?!
She's nothing but a crazy old witch!
It is told she spends her days and nights cowering in a cave– staring into fires!
I'm sure she *sees* all manner of things!
You would do best to listen to her, young one.
If not her, then trust the wisdom of Whakan. He would not lead the tribes astray.
Why put *our* tribes at risk, at all? Where are her people?
Maybe they are wiser than–
Dead.
They... are all dead.
They did *not* heed my warnings.
Even as a child I spoke with the buzzards and they shared with me the secrets of the dead.
Secrets carried to the graves.
As she will carry you...
...to Death's Door...

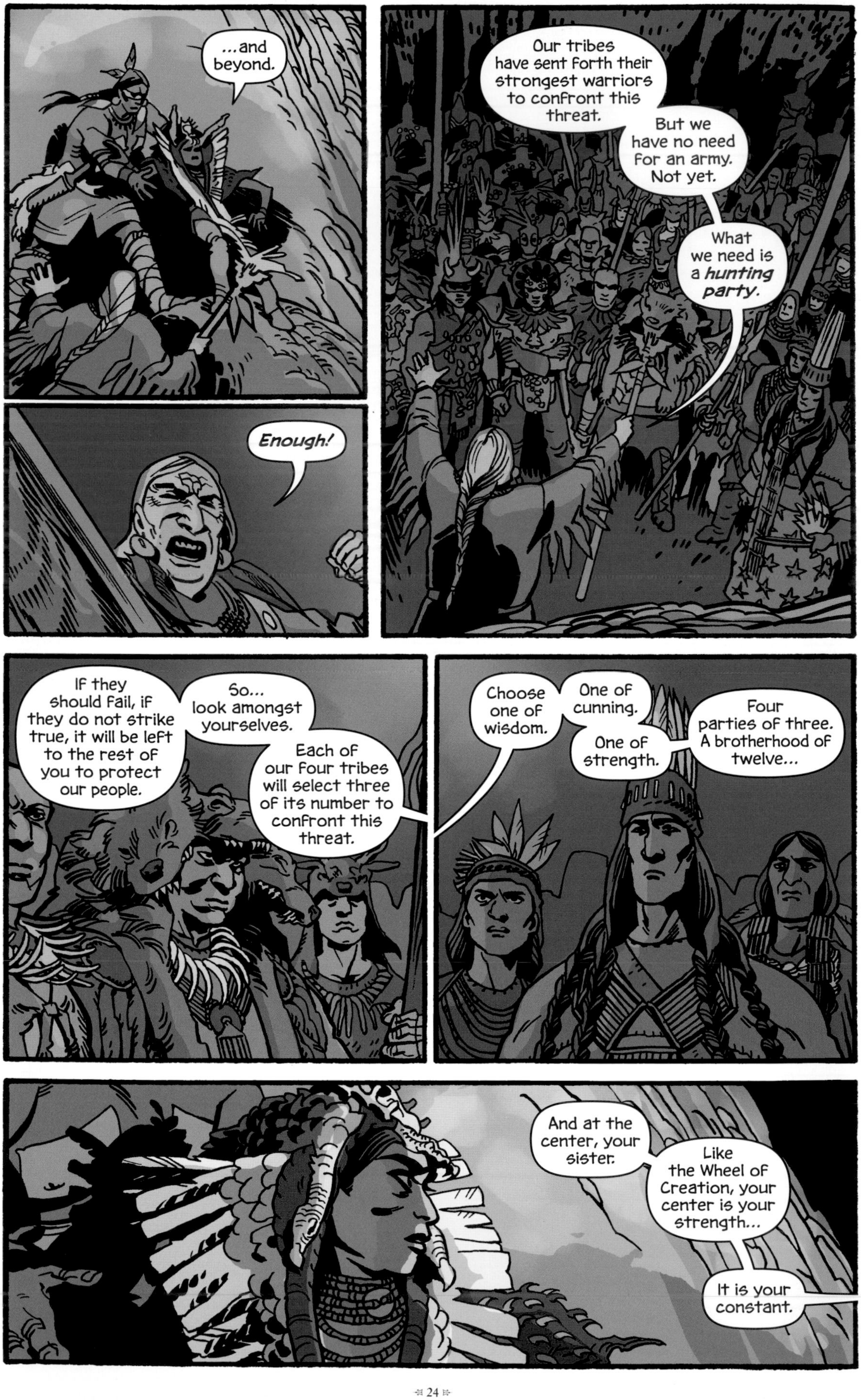
...and beyond.
Enough!
Our tribes have sent forth their strongest warriors to confront this threat.
But we have no need for an army. Not yet.
What we need is a *hunting party.*
If they should fail, if they do not strike true, it will be left to the rest of you to protect our people.
So... look amongst yourselves.
Each of our four tribes will select three of its number to confront this threat.
Choose one of wisdom.
One of cunning.
One of strength.
Four parties of three. A brotherhood of twelve...
And at the center, your sister.
Like the Wheel of Creation, your center is your strength...
It is your constant.

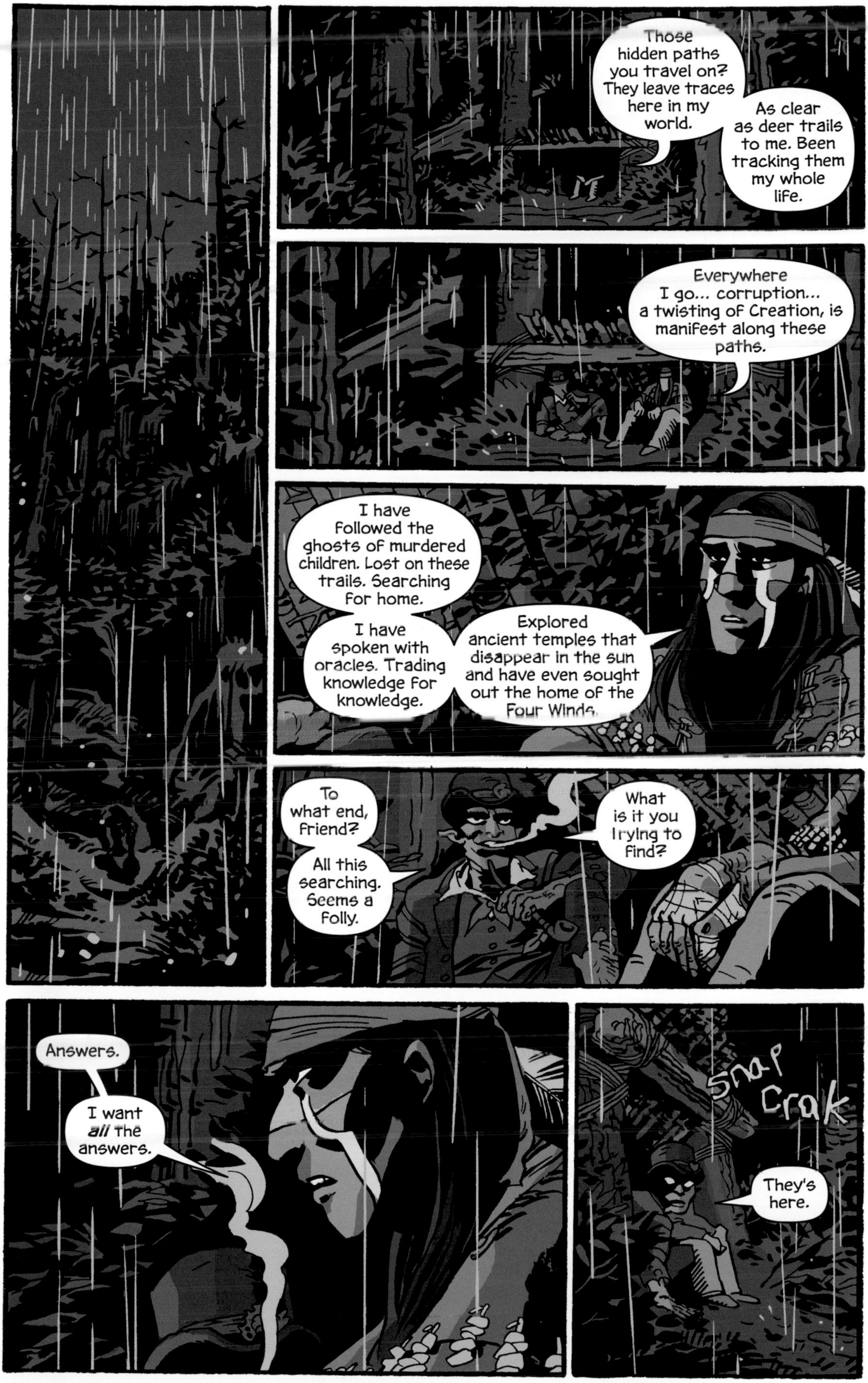
Those hidden paths you travel on? They leave traces here in my world.
As clear as deer trails to me. Been tracking them my whole life.
Everywhere I go... corruption... a twisting of Creation, is manifest along these paths.
I have followed the ghosts of murdered children. Lost on these trails. Searching for home.
I have spoken with oracles. Trading knowledge for knowledge.
Explored ancient temples that disappear in the sun and have even sought out the home of the Four Winds.
To what end, friend?
All this searching. Seems a folly.
What is it you trying to find?
Answers.
I want *all* the answers.
Snap
Crak
They's here.

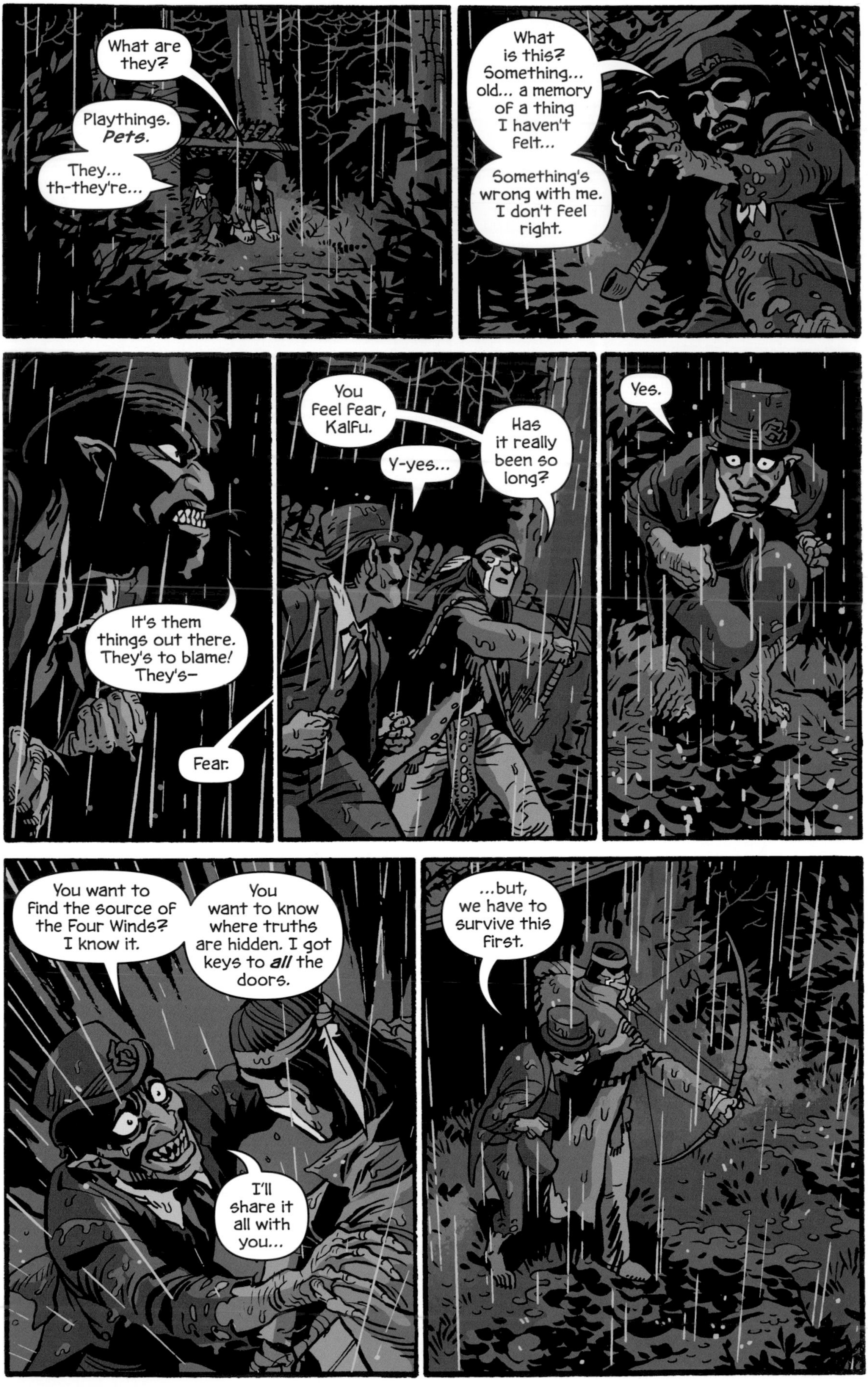
What are they?
Playthings. *Pets.*
They... th-they're...
What is this? Something... old... a memory of a thing I haven't felt...
Something's wrong with me. I don't feel right.
It's them things out there. They's to blame! They's–
Fear.
You feel Fear, Kalfu.
Y-yes...
Has it really been so long?
Yes.
You want to find the source of the Four Winds? I know it.
You want to know where truths are hidden. I got keys to *all* the doors.
I'll share it all with you...
...but, we have to survive this first.

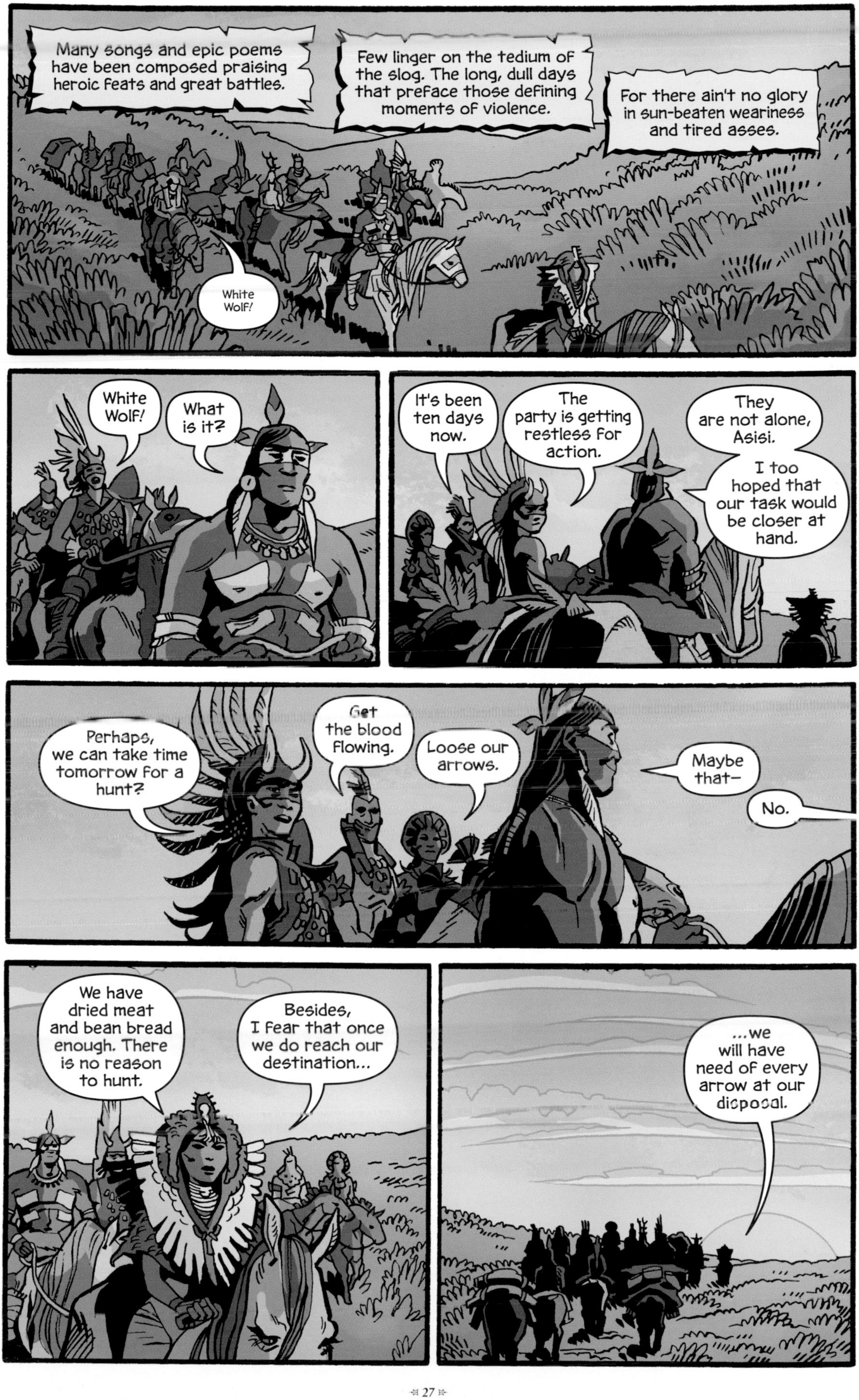
Many songs and epic poems have been composed praising heroic feats and great battles.
Few linger on the tedium of the slog. The long, dull days that preface those defining moments of violence.
For there ain't no glory in sun-beaten weariness and tired asses.
White Wolf!
White Wolf!
What is it?
It's been ten days now.
The party is getting restless for action.
They are not alone, Asisi.
I too hoped that our task would be closer at hand.
Perhaps, we can take time tomorrow for a hunt?
Get the blood flowing.
Loose our arrows.
Maybe that—
No.
We have dried meat and bean bread enough. There is no reason to hunt.
Besides, I fear that once we do reach our destination...
...we will have need of every arrow at our disposal.

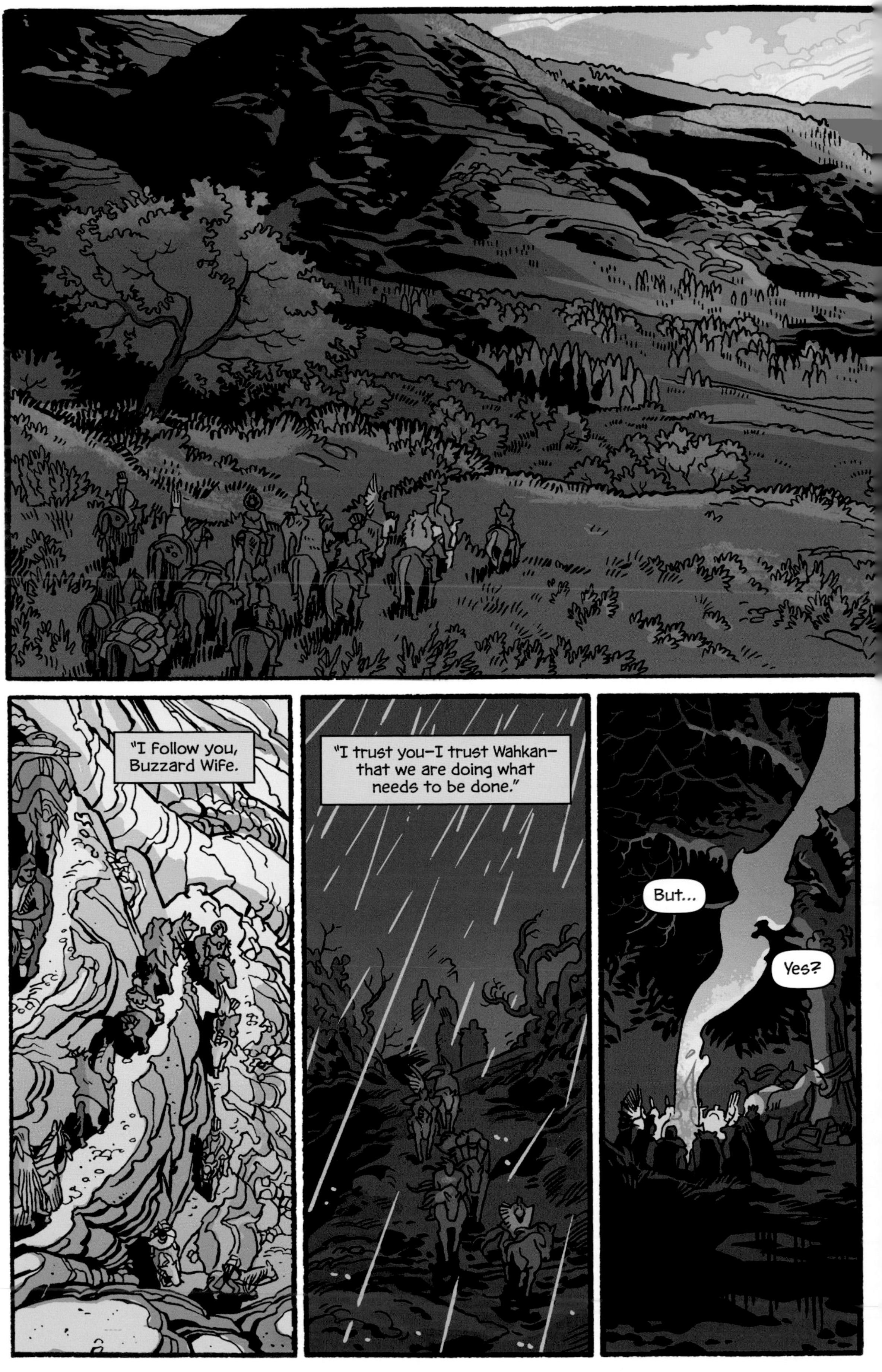
"I follow you, Buzzard Wife.
"I trust you—I trust Wahkan—that we are doing what needs to be done."
But...
Yes?

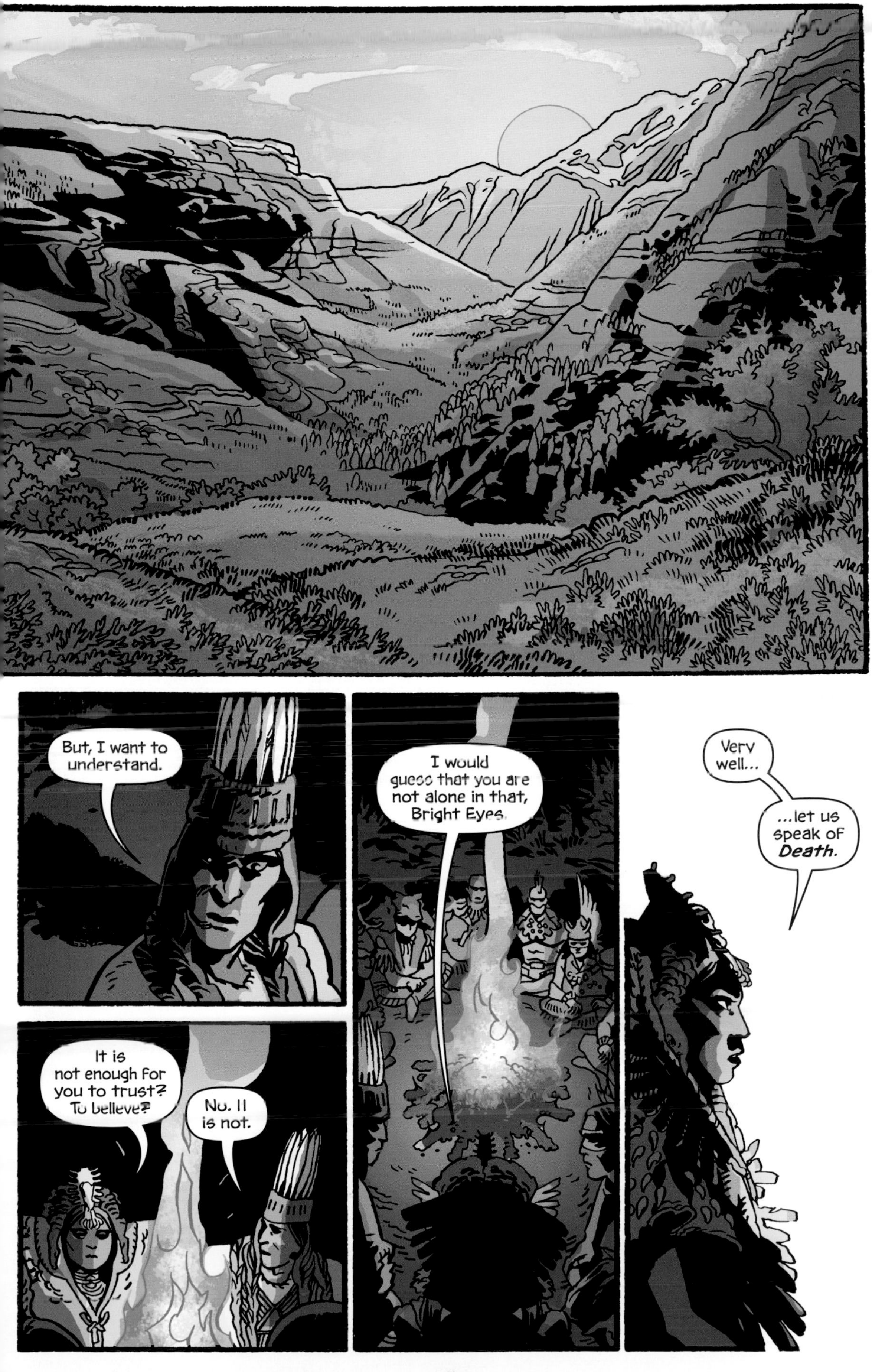
But, I want to understand.
I would guess that you are not alone in that, Bright Eyes.
Very well...
...let us speak of *Death*.
It is not enough for you to trust? To believe?
No. It is not.

"There were Others, there in the beginning. Spirits watching from the shadows as the Great Creator brought light to the darkness. Brought form to his creation."

"These Others, they saw creatures—men and animals—spring from the Creator's clay.

"There was, among these spirits, one who watched on with particular wonder... and understanding. And was not surprised when the Creator introduced Death.

"He alone comprehended the Creator's intent.

"His benevolence.

"*Finality*. Something the Great Creator and the lesser spirits did not have.

"A beginning... and an end. It wasn't life that was the Creator's greatest gift, it was purpose. Meaning.

"For it is hard to find any meaning in the infinite. This, the spirit knew too well."

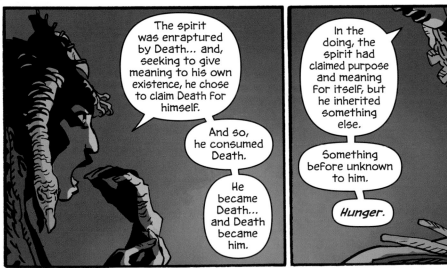

The spirit was enraptured by Death... and, seeking to give meaning to his own existence, he chose to claim Death for himself.

And so, he consumed Death.

He became Death... and Death became him.

In the doing, the spirit had claimed purpose and meaning for itself, but he inherited something else.

Something before unknown to him.

Hunger.

"This hunger knew no bounds.

"And so, Death set out to consume all life it could find."

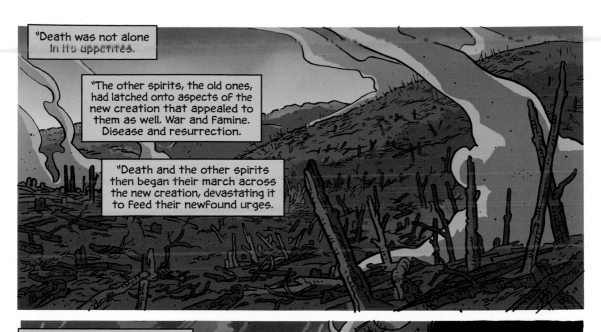

"Death was not alone in its appetites."

"The other spirits, the old ones, had latched onto aspects of the new creation that appealed to them as well. War and Famine. Disease and resurrection.

"Death and the other spirits then began their march across the new creation, devastating it to feed their newfound urges.

"The Great Creator was furious with their lack of restraint as they trampled his garden.

"As they were like brothers and sisters to him he could not find it in himself to destroy them."

Instead, he built a wall around what remained of his unmarred creation.

The spirits were each given their own realm to rule and barred from ever venturing into his garden again.

And there they dwelt, in the *Spirit Realms*.

Death, in his own realm, and with a constant hunger, could still smell all that life. Just on the other side of the veil.

Though he knew that all living things would eventually come to know him, he was impatient.

And he was clever.

"After many, many turns of the Great Wheel, he found a way. A door in the wall so old to have fallen out of memory of even the Gatekeepers themselves.

"And so, he slipped through this door, as wind through the branches."

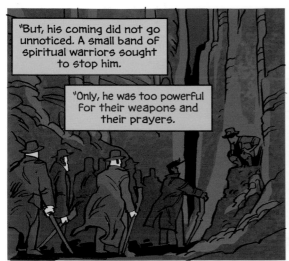

"But, his coming did not go unnoticed. A small band of spiritual warriors sought to stop him.

"Only, he was too powerful for their weapons and their prayers.

"They had to turn to older, darker magicks to stop him. To bind him.

"Blood magicks.

"Sacrifice.

"So much blood on his doorstep, he was lured back to the threshold of his realm.

"There, they defeated him. And they bound him.

"But their success bore unseen consequences.

"Their dark magicks had destroyed the door they stood upon.

"No longer is there a barrier between the Realm of Death and our own.

And now it is up to us to seal it.

You make it sound easy.

It won't be...

...but, I have a plan.

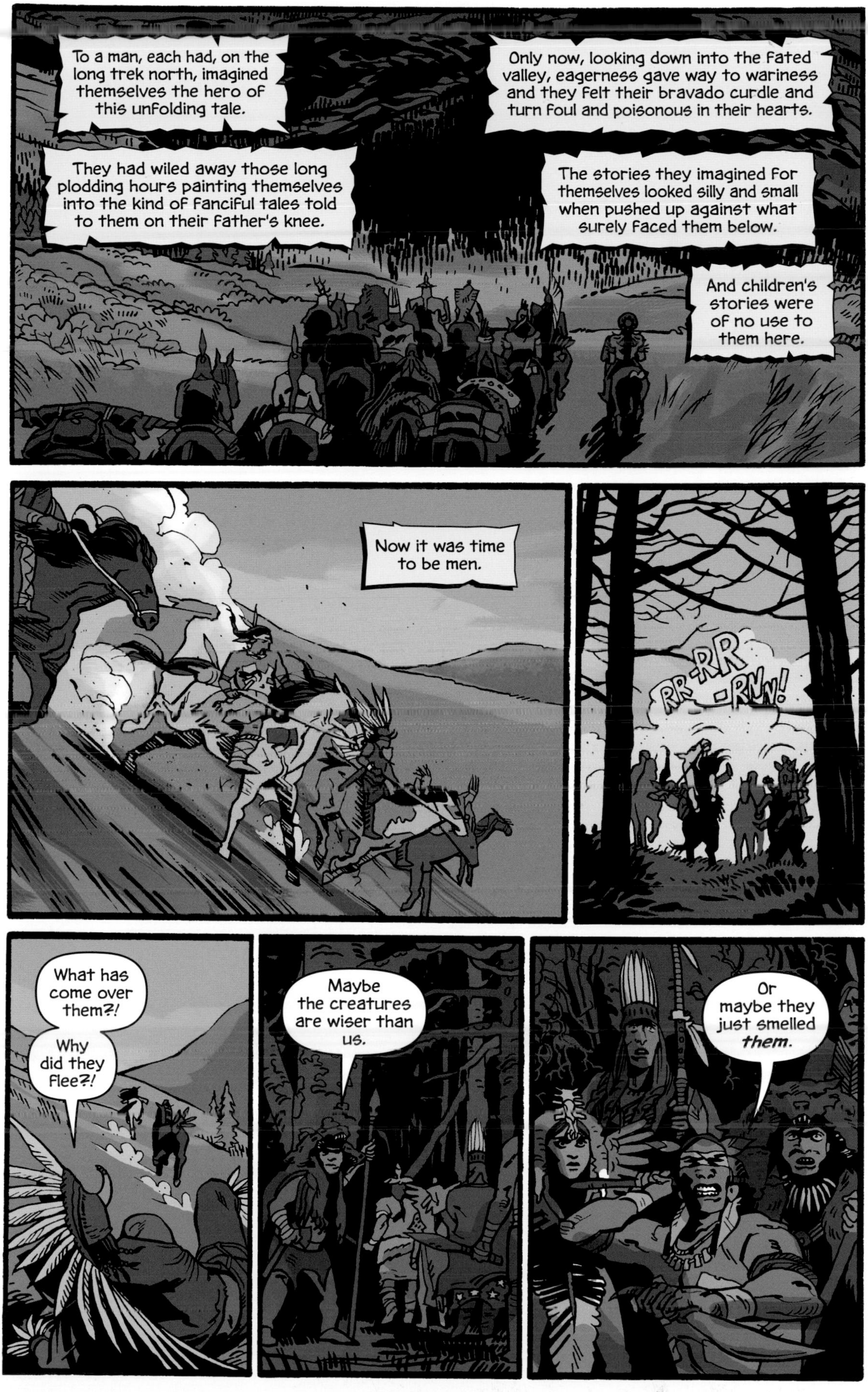
To a man, each had, on the long trek north, imagined themselves the hero of this unfolding tale.
They had wiled away those long plodding hours painting themselves into the kind of fanciful tales told to them on their father's knee.
Only now, looking down into the fated valley, eagerness gave way to wariness and they felt their bravado curdle and turn foul and poisonous in their hearts.
The stories they imagined for themselves looked silly and small when pushed up against what surely faced them below.
And children's stories were of no use to them here.
Now it was time to be men.
RR-RR-RNN!
What has come over them?!
Why did they flee?!
Maybe the creatures are wiser than us.
Or maybe they just smelled *them*.

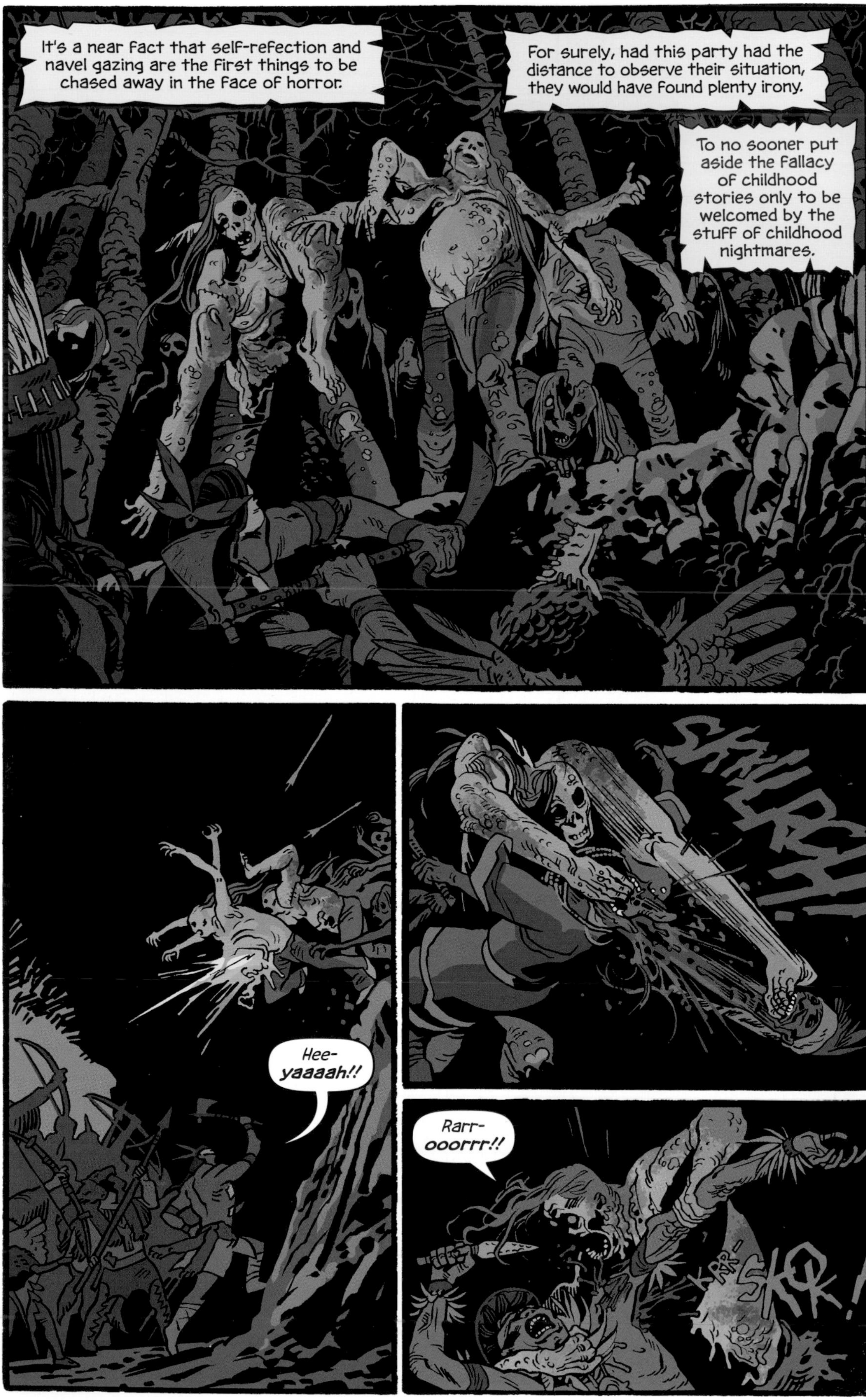
It's a near fact that self-refection and navel gazing are the first things to be chased away in the face of horror.
For surely, had this party had the distance to observe their situation, they would have found plenty irony.
To no sooner put aside the fallacy of childhood stories only to be welcomed by the stuff of childhood nightmares.
Hee-yaaaah!!
Rarr-ooorrr!!

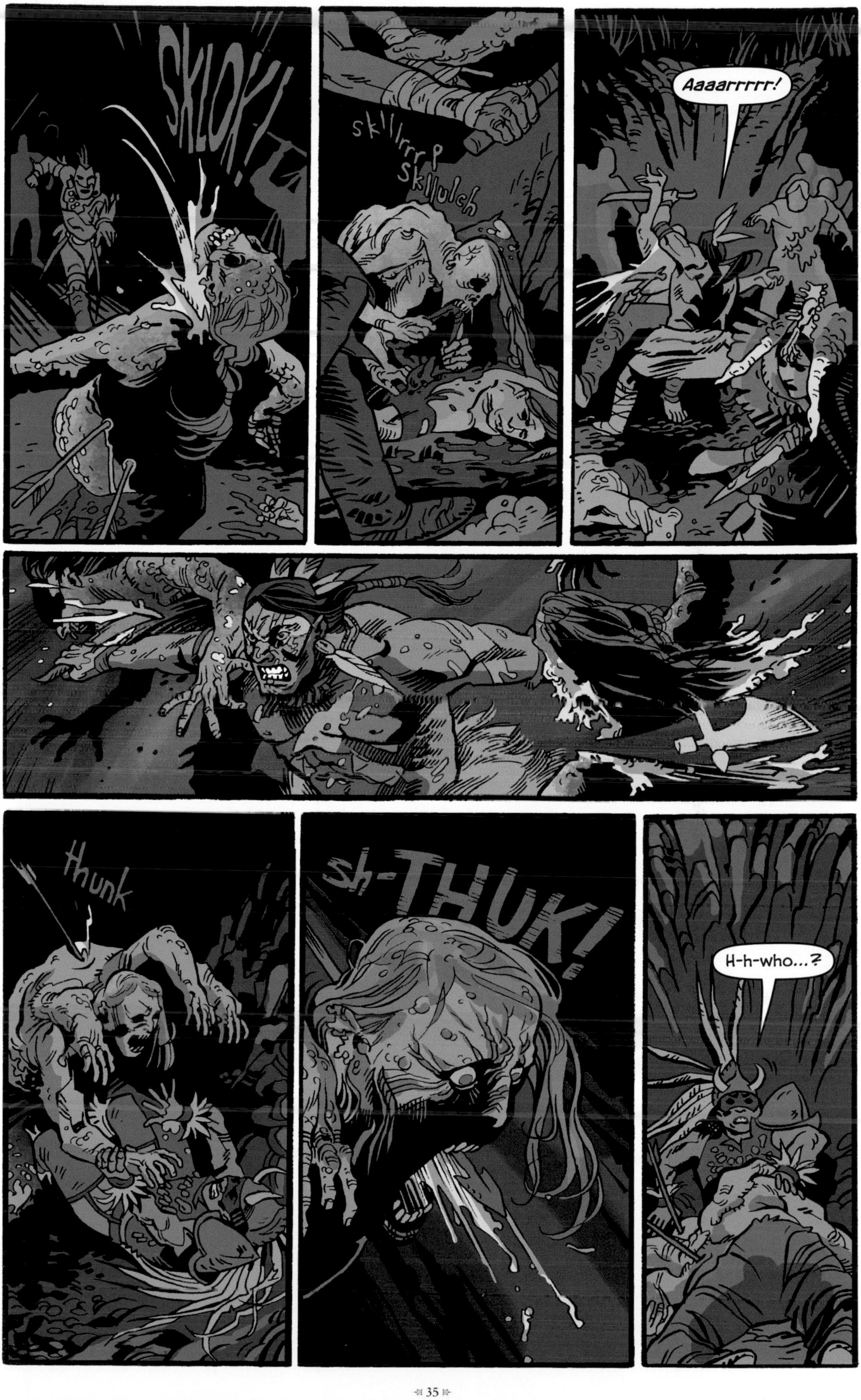
SKLOK!
skllrrrp
Skllulch
Aaaarrrrr!
thunk
sh-THUK!
H-h-who...?

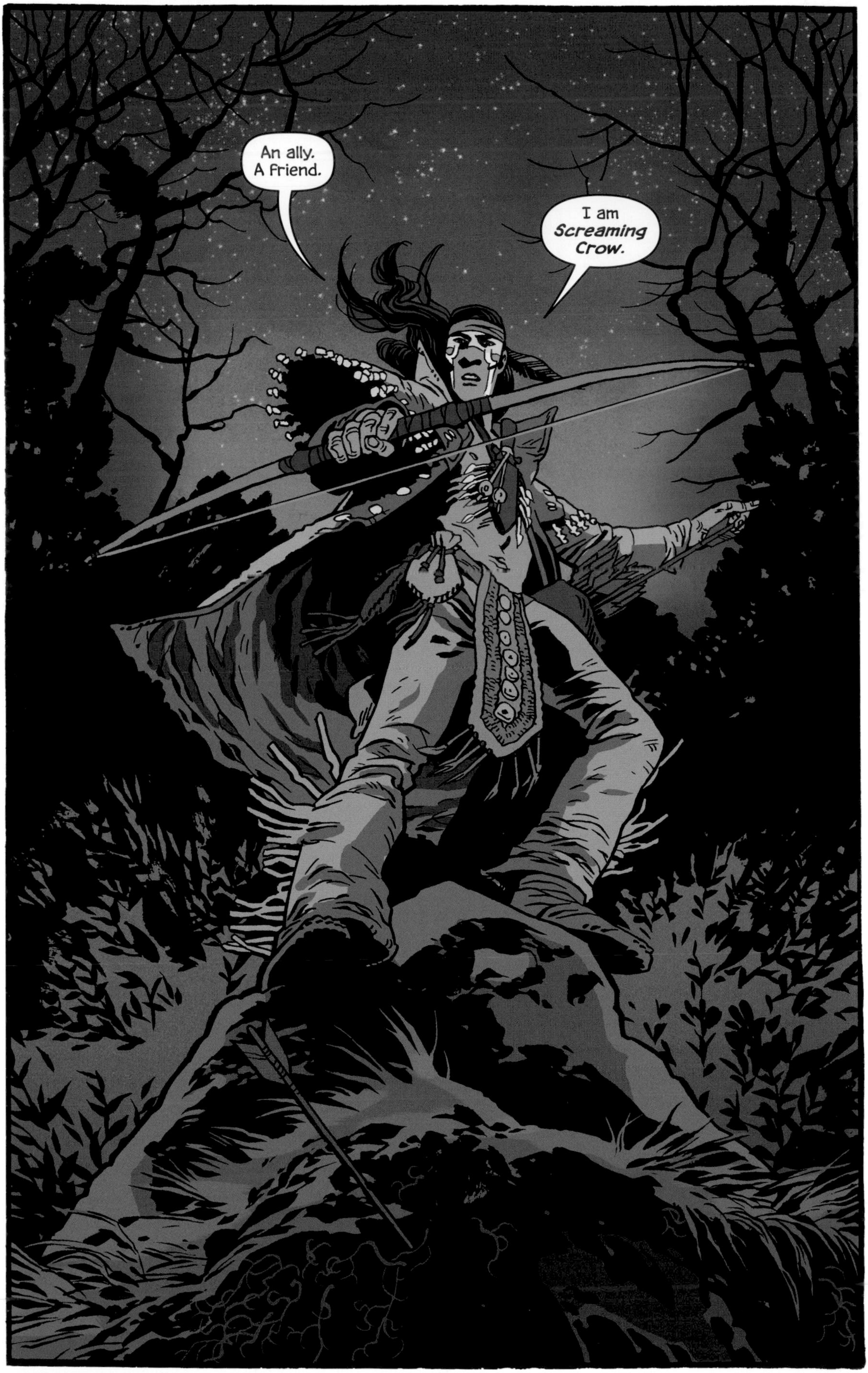
An ally. A friend.
I am *Screaming Crow.*

VALLEY OF DEATH

CHAPTER
TWO

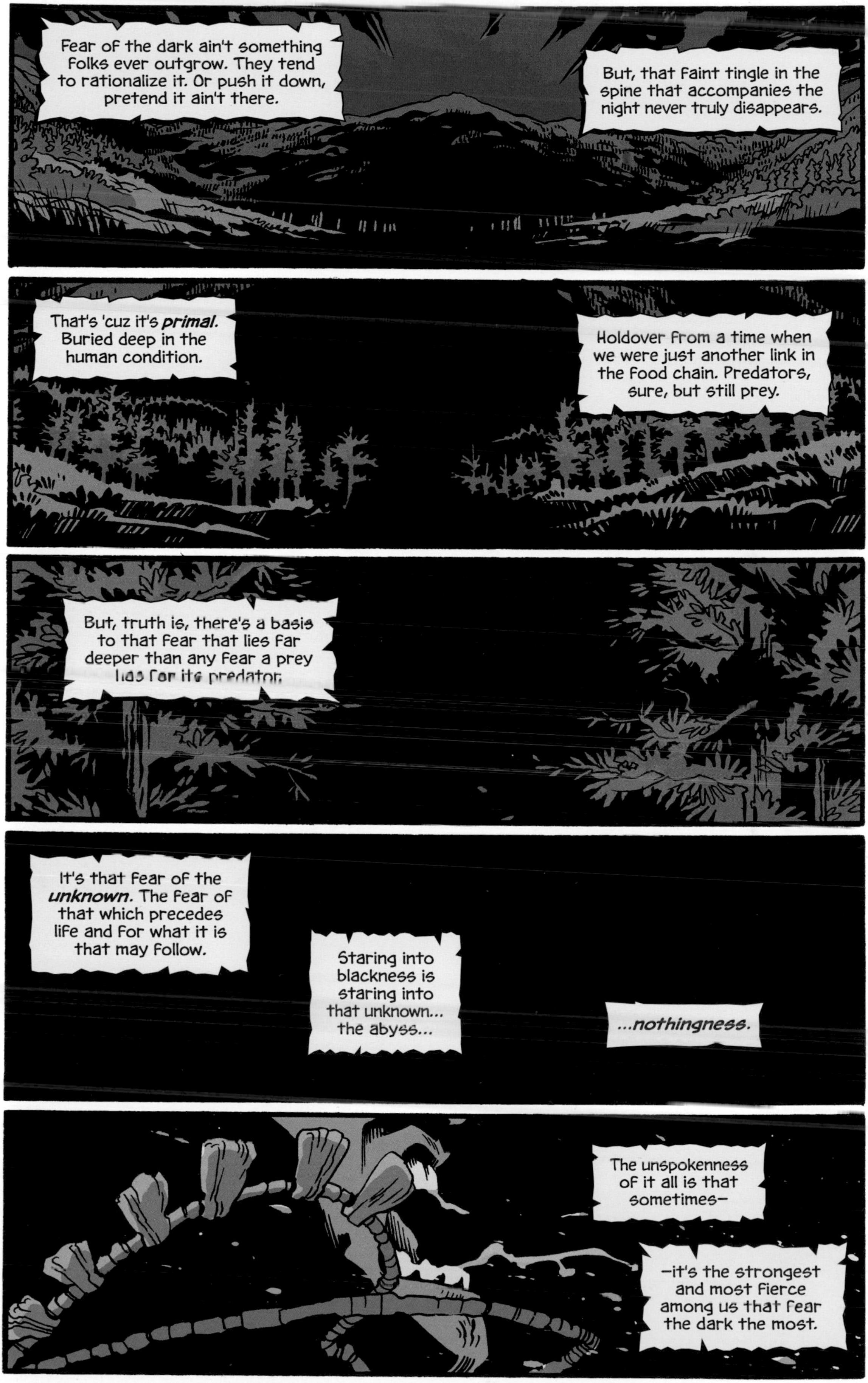
Fear of the dark ain't something folks ever outgrow. They tend to rationalize it. Or push it down, pretend it ain't there.
But, that faint tingle in the spine that accompanies the night never truly disappears.
That's 'cuz it's *primal.* Buried deep in the human condition.
Holdover from a time when we were just another link in the food chain. Predators, sure, but still prey.
But, truth is, there's a basis to that fear that lies far deeper than any fear a prey has for its predator.
It's that fear of the *unknown.* The fear of that which precedes life and for what it is that may follow.
Staring into blackness is staring into that unknown... the abyss...
...nothingness.
The unspokenness of it all is that sometimes—
—it's the strongest and most fierce among us that fear the dark the most.

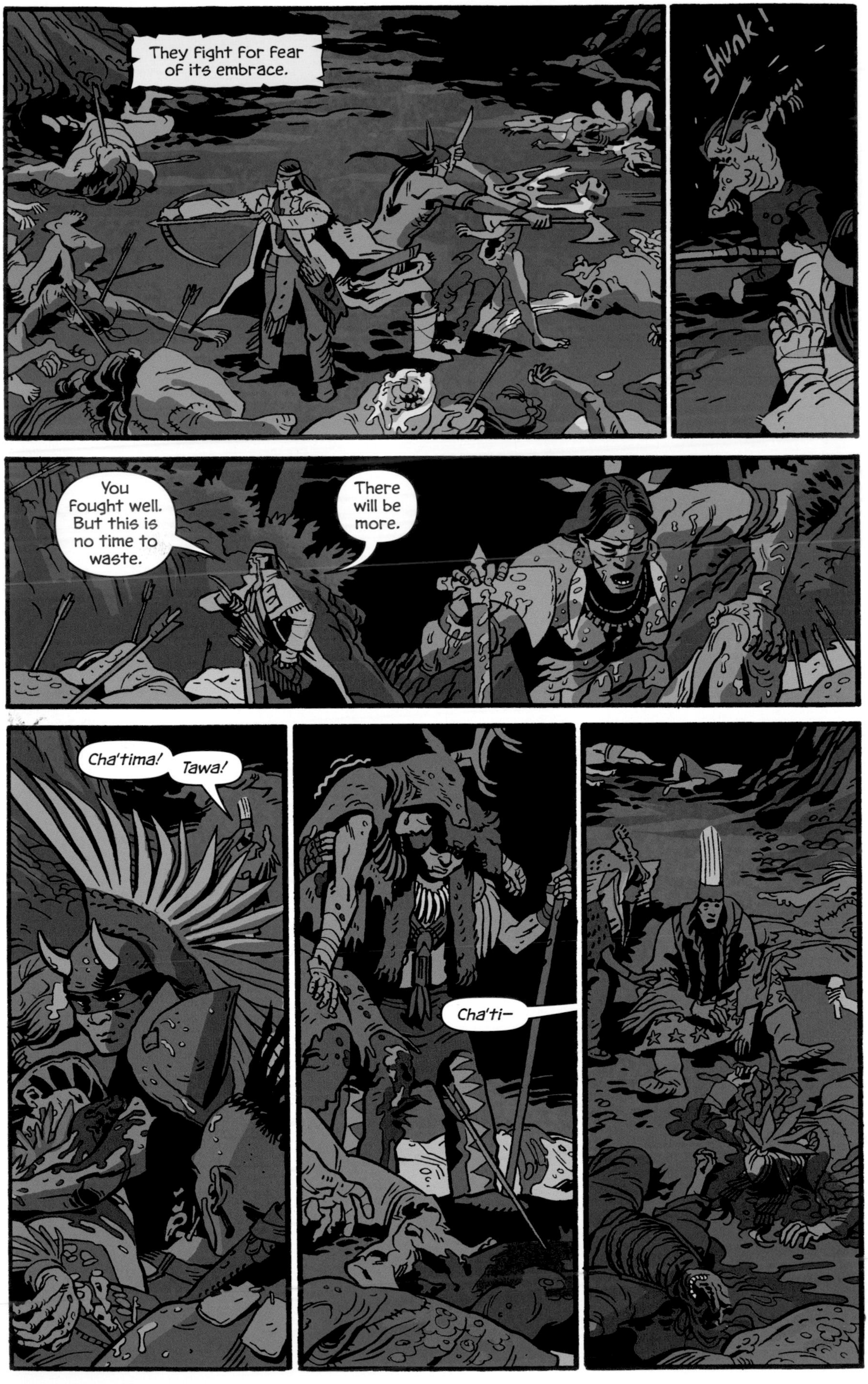

They fight for fear of its embrace.
shunk!
You fought well. But this is no time to waste.
There will be more.
Cha'tima!
Tawa!
Cha'ti—

You called yourself... *Screaming Crow?*

I did.

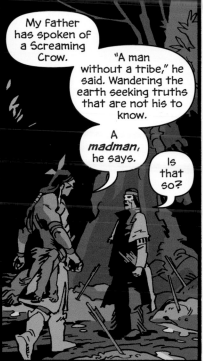

My Father has spoken of a Screaming Crow.

"A man without a tribe," he said. Wandering the earth seeking truths that are not his to know.

A *madman,* he says.

Is that so?

But my Father also said that this man is long dead.

It has been said many times before.

I begin to feel as though it is more a *wish* than an untruth.

But... we must hurry. More will be coming.

But the fallen...? We must honor them.

We have no time for rituals.

The bodies must be burned.

Burned?!

Unless you care to see the faces of your fallen amongst these abominations you will do as I say.

If not... I will not be the last warrior you meet on this journey that you once thought dead.

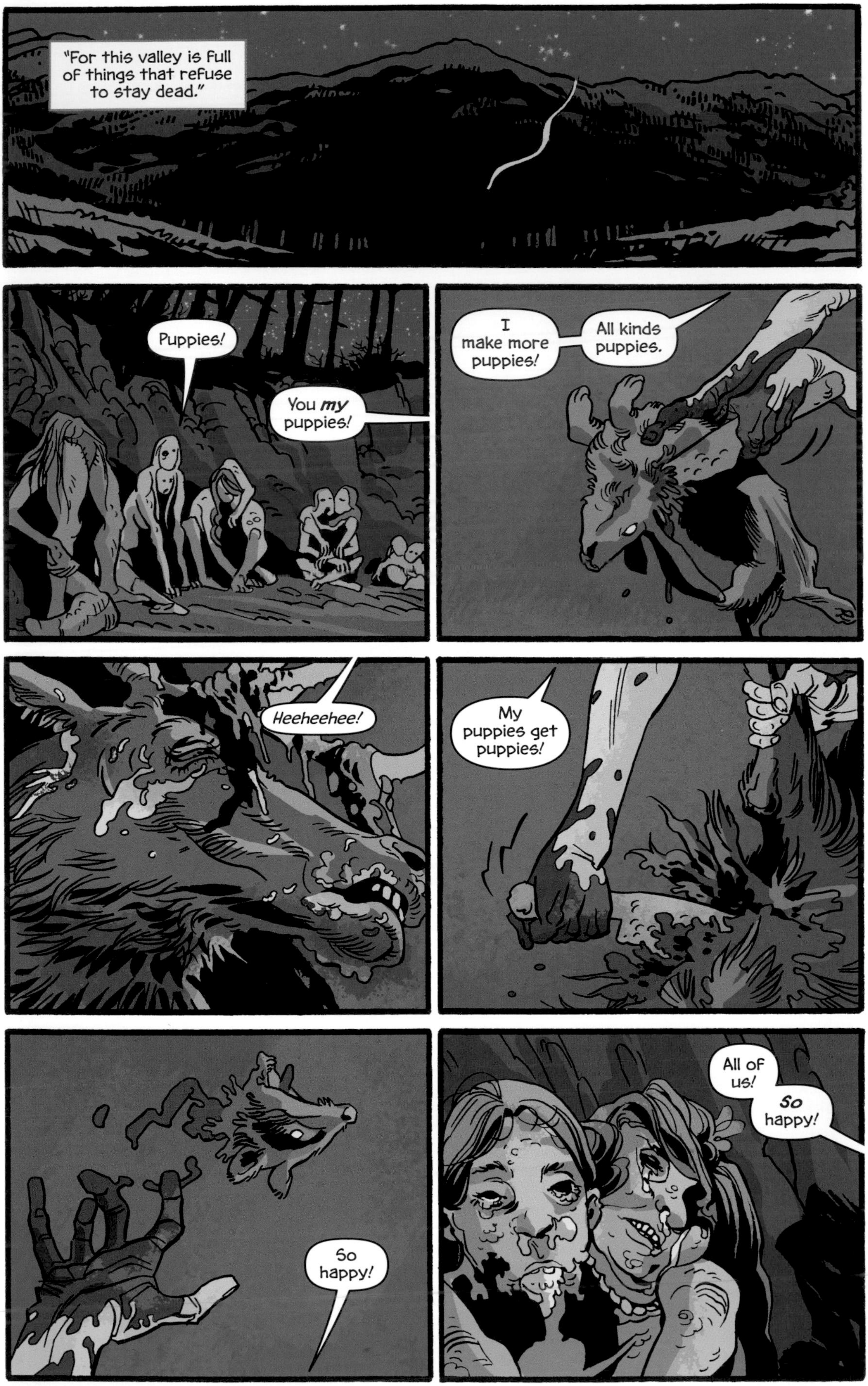
"For this valley is full of things that refuse to stay dead."
Puppies!
You *my* puppies!
I make more puppies!
All kinds puppies.
Heeheehee!
My puppies get puppies!
So happy!
All of us!
So happy!

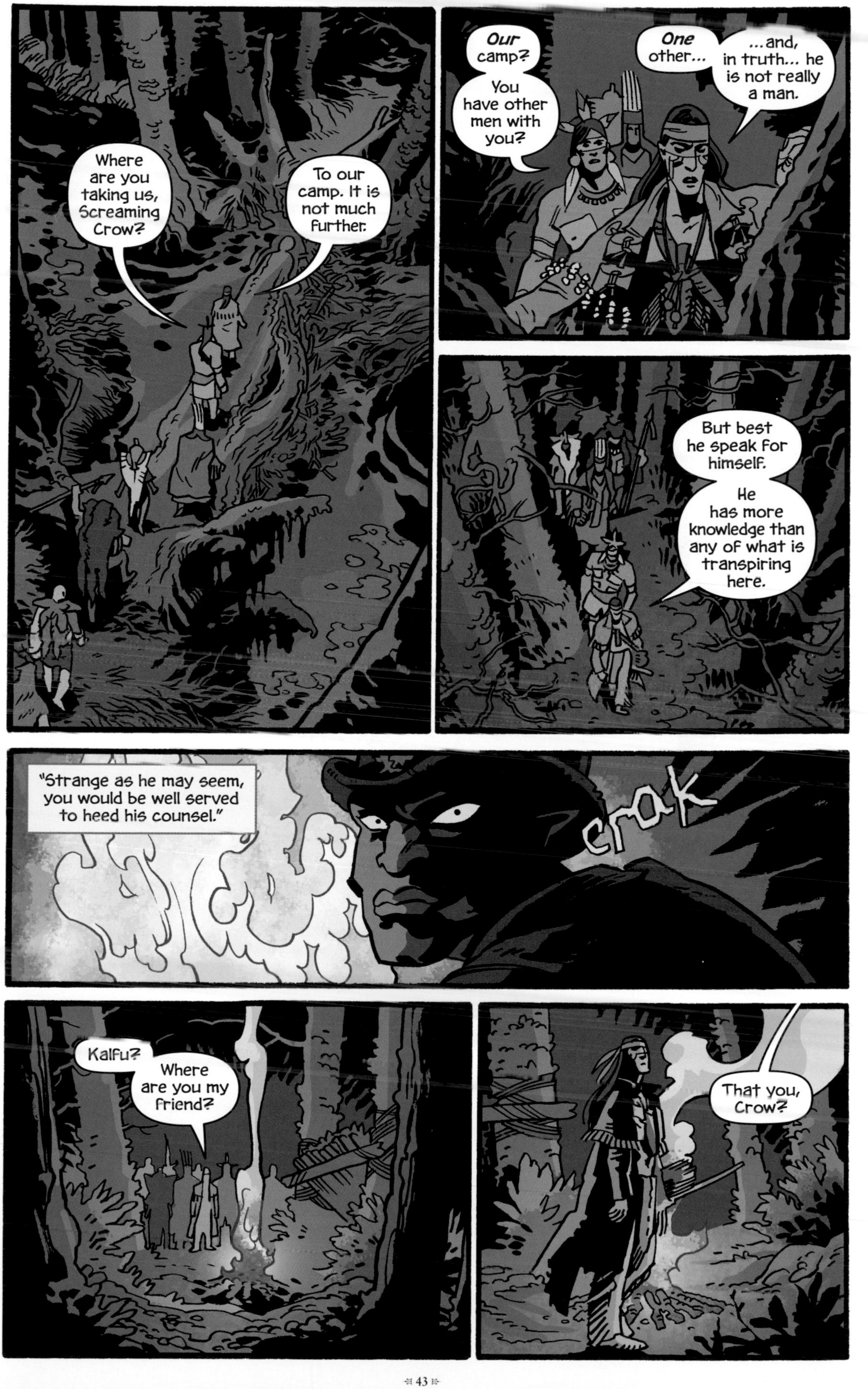
Where are you taking us, Screaming Crow?
To our camp. It is not much further.
Our camp?
You have other men with you?
One other...
...and, in truth... he is not really a man.
But best he speak for himself.
He has more knowledge than any of what is transpiring here.
"Strange as he may seem, you would be well served to heed his counsel."
CRAK
Kalfu?
Where are you my friend?
That you, Crow?

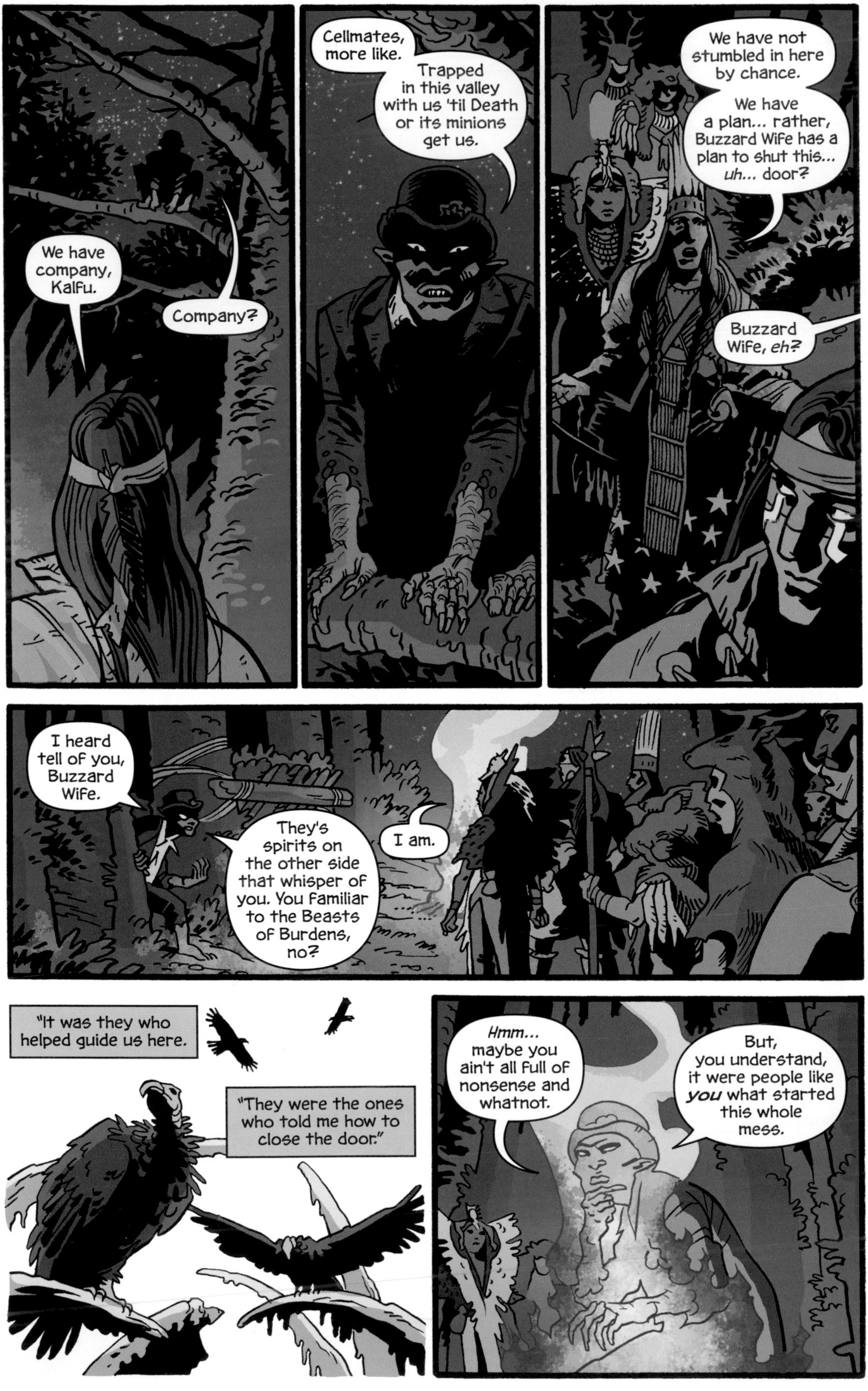
We have company, Kalfu.
Company?
Cellmates, more like.
Trapped in this valley with us 'til Death or its minions get us.
We have not stumbled in here by chance.
We have a plan... rather, Buzzard Wife has a plan to shut this... *uh...* door?
Buzzard Wife, *eh?*
I heard tell of you, Buzzard Wife.
I am.
They's spirits on the other side that whisper of you. You familiar to the Beasts of Burdens, no?
"It was they who helped guide us here.
"They were the ones who told me how to close the door."
Hmm... maybe you ain't all full of nonsense and whatnot.
But, you understand, it were people like ***you*** what started this whole mess.

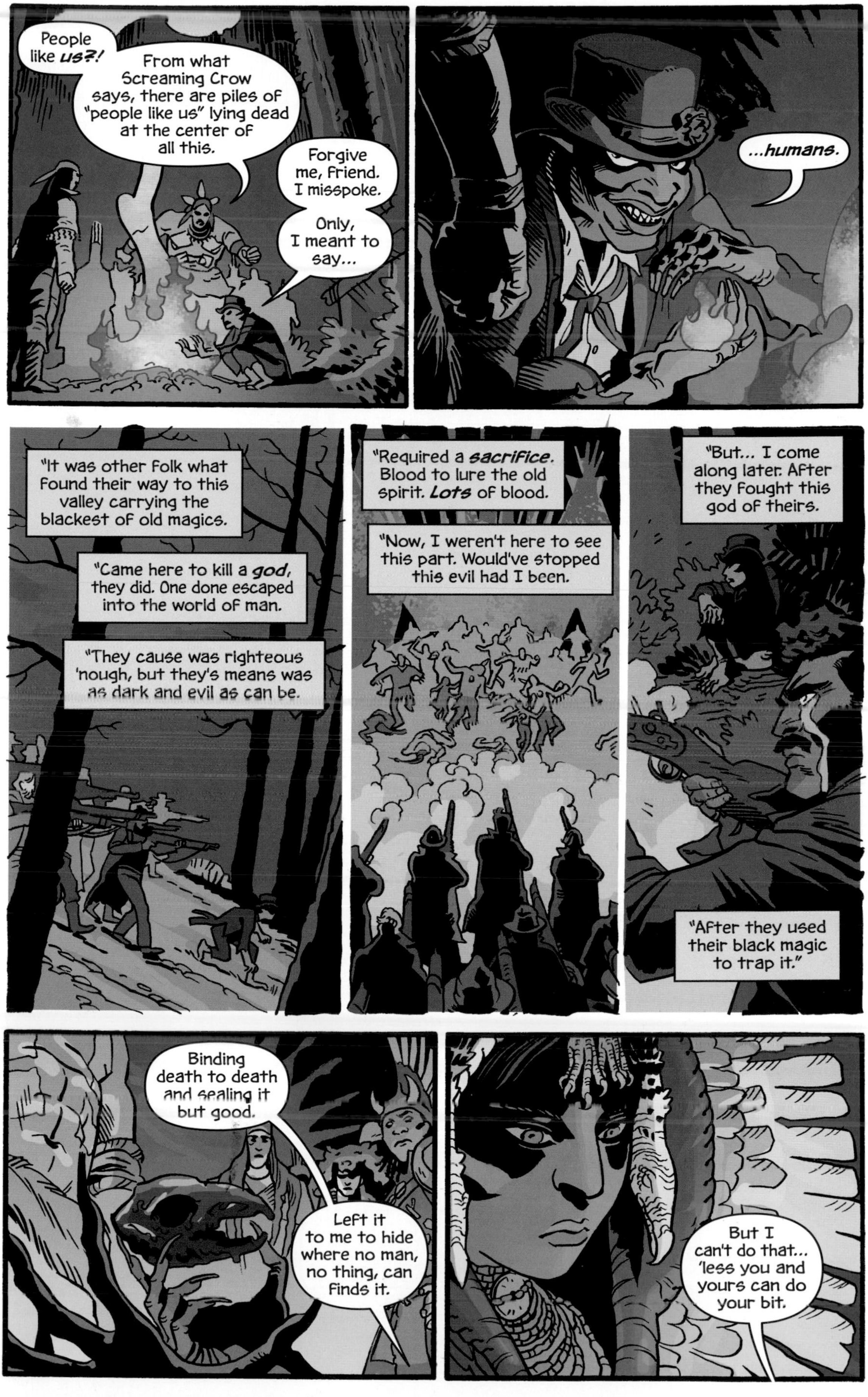
People like *us?!*
From what Screaming Crow says, there are piles of "people like us" lying dead at the center of all this.
Forgive me, Friend. I misspoke.
Only, I meant to say...
...*humans.*
"It was other folk what found their way to this valley carrying the blackest of old magics.
"Came here to kill a *god*, they did. One done escaped into the world of man.
"They cause was righteous 'nough, but they's means was as dark and evil as can be.
"Required a *sacrifice*. Blood to lure the old spirit. *Lots* of blood.
"Now, I weren't here to see this part. Would've stopped this evil had I been.
"But... I come along later. After they fought this god of theirs.
"After they used their black magic to trap it."
Binding death to death and sealing it but good.
Left it to me to hide where no man, no thing, can finds it.
But I can't do that... 'less you and yours can do your bit.

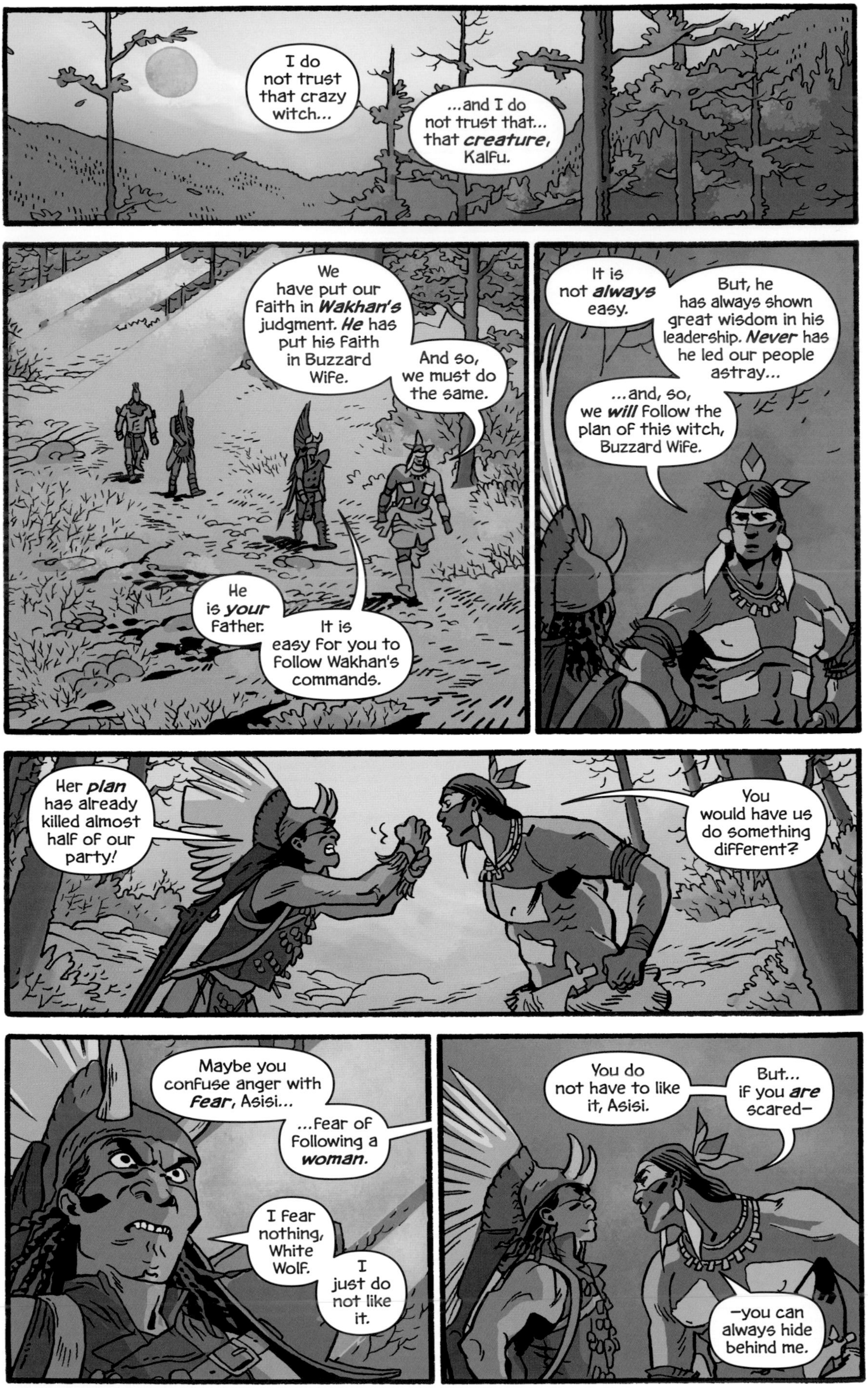
I do not trust that crazy witch...
...and I do not trust that... that *creature*, Kalfu.
We have put our faith in *Wakhan's* judgment. *He* has put his faith in Buzzard Wife.
And so, we must do the same.
He is *your* father.
It is easy for you to follow Wakhan's commands.
It is not *always* easy.
But, he has always shown great wisdom in his leadership. *Never* has he led our people astray...
...and, so, we *will* follow the plan of this witch, Buzzard Wife.
Her *plan* has already killed almost half of our party!
You would have us do something different?
Maybe you confuse anger with *fear*, Asisi...
...fear of following a *woman*.
I fear nothing, White Wolf.
I just do not like it.
You do not have to like it, Asisi.
But... if you *are* scared—
—you can always hide behind me.

SKREEEARRRGGHH!!!

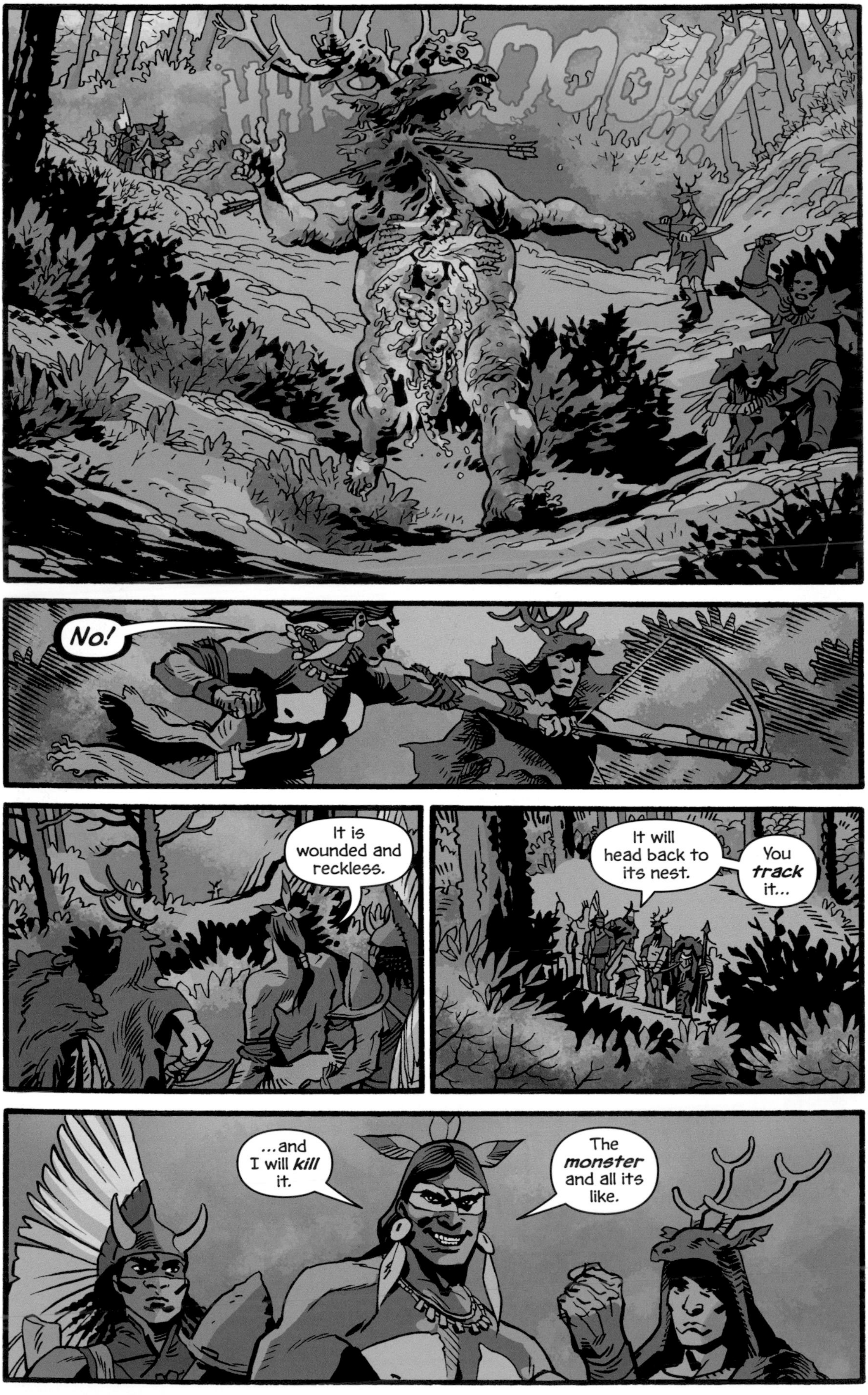

HHRROOOO!!!
No!
It is wounded and reckless.
It will head back to its nest.
You *track* it...
...and I will *kill* it.
The *monster* and all its like.

"It is as told.

"Death is spreading. Consuming everything."

It will not be long before it has taken its hold over the whole valley—

And *beyond*, sister.

Death's hunger ain't never satisfied.

Seems less like hunger... more like a *sickness*.

Sickness and plague are their own kind of hunger, Star Eyes.

Well then...

...I hope you three brought some *strong* medicine.

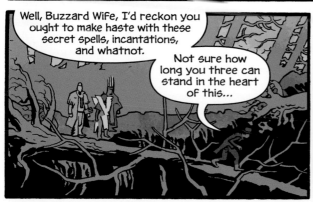

Well, Buzzard Wife, I'd reckon you ought to make haste with these secret spells, incantations, and whatnot.

Not sure how long you three can stand in the heart of this...

...'fore Death lay claim to you as well.

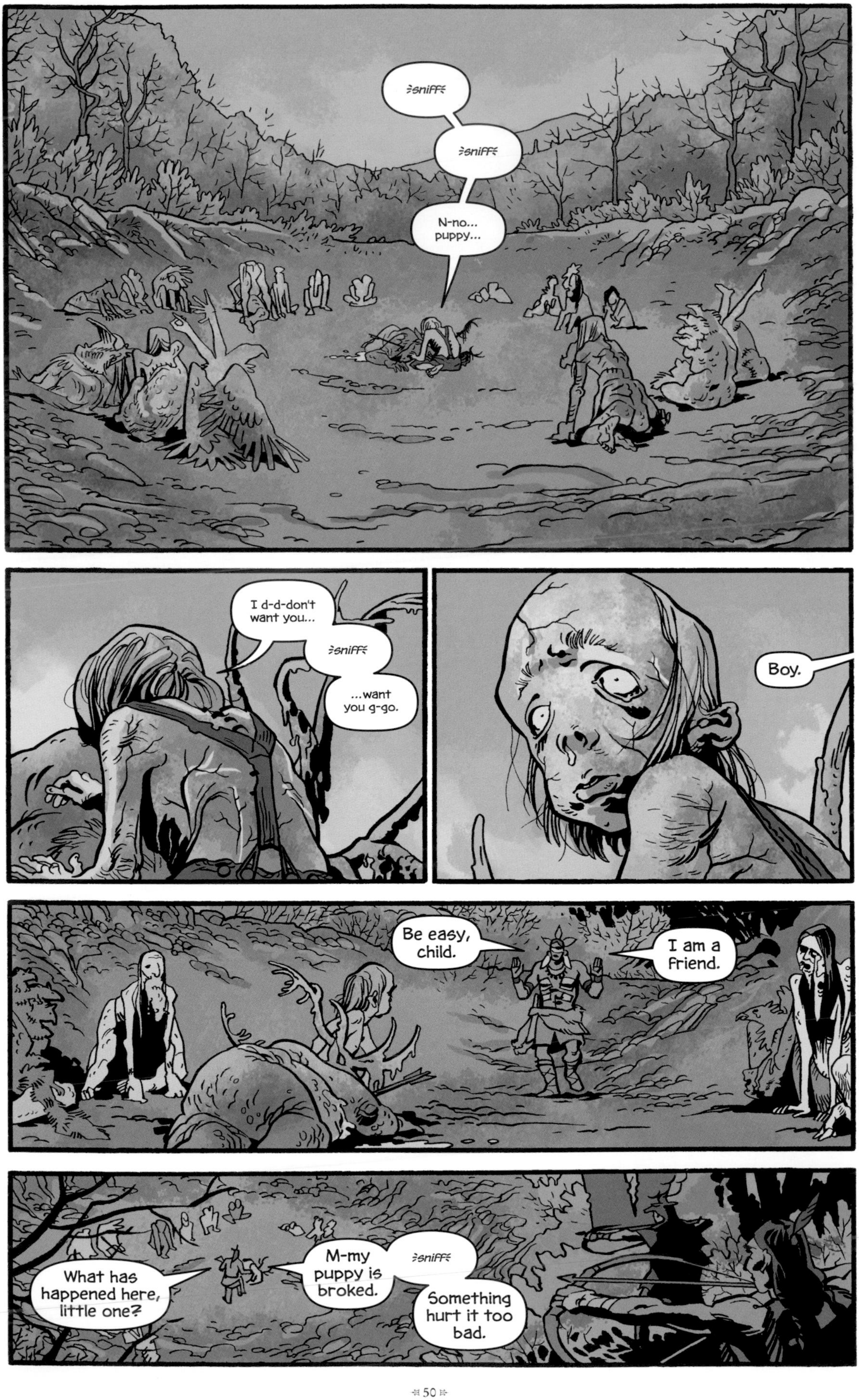

≈sniff≈
≈sniff≈
N-no... puppy...
I d-d-don't want you...
≈sniff≈
...want you g-go.
Boy.
Be easy, child.
I am a friend.
What has happened here, little one?
M-my puppy is broked.
≈sniff≈
Something hurt it too bad.

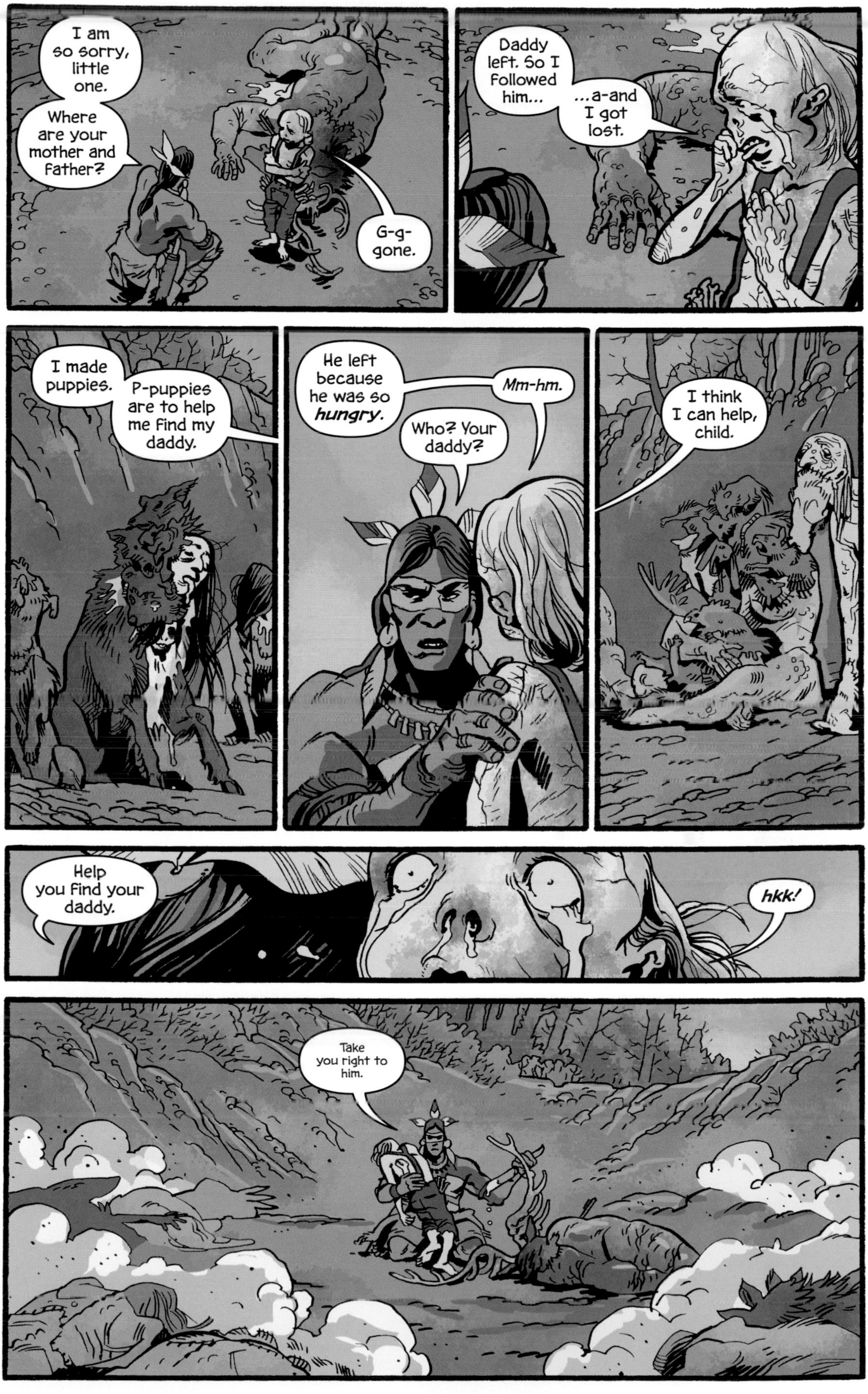
I am so sorry, little one.
Where are your mother and father?
G-g-gone.
Daddy left. So I followed him...
...a-and I got lost.
I made puppies.
P-puppies are to help me find my daddy.
He left because he was so *hungry*.
Mm-hm.
Who? Your daddy?
I think I can help, child.
Help you find your daddy.
hkk!
Take you right to him.

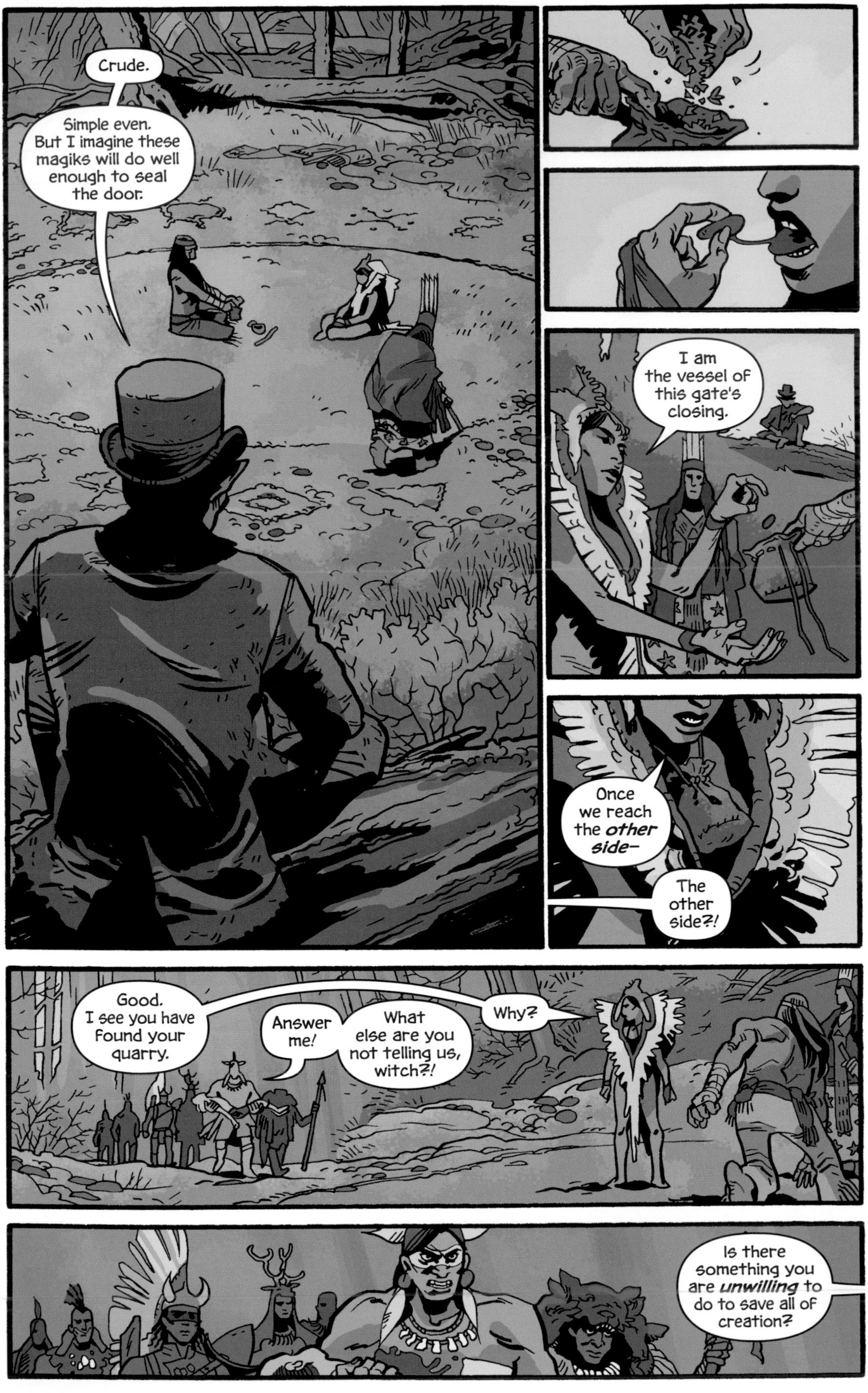
Crude.
Simple even. But I imagine these magiks will do well enough to seal the door.
I am the vessel of this gate's closing.
Once we reach the *other side*—
The other side?!
Good. I see you have found your quarry.
Answer me!
What else are you not telling us, witch?!
Why?
Is there something you are *unwilling* to do to save all of creation?

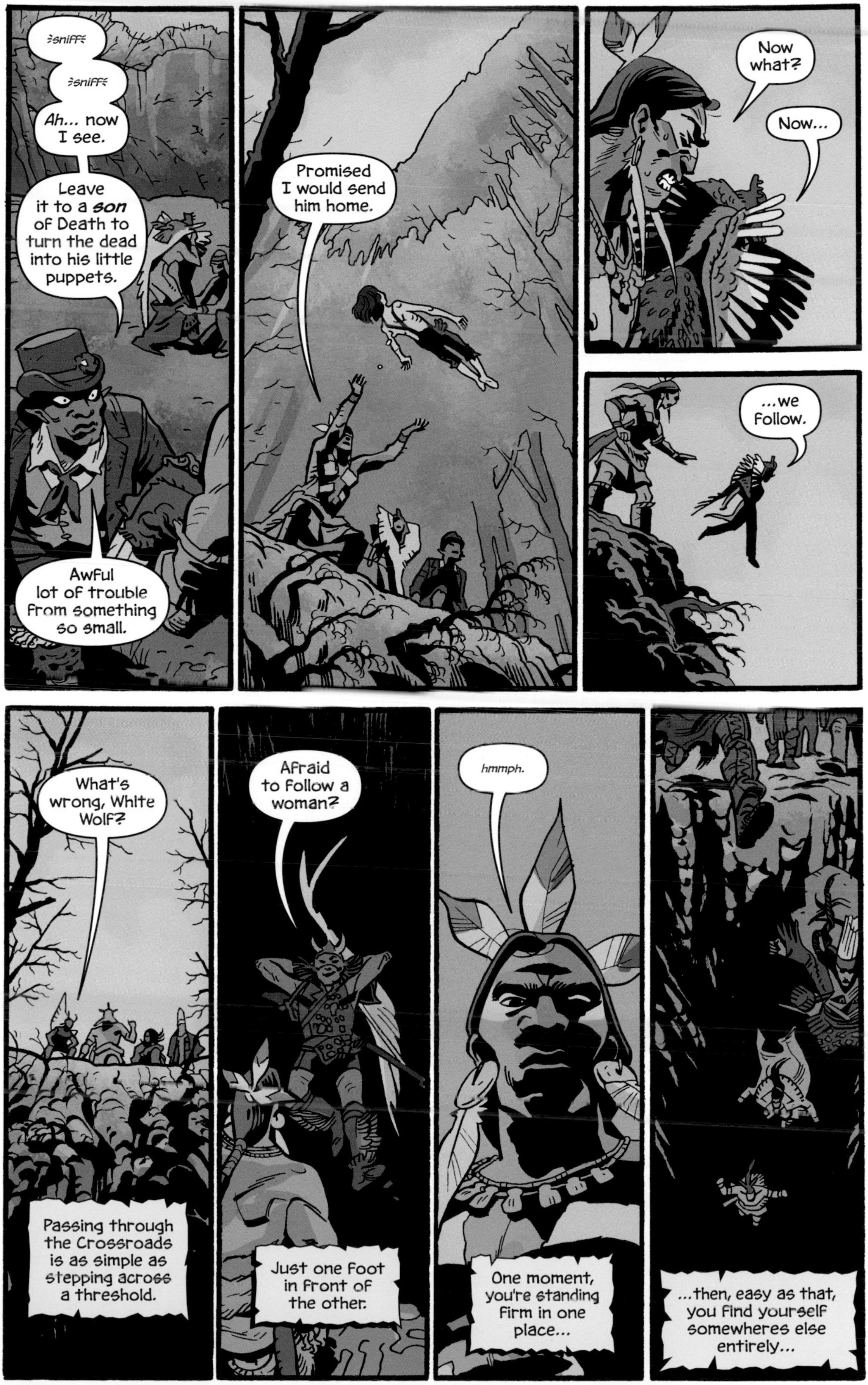

sniff
sniff
Ah... now I see.
Leave it to a *son* of Death to turn the dead into his little puppets.
Awful lot of trouble from something so small.
Promised I would send him home.
Now what?
Now...
...we follow.
What's wrong, White Wolf?
Passing through the Crossroads is as simple as stepping across a threshold.
Afraid to follow a woman?
Just one foot in front of the other.
hmmph.
One moment, you're standing firm in one place...
...then, easy as that, you find yourself somewheres else entirely...

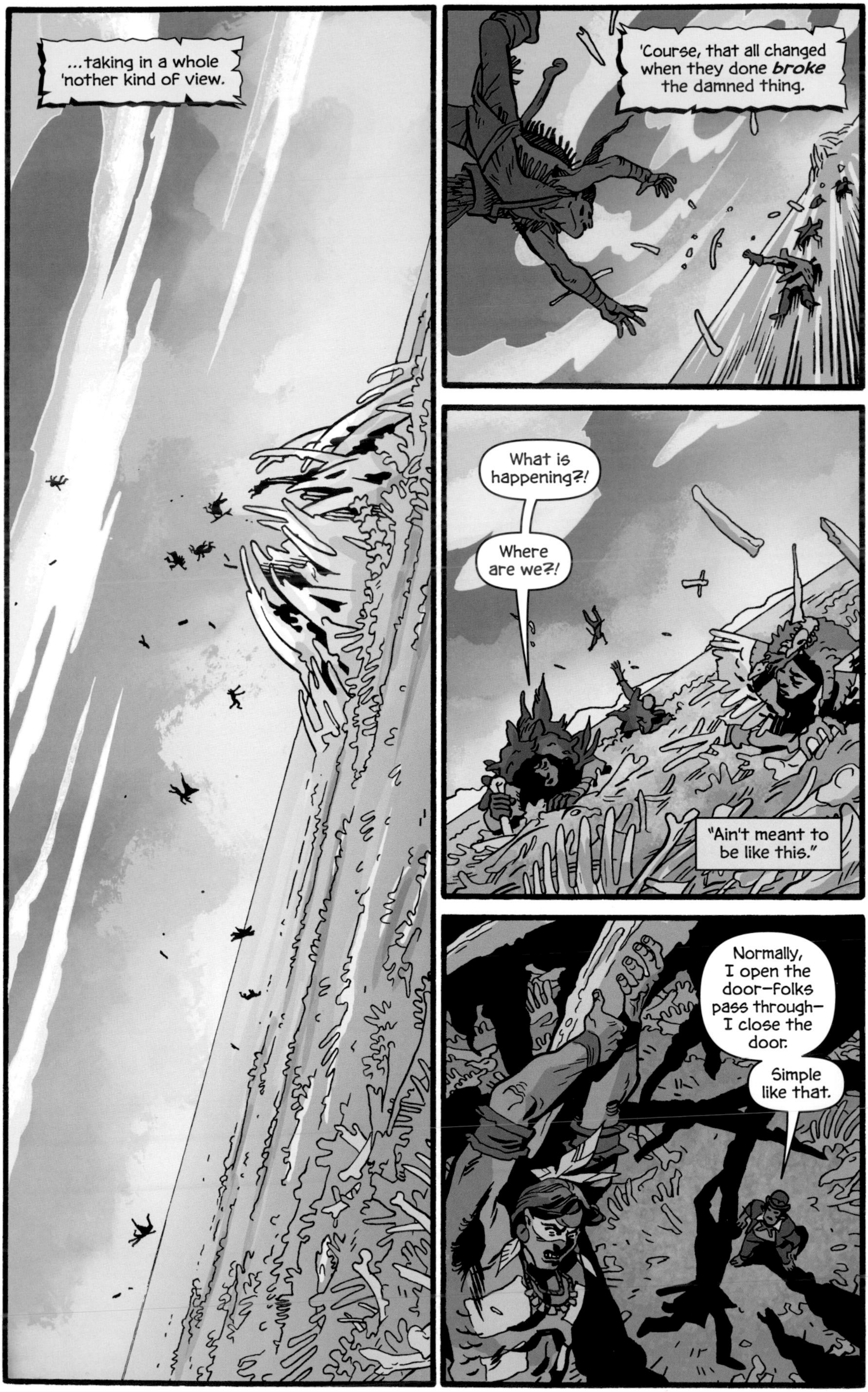
...taking in a whole 'nother kind of view.
'Course, that all changed when they done *broke* the damned thing.
What is happening?!
Where are we?!
"Ain't meant to be like this."
Normally, I open the door—folks pass through— I close the door.
Simple like that.

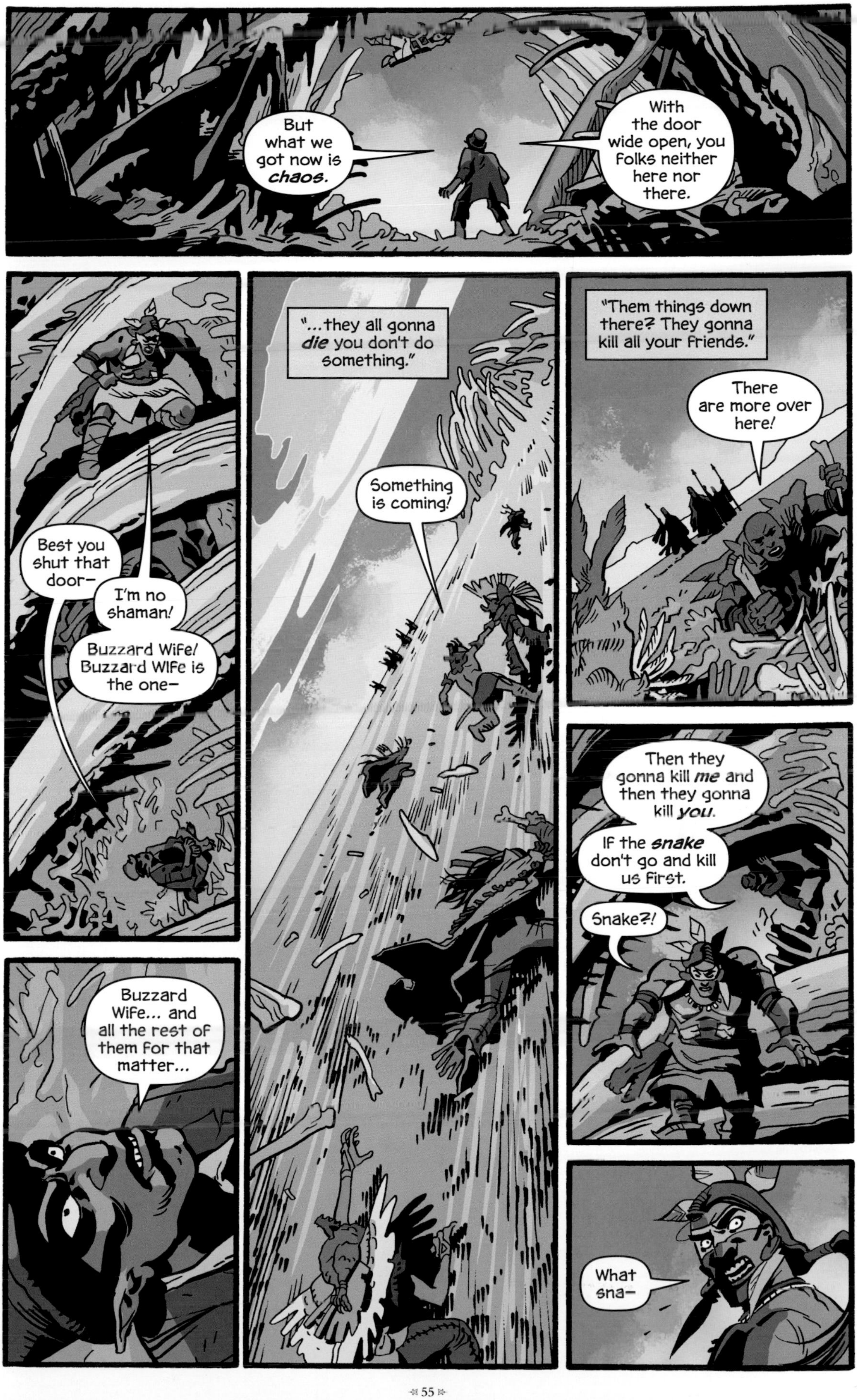
But what we got now is *chaos.*
With the door wide open, you folks neither here nor there.
Best you shut that door—
I'm no shaman!
Buzzard Wife! Buzzard Wife is the one—
"...they all gonna *die* you don't do something."
Something is coming!
"Them things down there? They gonna kill all your friends."
There are more over here!
Then they gonna kill *me* and then they gonna kill *you*.
If the *snake* don't go and kill us first.
Snake?!
Buzzard Wife... and all the rest of them for that matter...
What sna—

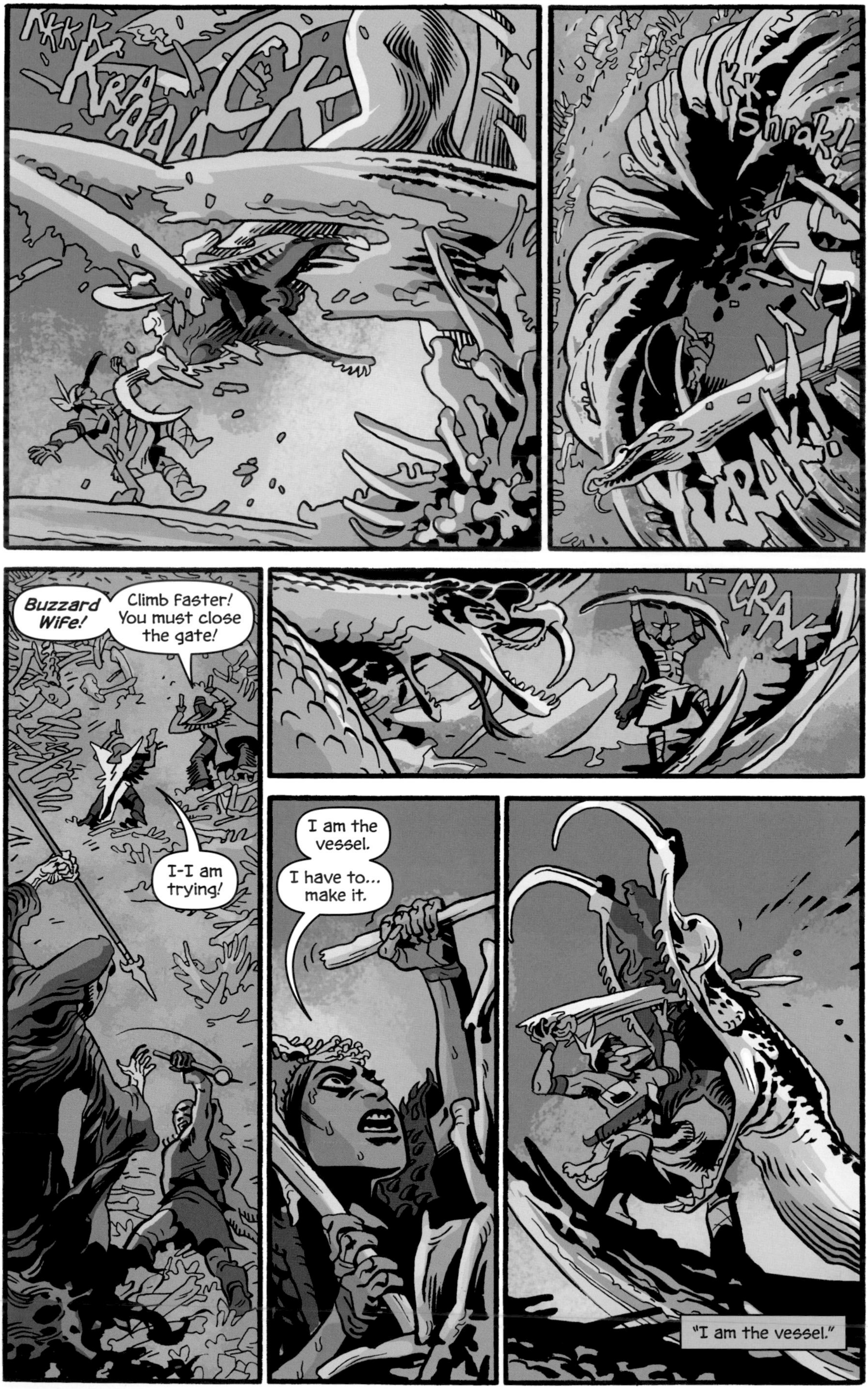
KKK KRAAACK
KK-SHRAK!
KRAK!
Buzzard Wife!
Climb faster! You must close the gate!
I-I am trying!
R-CRAK!
I am the vessel.
I have to... make it.
"I am the vessel."

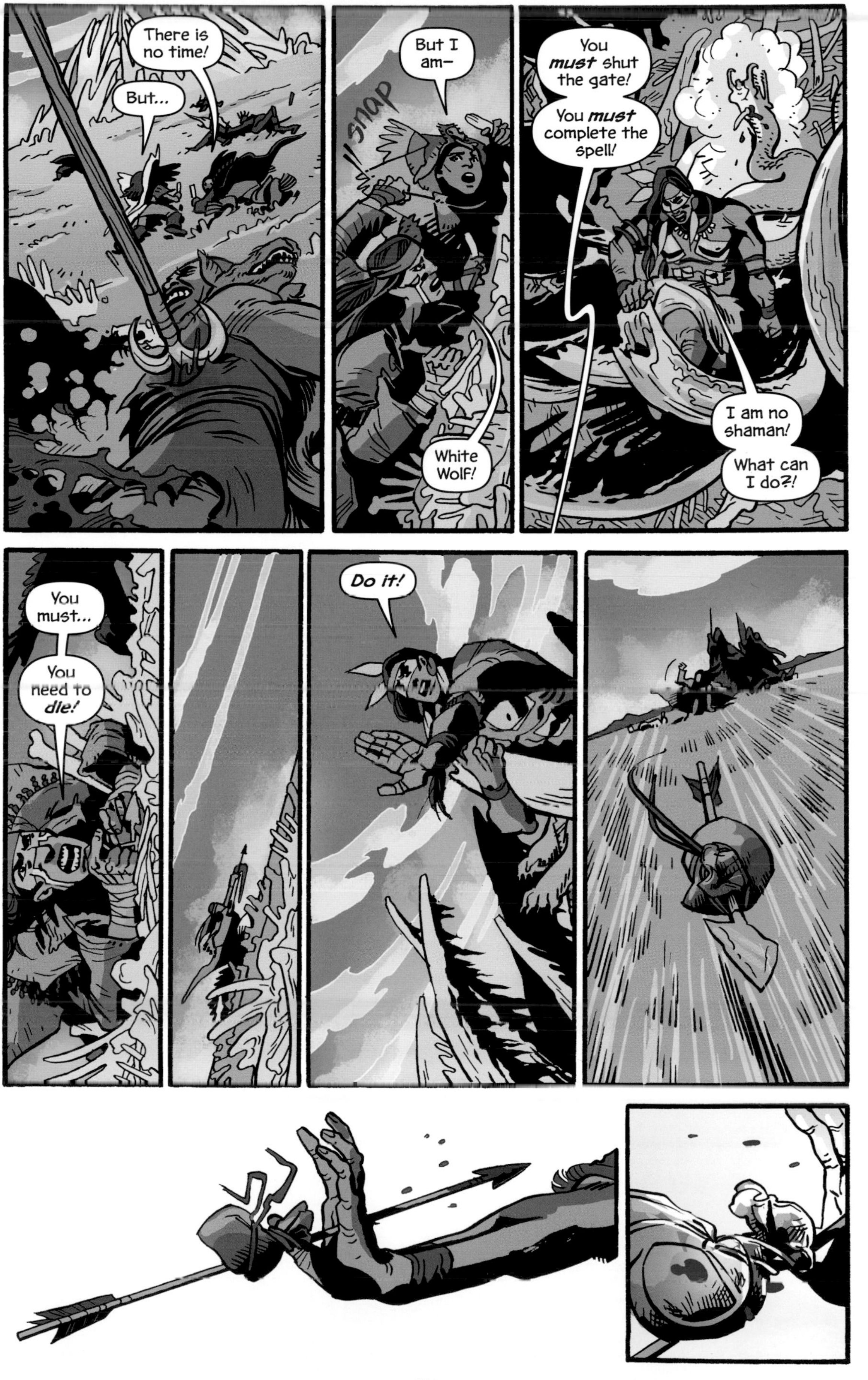

There is no time!
But...
But I am—
snap
White Wolf!
You must shut the gate!
You must complete the spell!
I am no shaman!
What can I do?!
You must...
You need to die!
Do it!

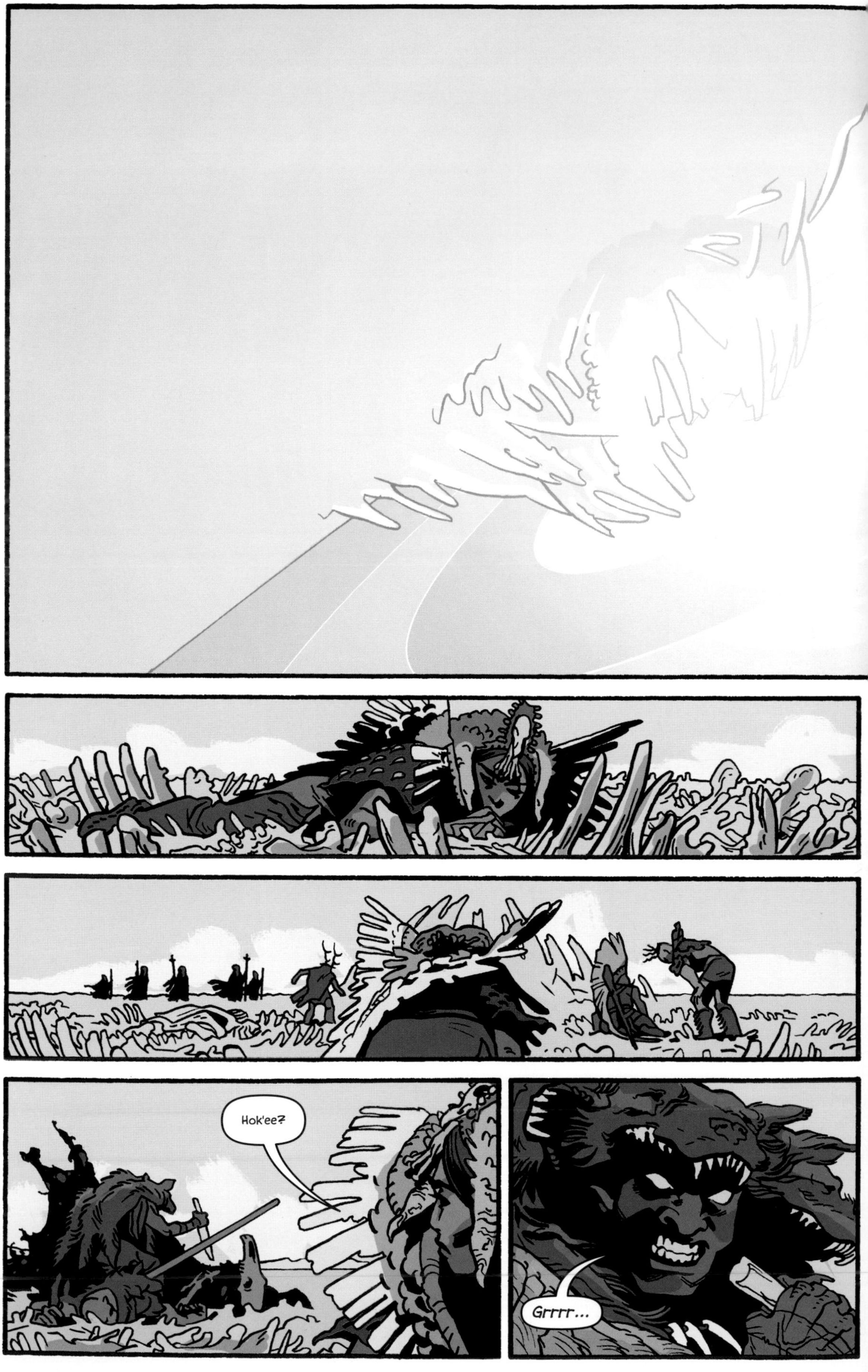
Hok'ee?
Grrrr...

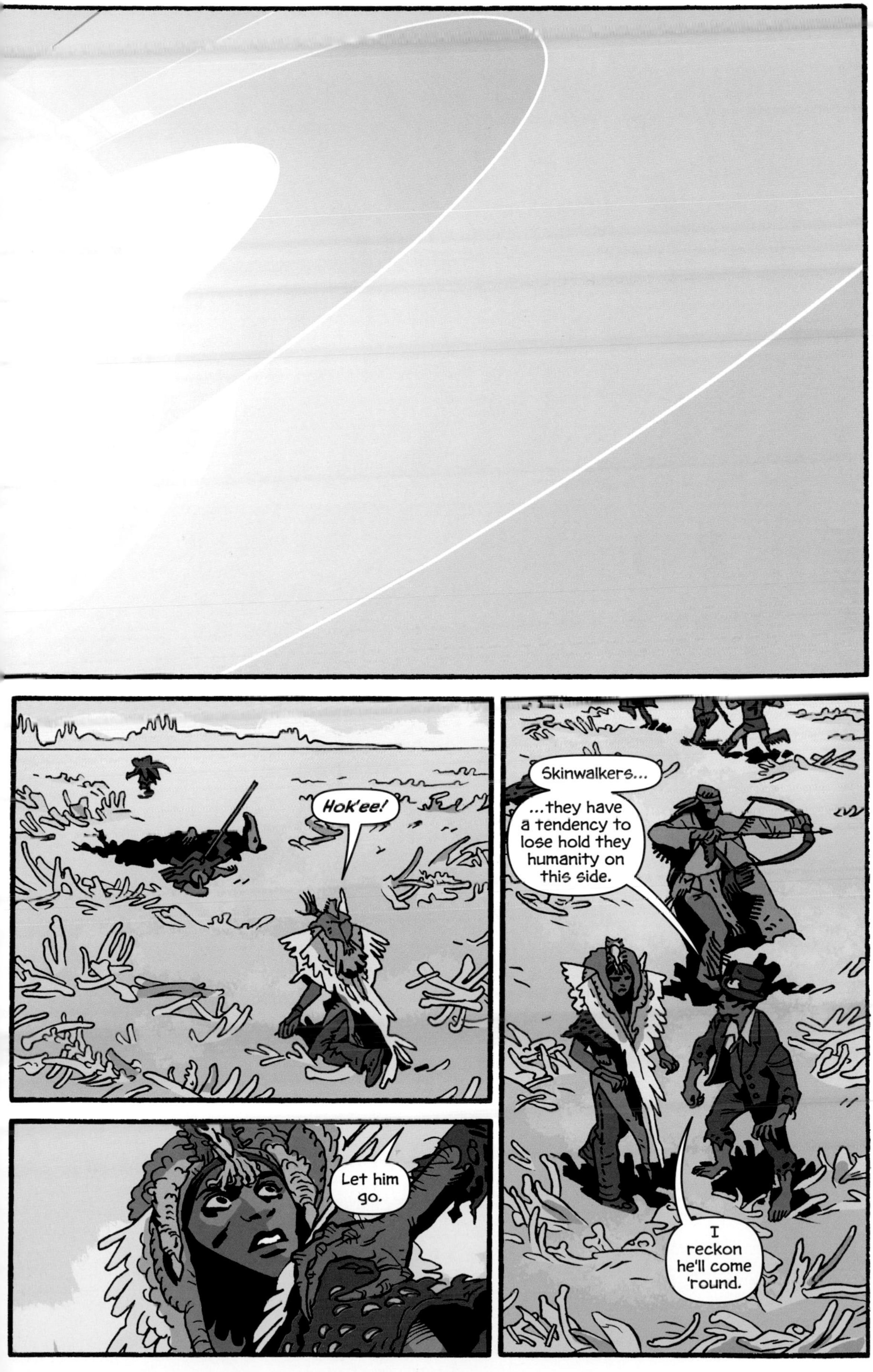
Hok'ee!
Let him go.
Skinwalkers...
...they have a tendency to lose hold they humanity on this side.
I reckon he'll come 'round.

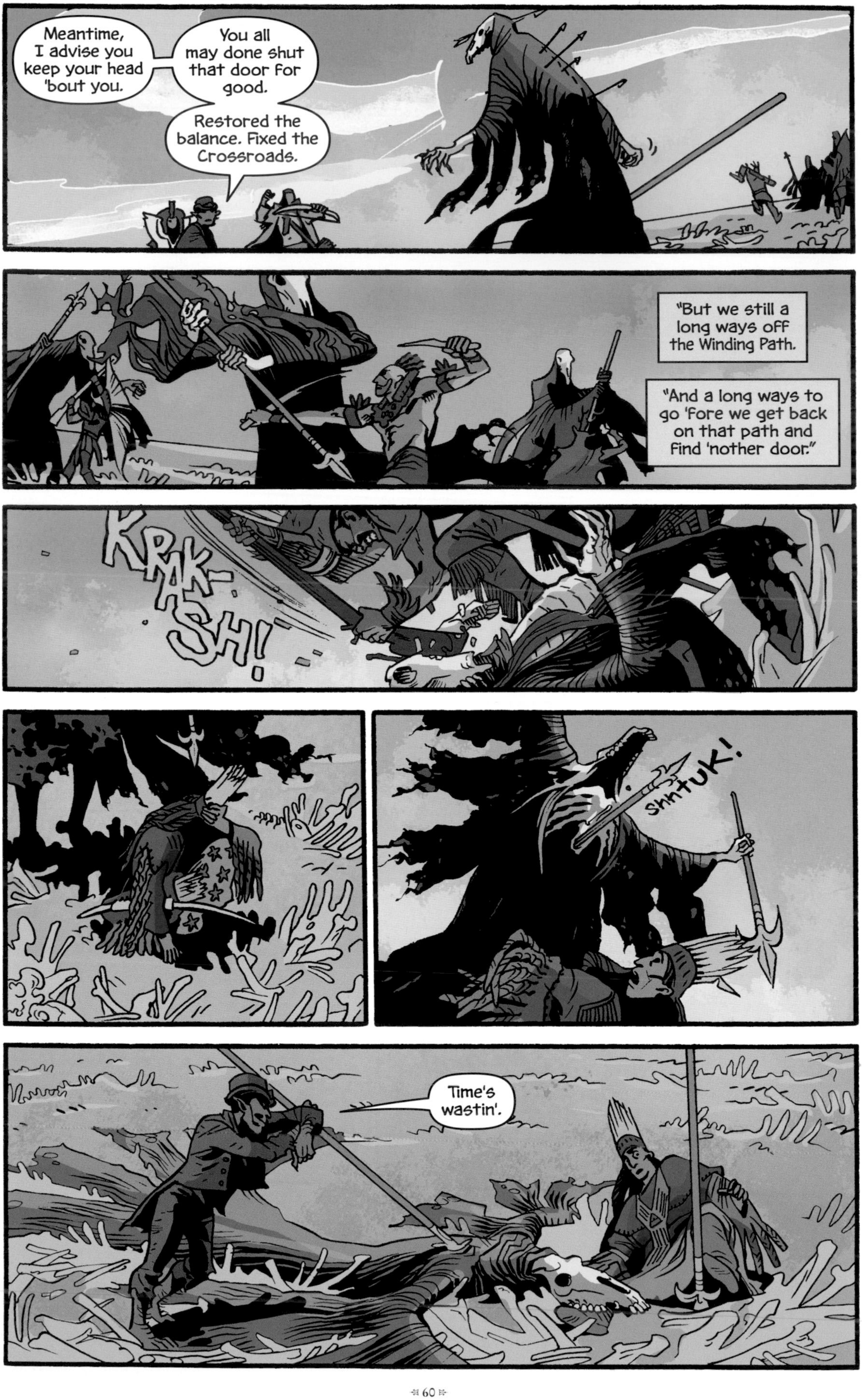

Meantime, I advise you keep your head 'bout you.
You all may done shut that door for good.
Restored the balance. Fixed the Crossroads.
"But we still a long ways off the Winding Path.
"And a long ways to go 'fore we get back on that path and find 'nother door."
KRAK-SH!
shhTUK!
Time's wastin'.

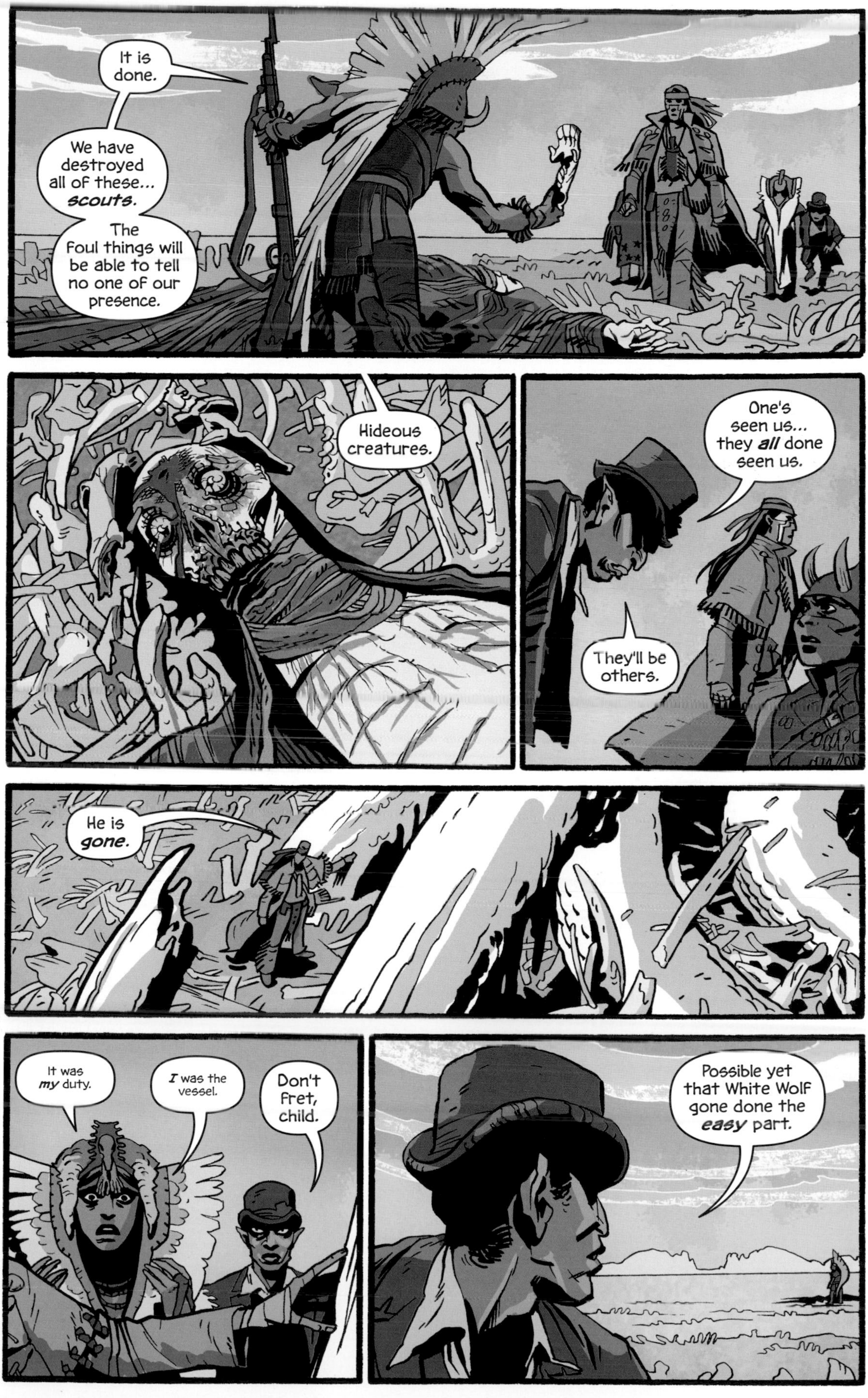
It is done.
We have destroyed all of these... *scouts*.
The foul things will be able to tell no one of our presence.
Hideous creatures.
One's seen us... they *all* done seen us.
They'll be others.
He is *gone*.
It was *my* duty.
I was the vessel.
Don't fret, child.
Possible yet that White Wolf gone done the *easy* part.

The *Winding Path* and its multitude of arteries spider out across all of creation.

Hidden there, in its mysterious pattern, is a place, a beginning and an ending point, all in one.

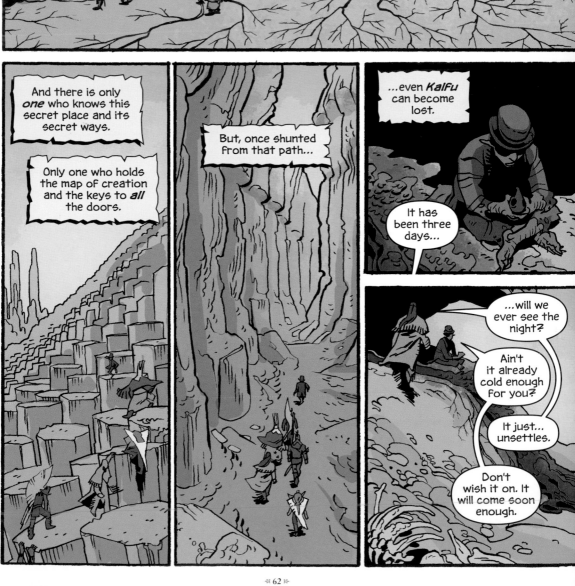

And there is only *one* who knows this secret place and its secret ways.

Only one who holds the map of creation and the keys to *all* the doors.

But, once shunted from that path...

...even *Kalfu* can become lost.

It has been three days...

...will we ever see the night?

Ain't it already cold enough for you?

It just... unsettles.

Don't wish it on. It will come soon enough.

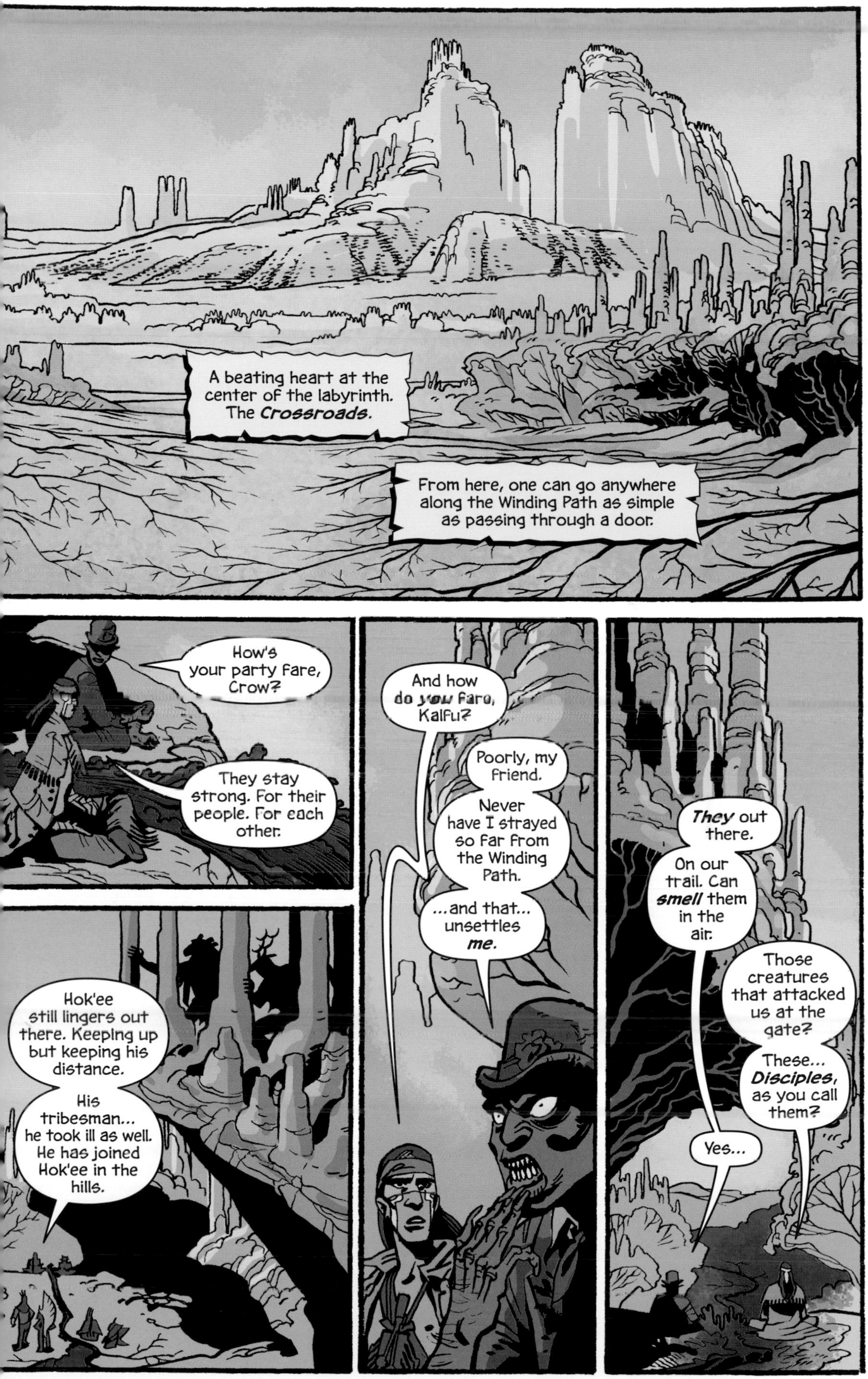
A beating heart at the center of the labyrinth. The *Crossroads.*
From here, one can go anywhere along the Winding Path as simple as passing through a door.
How's your party fare, Crow?
They stay strong. For their people. For each other.
Hok'ee still lingers out there. Keeping up but keeping his distance.
His tribesman... he took ill as well. He has joined Hok'ee in the hills.
And how do *you* fare, Kalfu?
Poorly, my friend.
Never have I strayed so far from the Winding Path.
...and that... unsettles *me.*
They out there.
On our trail. Can *smell* them in the air.
Those creatures that attacked us at the gate?
These... *Disciples,* as you call them?
Yes...

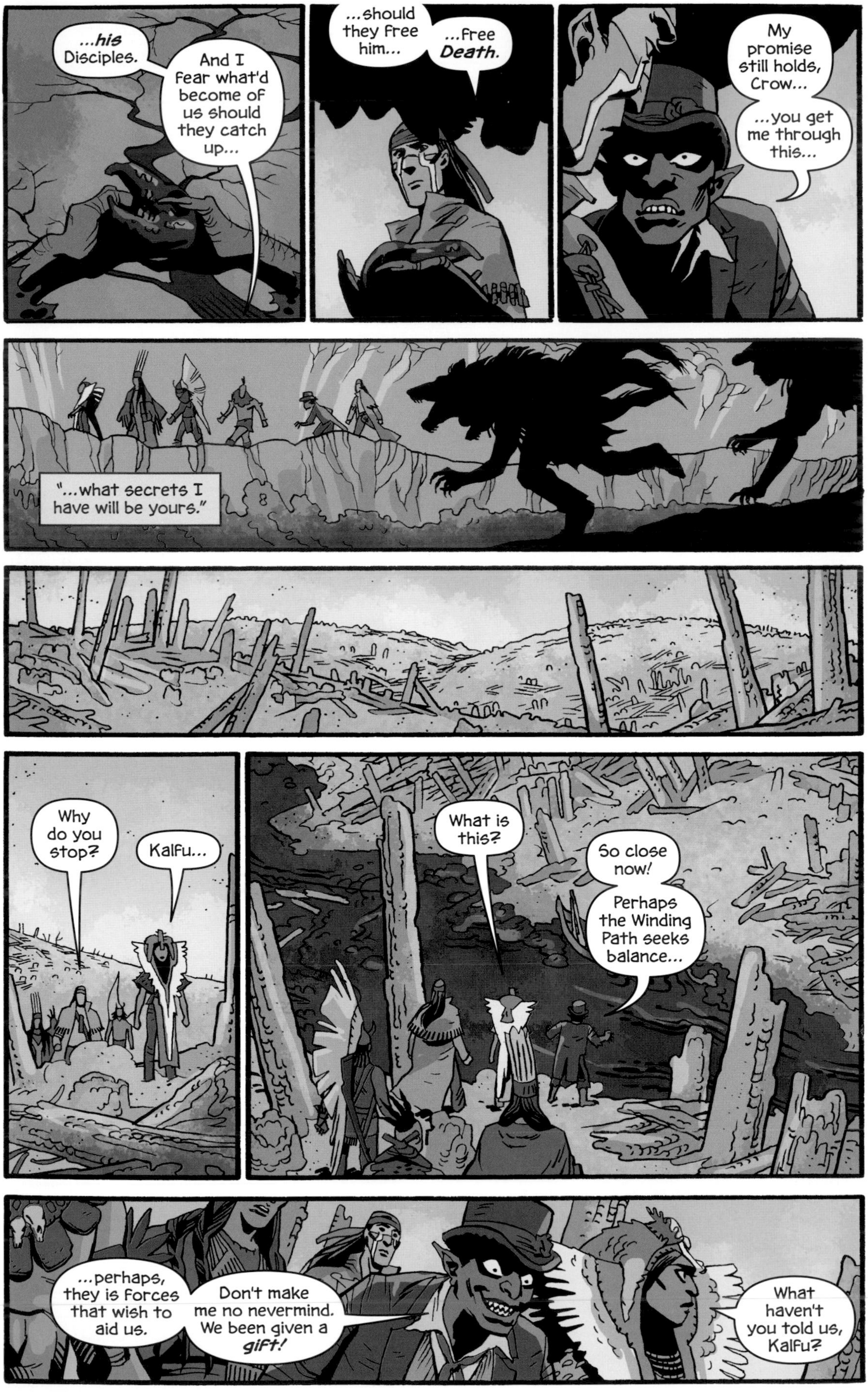
...*his* Disciples.
And I fear what'd become of us should they catch up...
...should they free him...
...free *Death*.
My promise still holds, Crow...
...you get me through this...
"...what secrets I have will be yours."
Why do you stop?
Kalfu...
What is this?
So close now!
Perhaps the Winding Path seeks balance...
...perhaps, they is forces that wish to aid us.
Don't make me no nevermind. We been given a *gift!*
What haven't you told us, Kalfu?

What tribe would call this place home?

What tribe?

None!

What you on about?

The *canoes*. The *longhouse*.

That is the place of a great chieftain.

Canoes? Longhouse?

That what you see?

Curious...

All's I see is the House of Death, himself.

Even though no one's home, I'd still like to get down river.

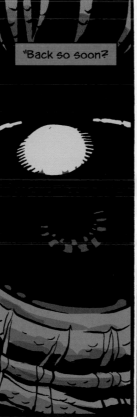

"Back so soon?

"Truly, it is a poor substitute for the real thing.

"Yet, I cannot seem to get enough of you dying."

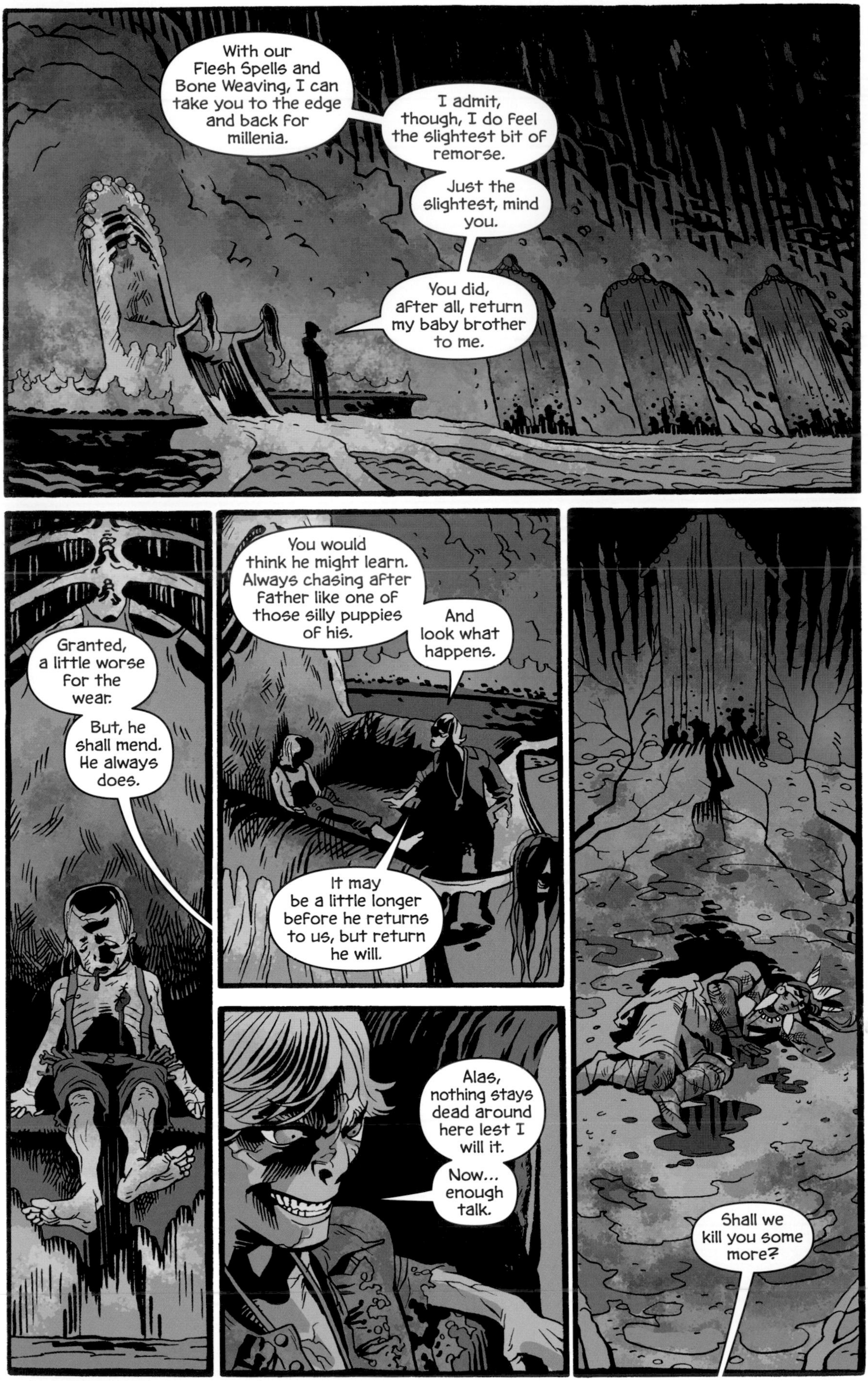
With our Flesh Spells and Bone Weaving, I can take you to the edge and back for millenia.
I admit, though, I do feel the slightest bit of remorse.
Just the slightest, mind you.
You did, after all, return my baby brother to me.
Granted, a little worse for the wear.
But, he shall mend. He always does.
You would think he might learn. Always chasing after Father like one of those silly puppies of his.
And look what happens.
It may be a little longer before he returns to us, but return he will.
Alas, nothing stays dead around here lest I will it.
Now... enough talk.
Shall we kill you some more?

VALLEY OF DEATH

CHAPTER
THREE

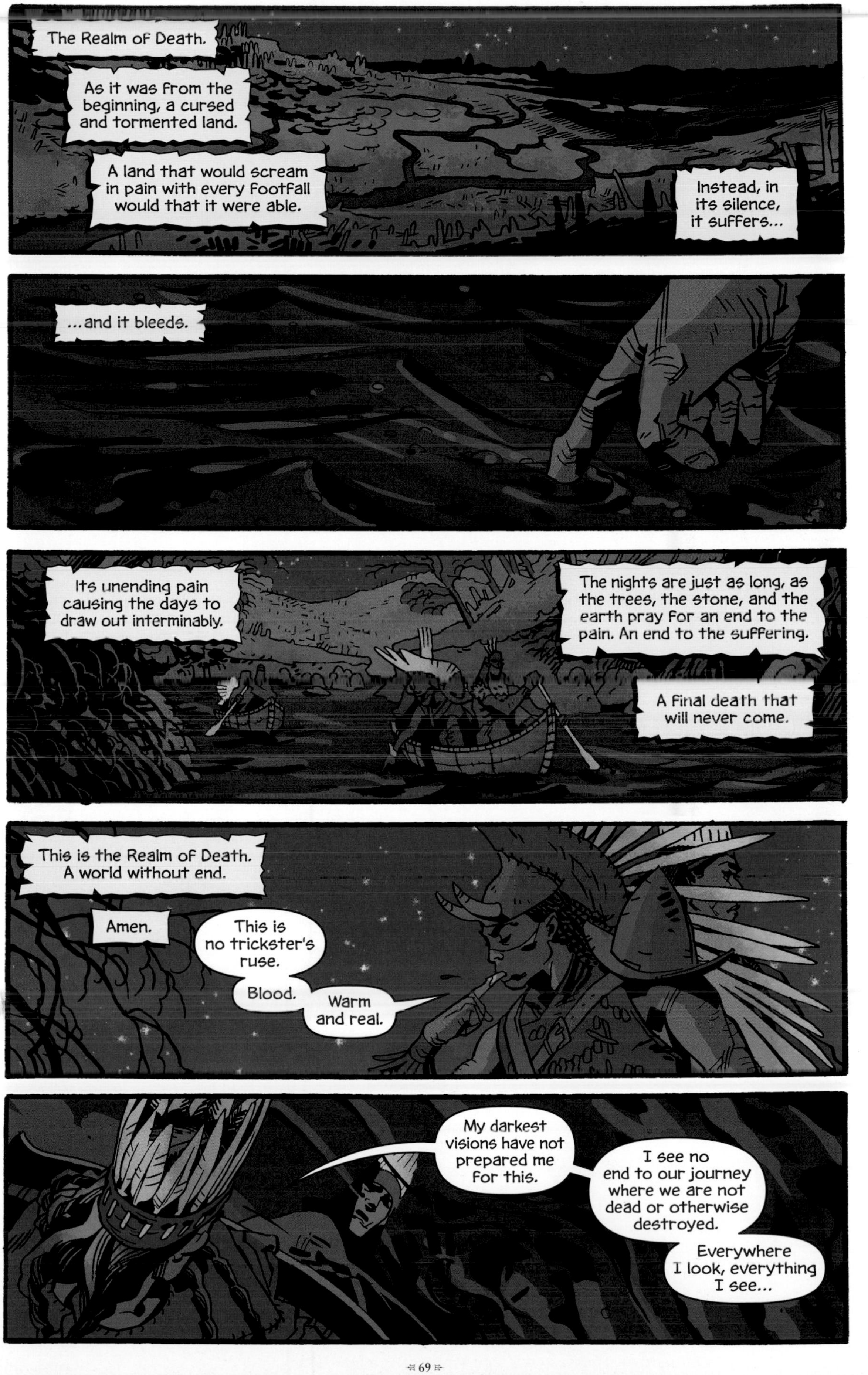
The Realm of Death.
As it was from the beginning, a cursed and tormented land.
A land that would scream in pain with every footfall would that it were able.
Instead, in its silence, it suffers...
...and it bleeds.
Its unending pain causing the days to draw out interminably.
The nights are just as long, as the trees, the stone, and the earth pray for an end to the pain. An end to the suffering.
A final death that will never come.
This is the Realm of Death. A world without end.
Amen.
This is no trickster's ruse.
Blood.
Warm and real.
My darkest visions have not prepared me for this.
I see no end to our journey where we are not dead or otherwise destroyed.
Everywhere I look, everything I see...

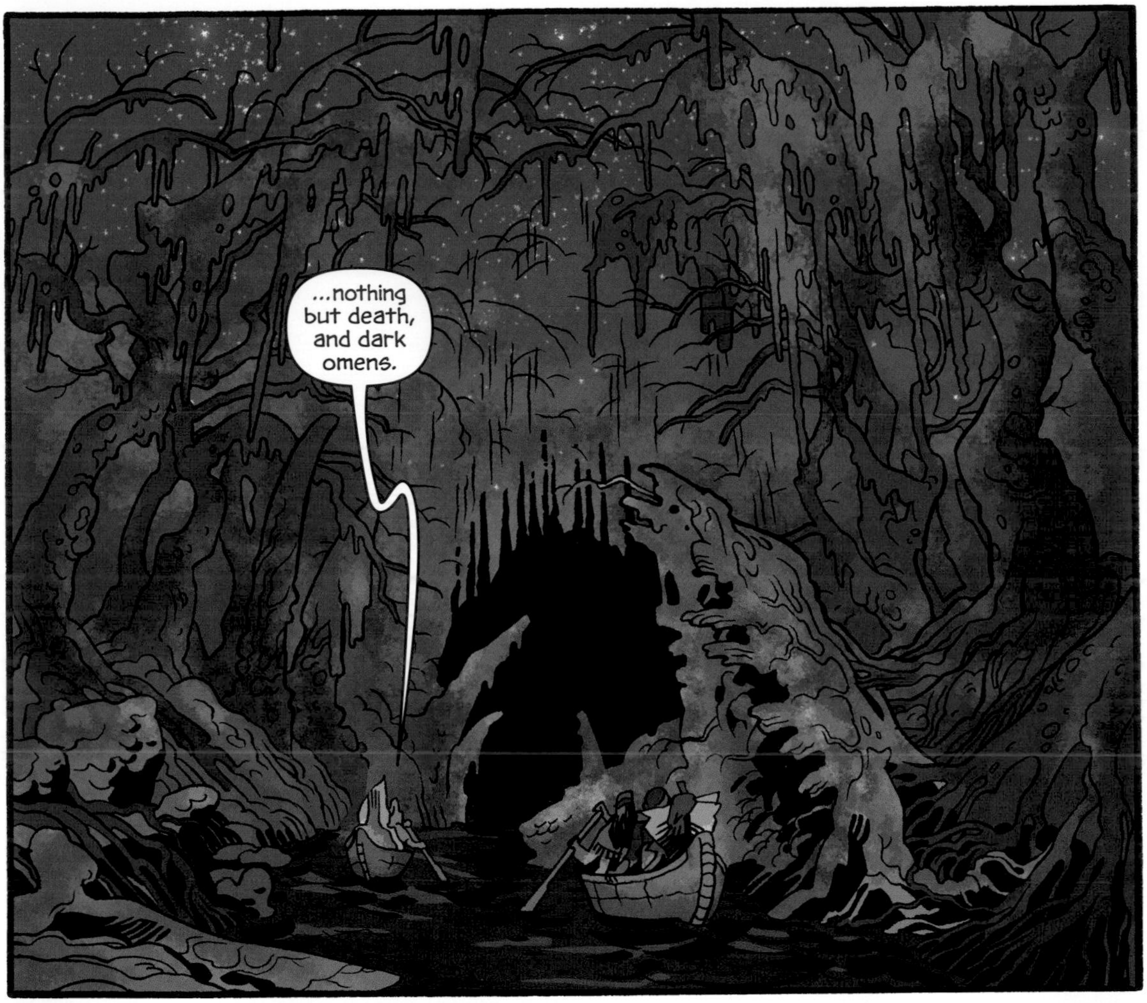
...nothing but death, and dark omens.

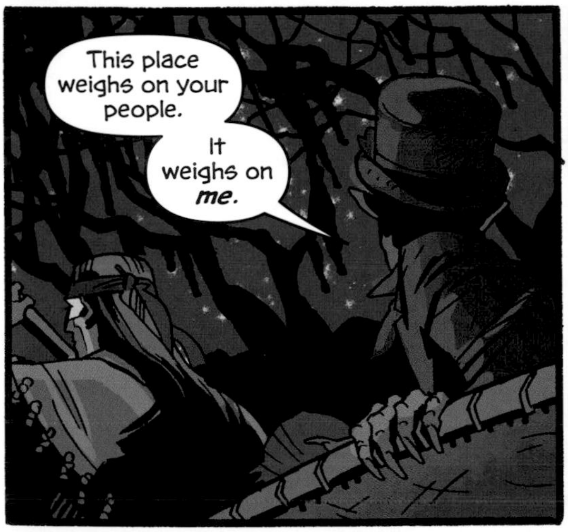
This place weighs on your people.
It weighs on *me*.

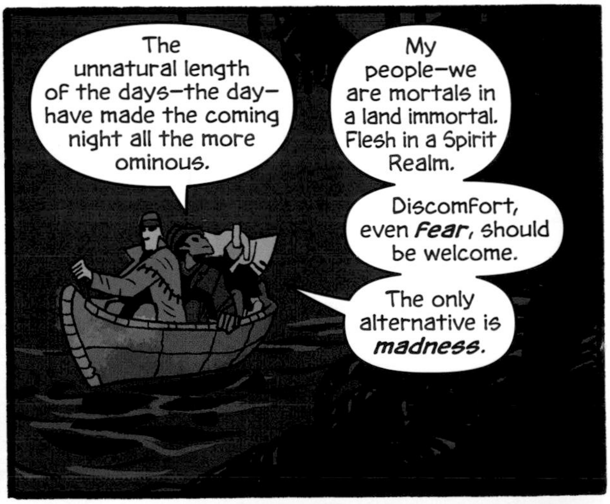
The unnatural length of the days—the day—have made the coming night all the more ominous.
My people—we are mortals in a land immortal. Flesh in a Spirit Realm.
Discomfort, even *Fear*, should be welcome.
The only alternative is *madness*.

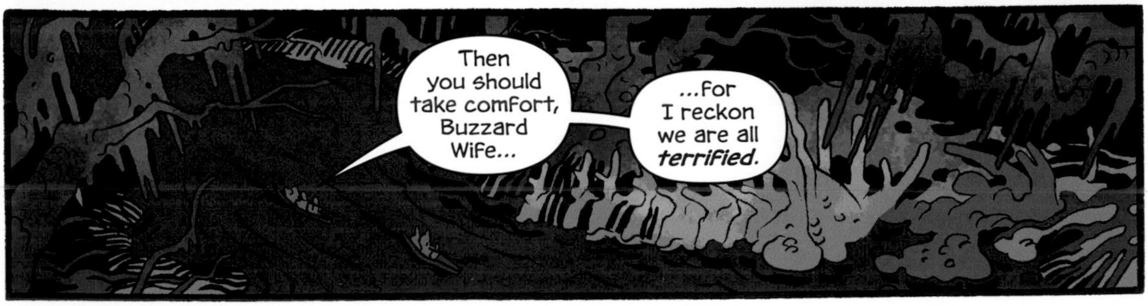
Then you should take comfort, Buzzard Wife...
...for I reckon we are all *terrified*.

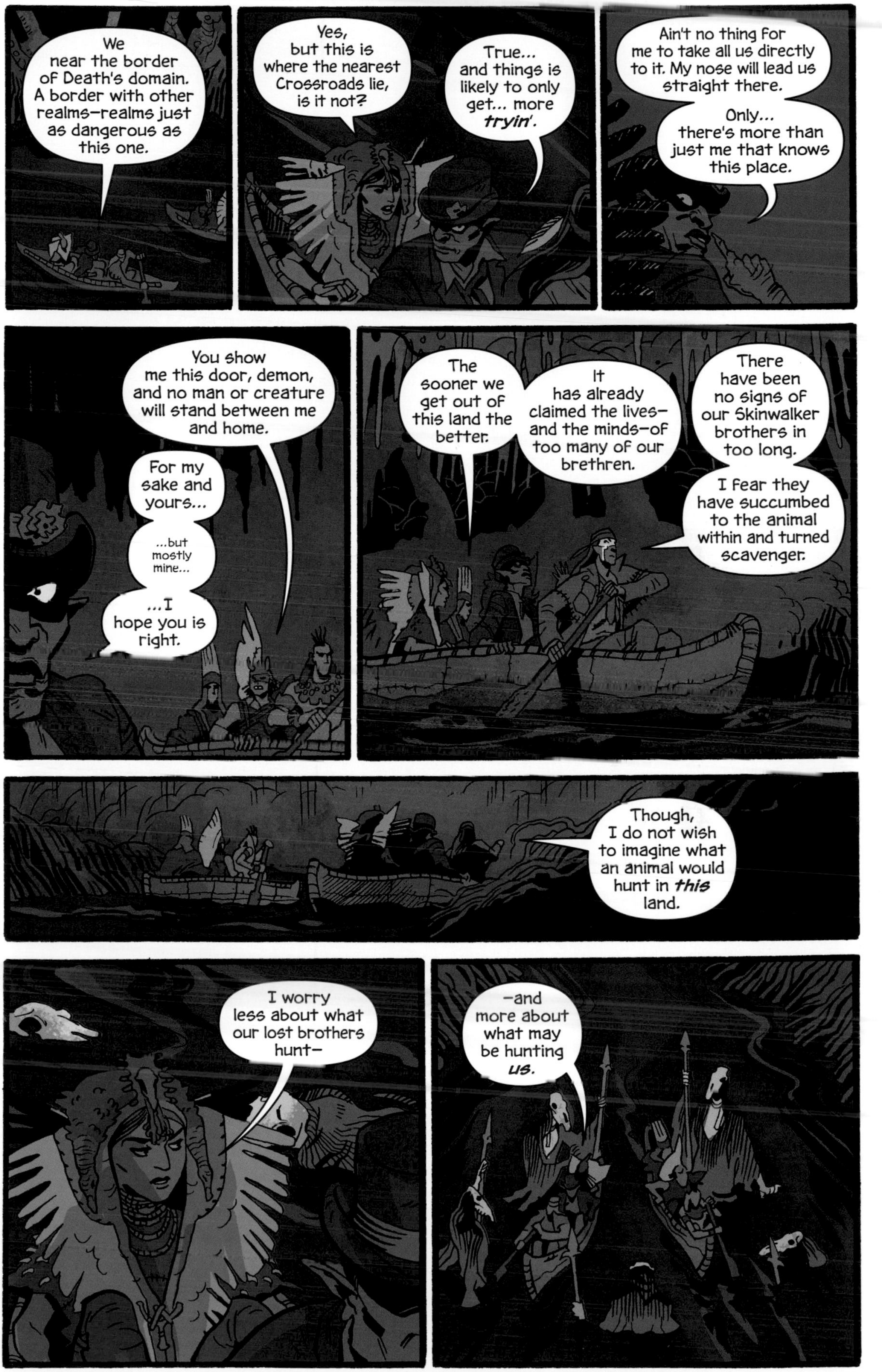
We near the border of Death's domain. A border with other realms—realms just as dangerous as this one.
Yes, but this is where the nearest Crossroads lie, is it not?
True... and things is likely to only get... more *tryin'*.
Ain't no thing for me to take all us directly to it. My nose will lead us straight there.
Only... there's more than just me that knows this place.
You show me this door, demon, and no man or creature will stand between me and home.
For my sake and yours...
...but mostly mine...
...I hope you is right.
The sooner we get out of this land the better.
It has already claimed the lives—and the minds—of too many of our brethren.
There have been no signs of our Skinwalker brothers in too long.
I fear they have succumbed to the animal within and turned scavenger.
Though, I do not wish to imagine what an animal would hunt in *this* land.
I worry less about what our lost brothers hunt—
—and more about what may be hunting *us*.

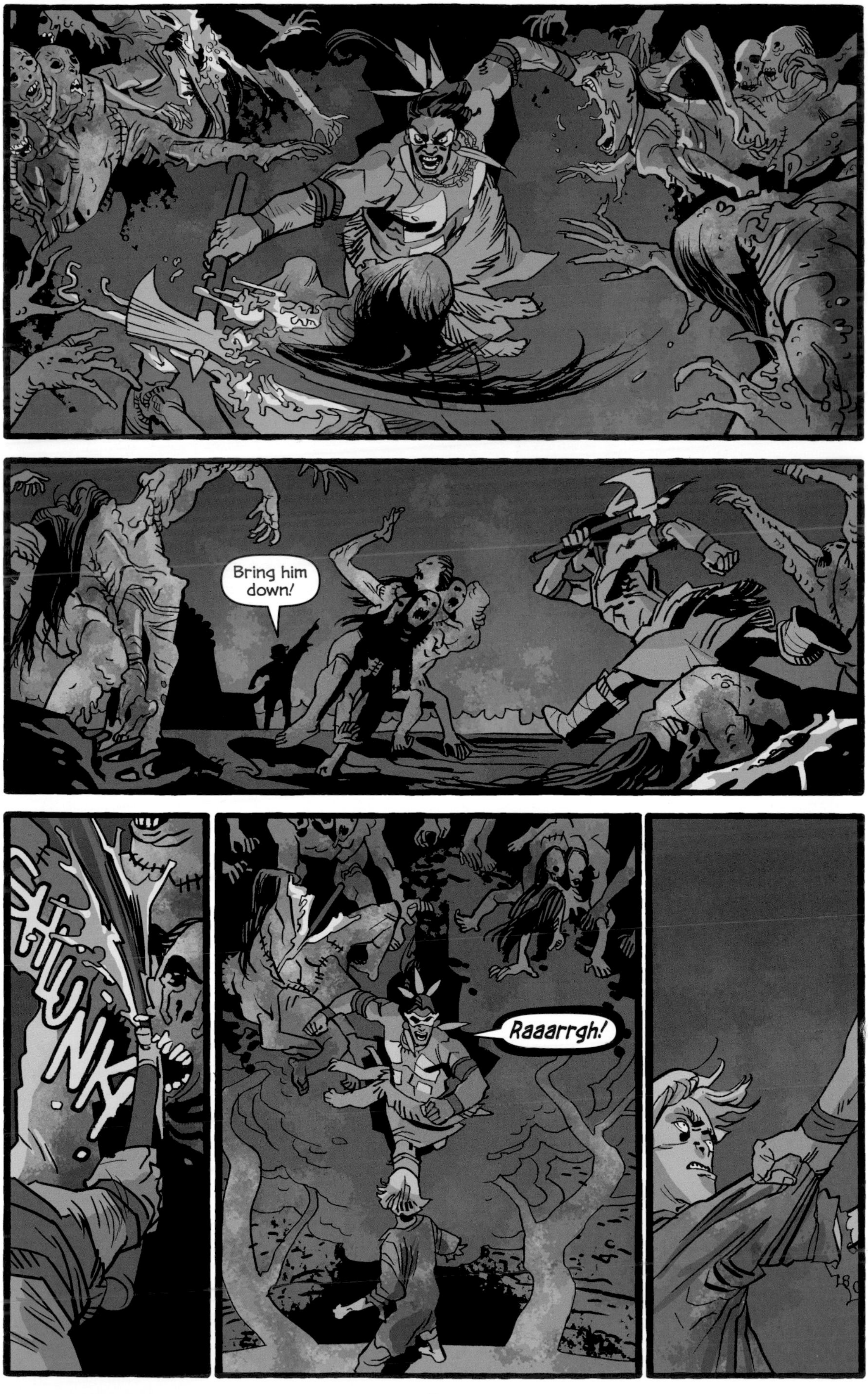
Bring him down!
SHLUNK!
Raaarrgh!

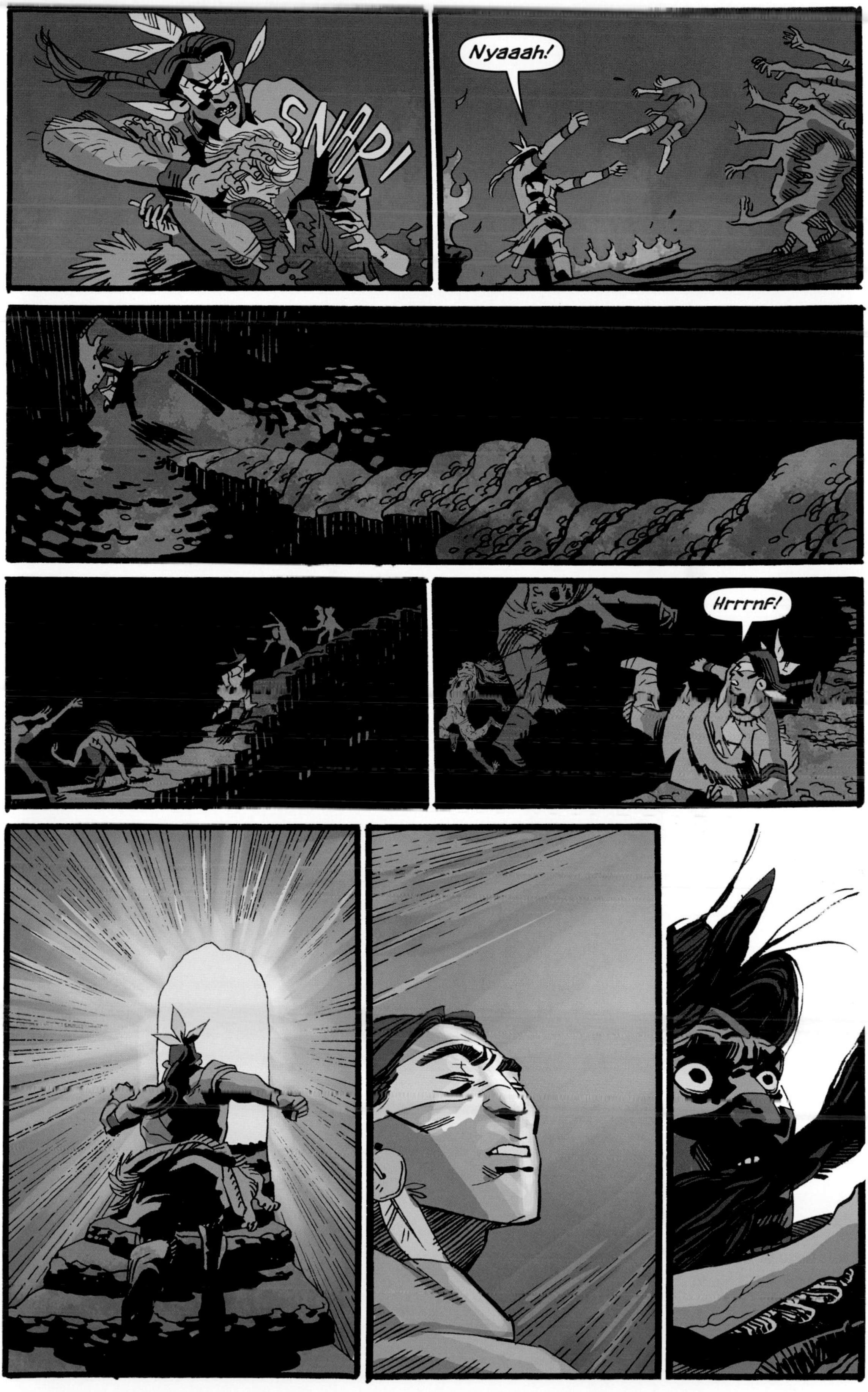
SNAP!
Nyaaah!
Hrrrnf!

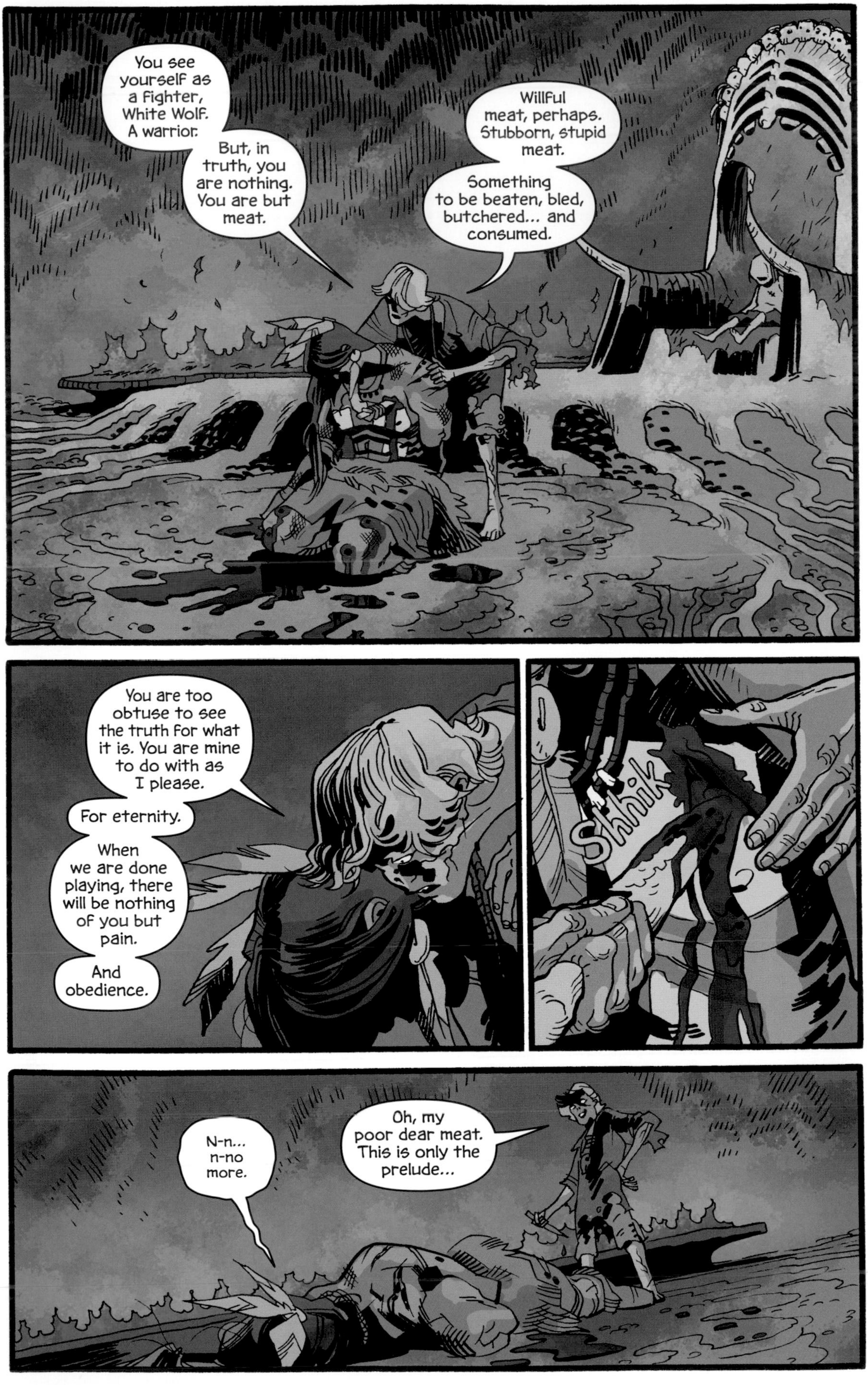
You see yourself as a fighter, White Wolf. A warrior.
But, in truth, you are nothing. You are but meat.
Willful meat, perhaps. Stubborn, stupid meat.
Something to be beaten, bled, butchered... and consumed.
You are too obtuse to see the truth for what it is. You are mine to do with as I please.
For eternity.
When we are done playing, there will be nothing of you but pain.
And obedience.
Shhik
N-n... n-no more.
Oh, my poor dear meat. This is only the prelude...

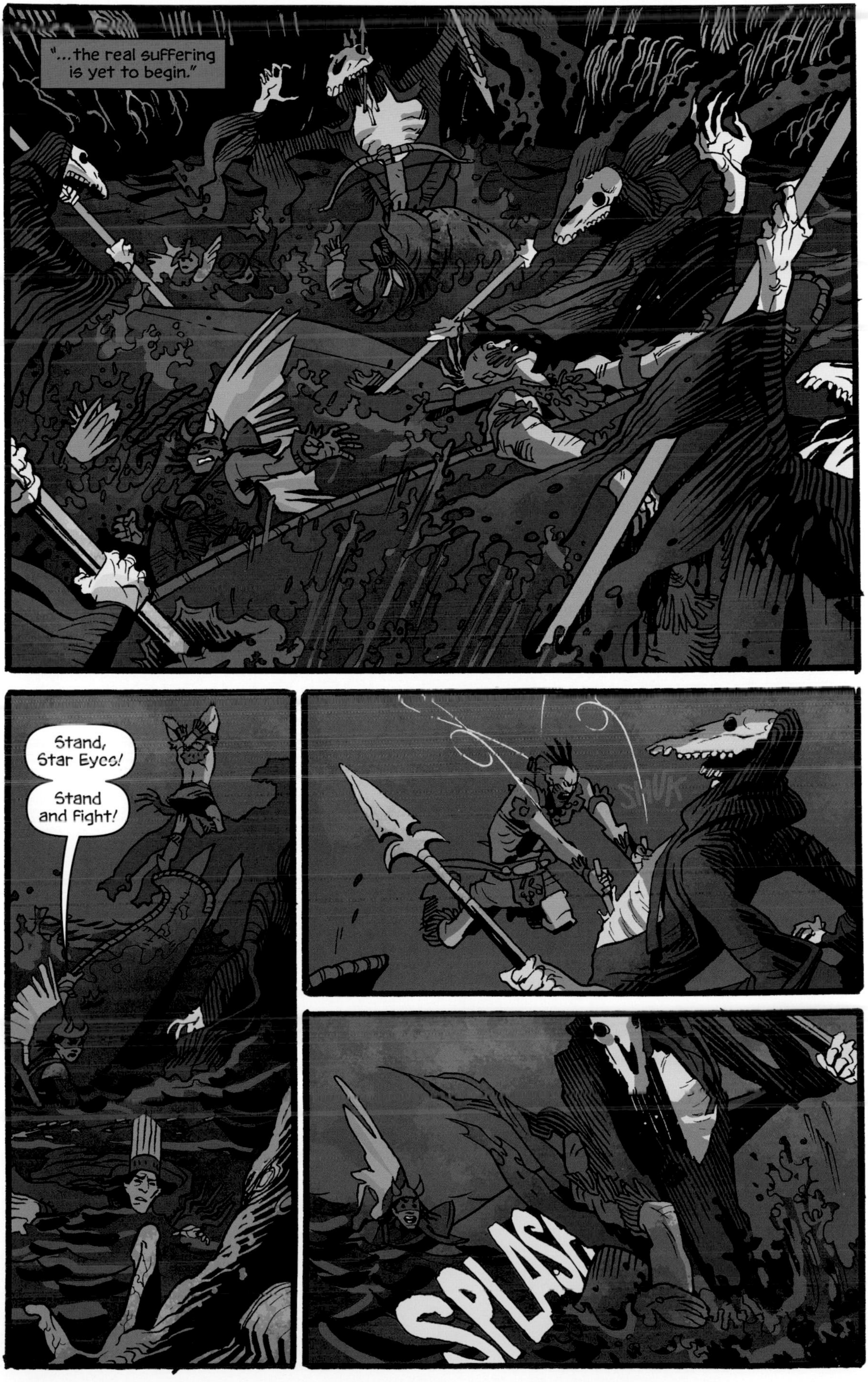
"...the real suffering is yet to begin."
Stand, Star Eyes!
Stand and Fight!
SHUK
SPLAS

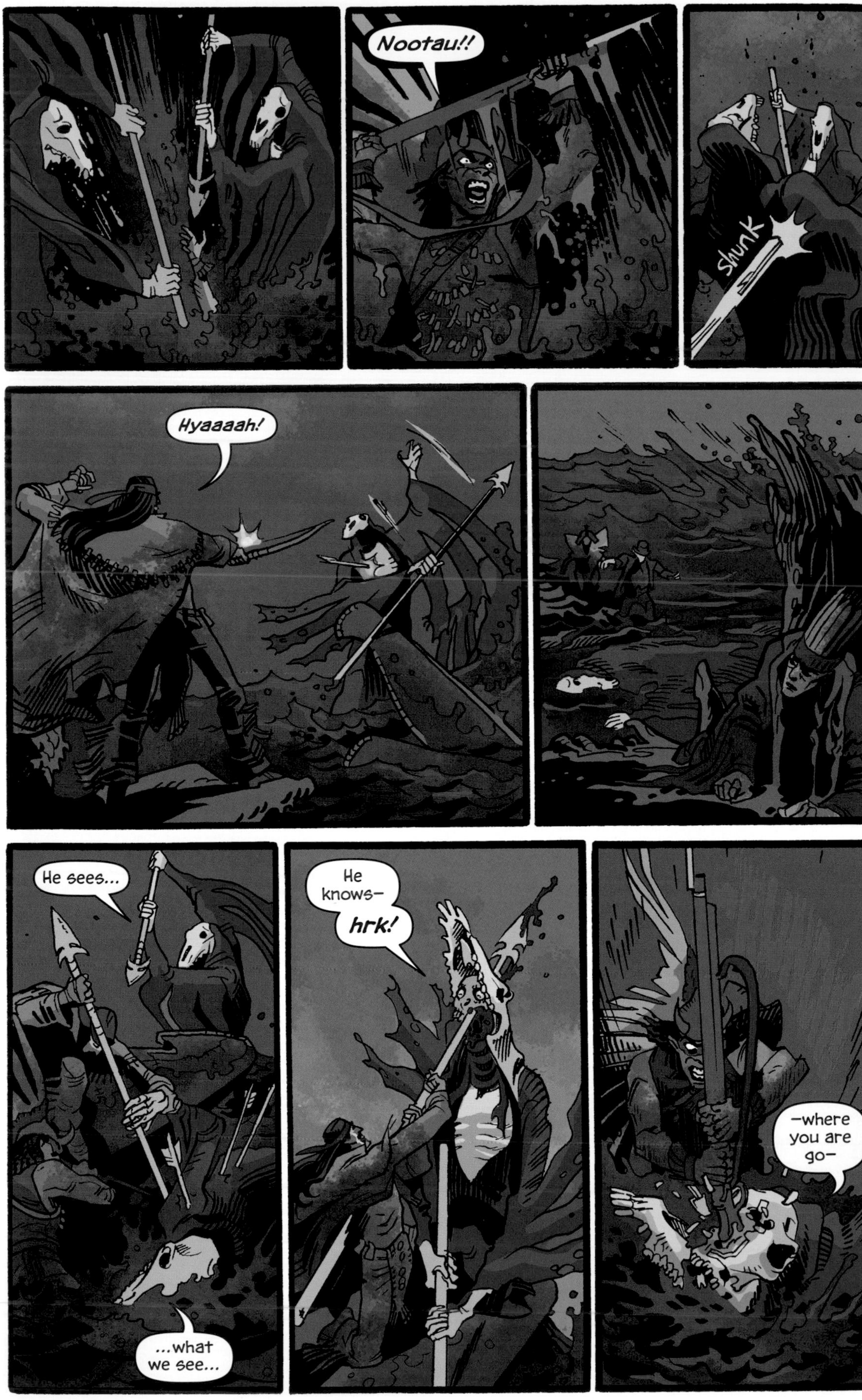
Nootau!!
shunk
Hyaaaah!
He sees...
...what we see...
He knows—
hrk!
—where you are go—

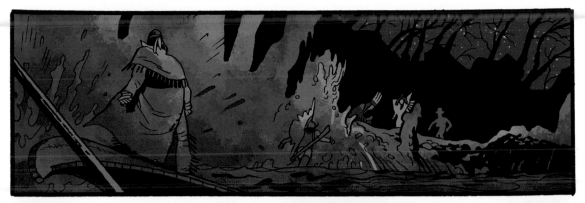

You! What use are **you?!**

What use are your magiks?!

I-I had no time...

...no time to prepare—

You two only live because great men—**warriors**—have stood between you and death!

Stood for you!

Fell for you!

When the last of **us** dies—what then?!

What becomes of **you?!**

Asisi. Enough. There is not time for this.

No...

...but there will be.

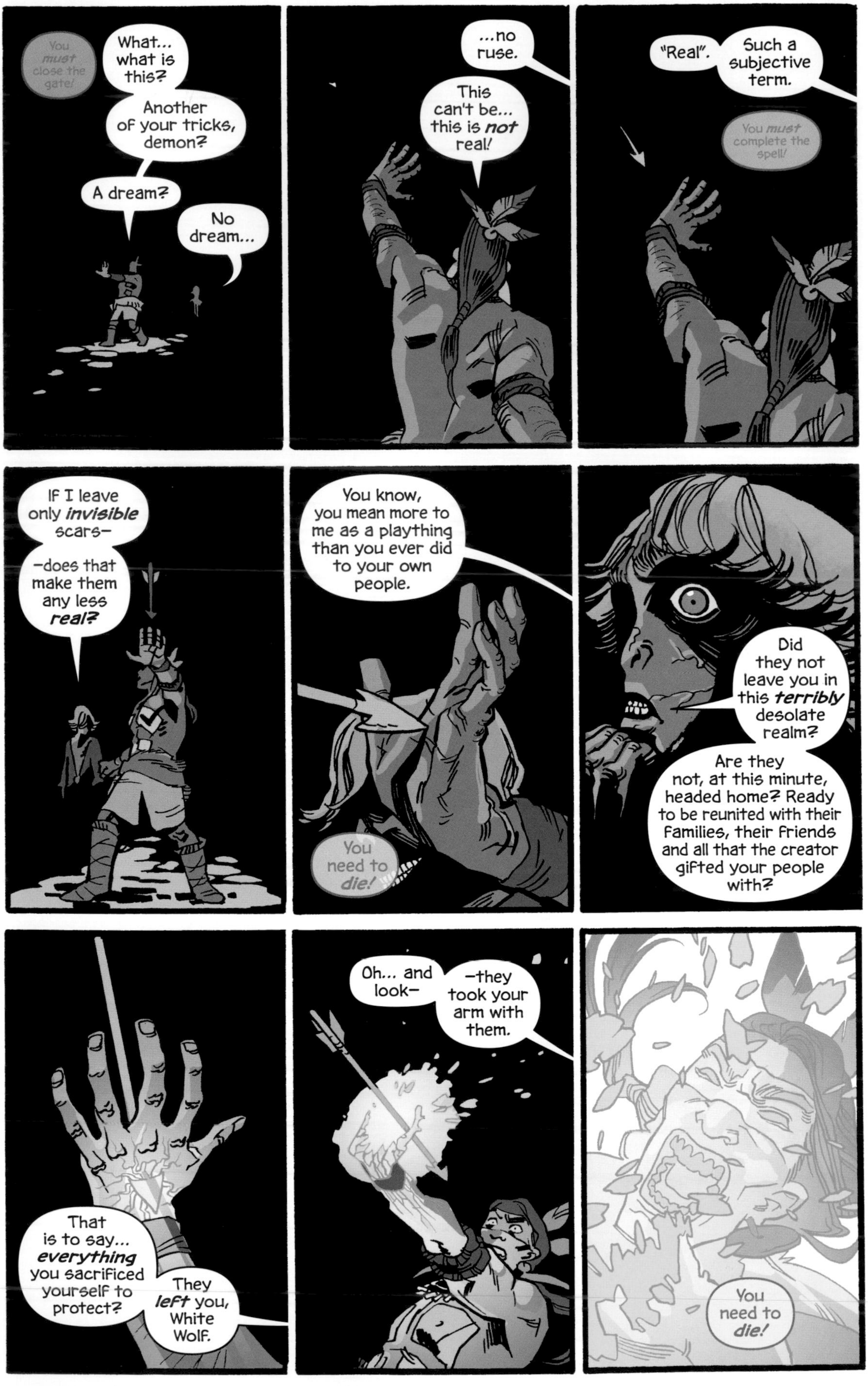
You must close the gate!
What... what is this?
Another of your tricks, demon?
A dream?
No dream...
...no ruse.
This can't be... this is not real!
"Real".
Such a subjective term.
You must complete the spell!
If I leave only invisible scars—
—does that make them any less real?
You know, you mean more to me as a plaything than you ever did to your own people.
You need to die!
Did they not leave you in this terribly desolate realm?
Are they not, at this minute, headed home? Ready to be reunited with their families, their friends and all that the creator gifted your people with?
That is to say... everything you sacrificed yourself to protect?
They left you, White Wolf.
Oh... and look—
—they took your arm with them.
You need to die!

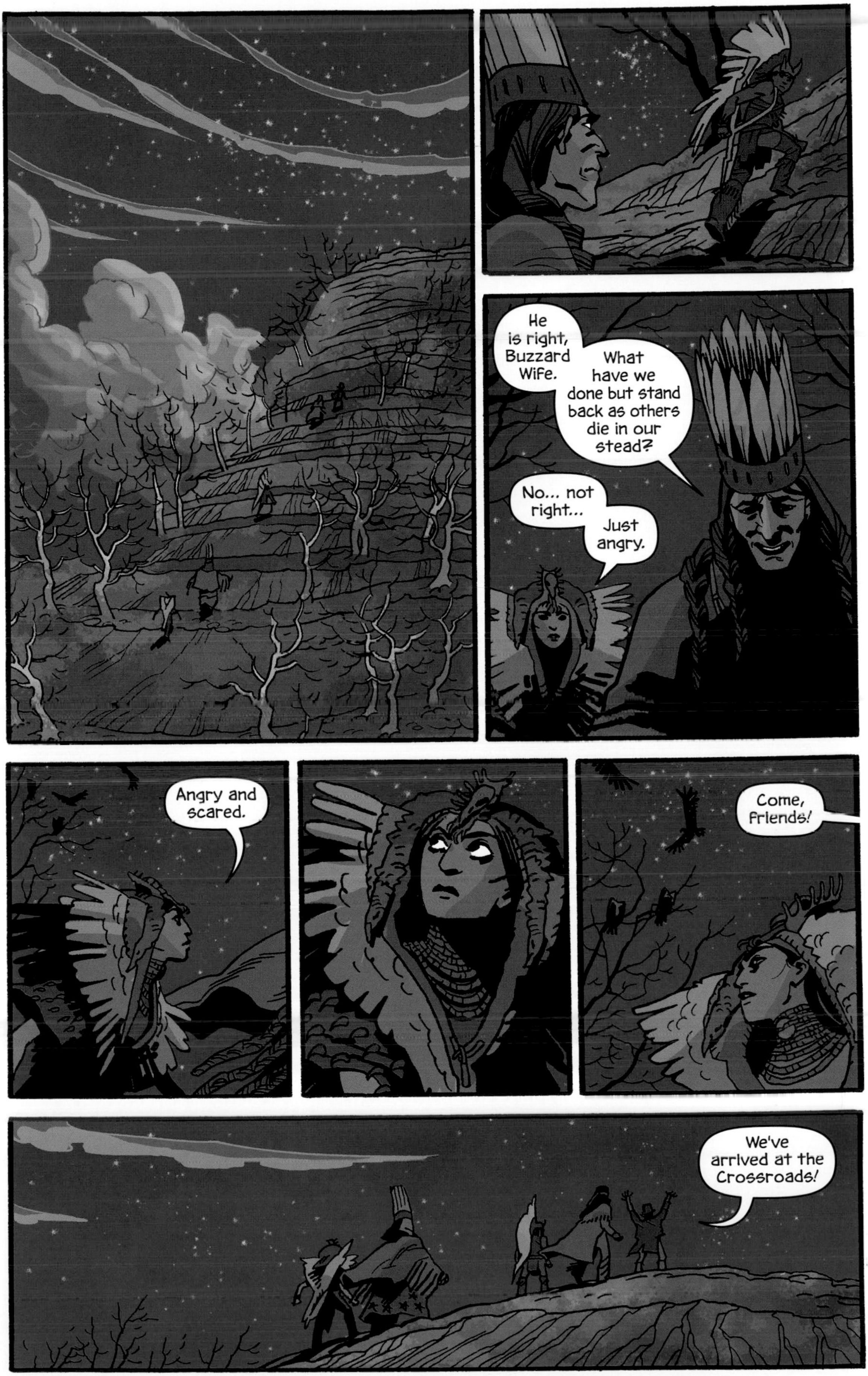
He is right, Buzzard Wife.
What have we done but stand back as others die in our stead?
No... not right...
Just angry.
Angry and scared.
Come, friends!
We've arrived at the Crossroads!

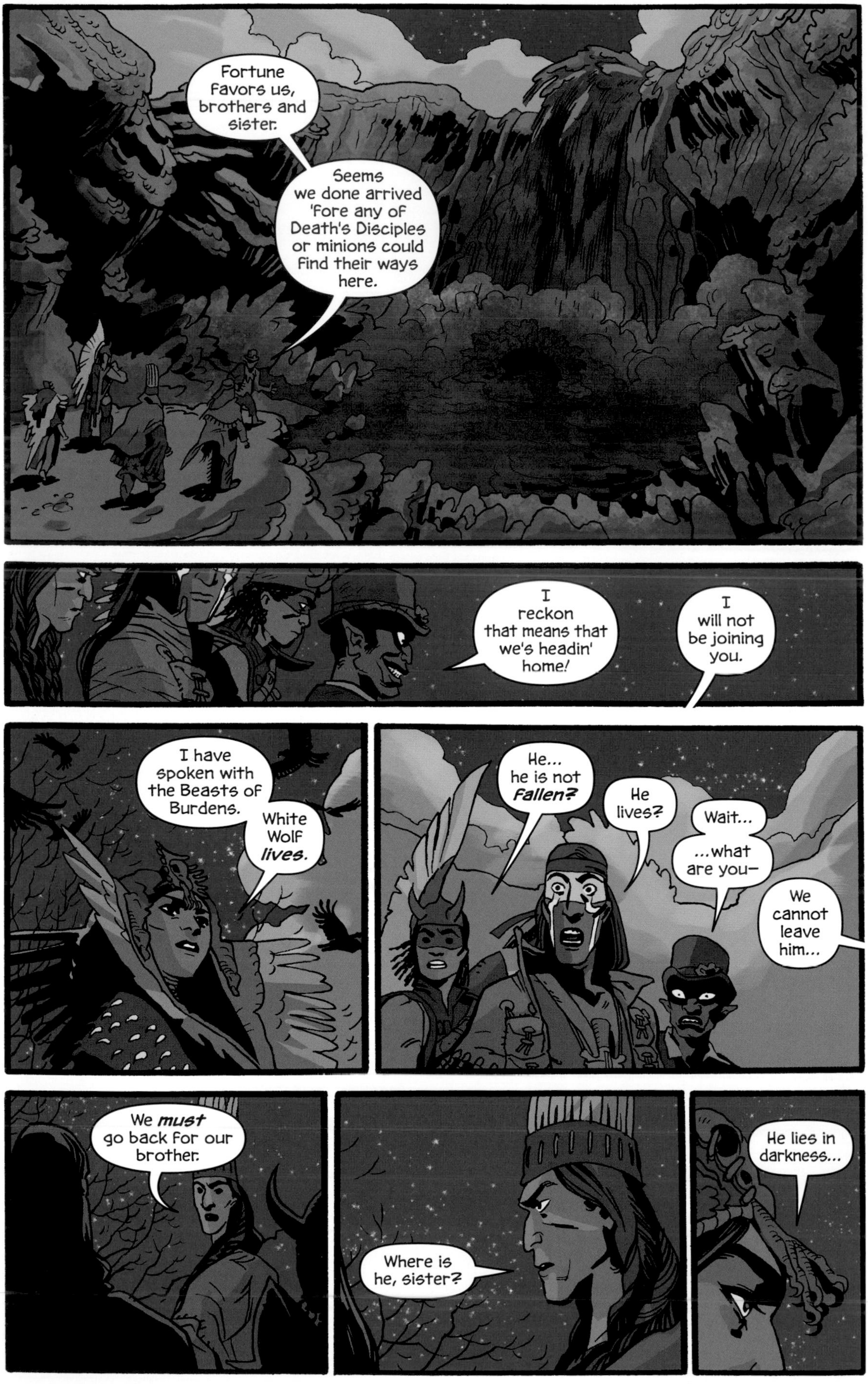

Fortune favors us, brothers and sister.
Seems we done arrived 'fore any of Death's Disciples or minions could find their ways here.
I reckon that means that we's headin' home!
I will not be joining you.
I have spoken with the Beasts of Burdens.
White Wolf *lives.*
He... he is not *fallen?*
He lives?
Wait...
...what are you–
We cannot leave him...
We *must* go back for our brother.
Where is he, sister?
He lies in darkness...

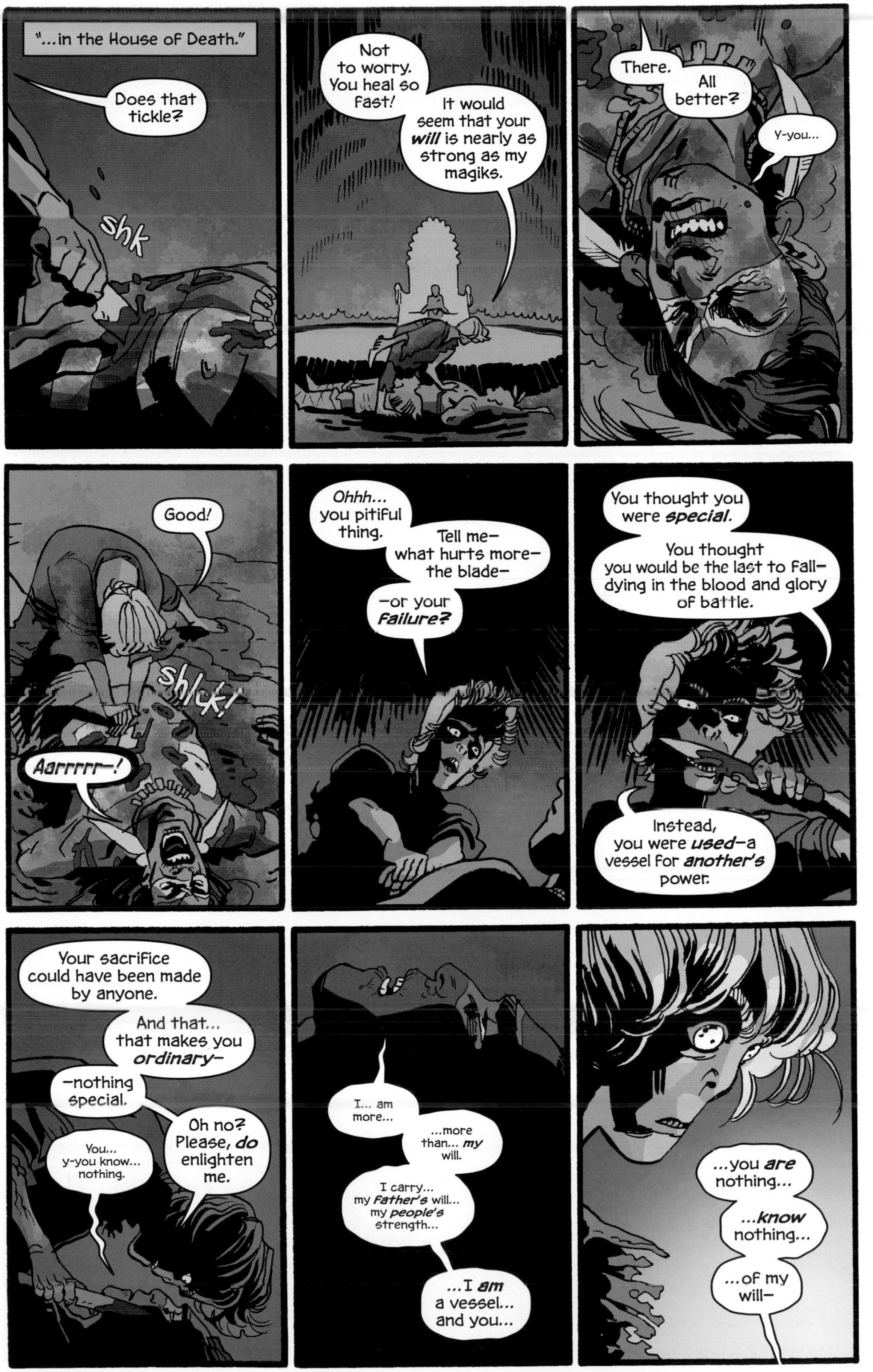
"...in the House of Death."
Does that tickle?
shk
Not to worry. You heal so fast!
It would seem that your *will* is nearly as strong as my magiks.
There.
All better?
Y-you...
Good!
shlck!
Aarrrrr—!
Ohhh... you pitiful thing.
Tell me— what hurts more— the blade—
—or your *failure?*
You thought you were *special.*
You thought you would be the last to fall— dying in the blood and glory of battle.
Instead, you were *used*—a vessel for *another's* power.
Your sacrifice could have been made by anyone.
And that... that makes you *ordinary*—
—nothing special.
Oh no? Please, *do* enlighten me.
You... y-you know... nothing.
I... am more...
...more than... *my* will.
I carry... my *father's* will... my *people's* strength...
...I *am* a vessel... and you...
...you *are* nothing...
...*know* nothing...
...of my will—

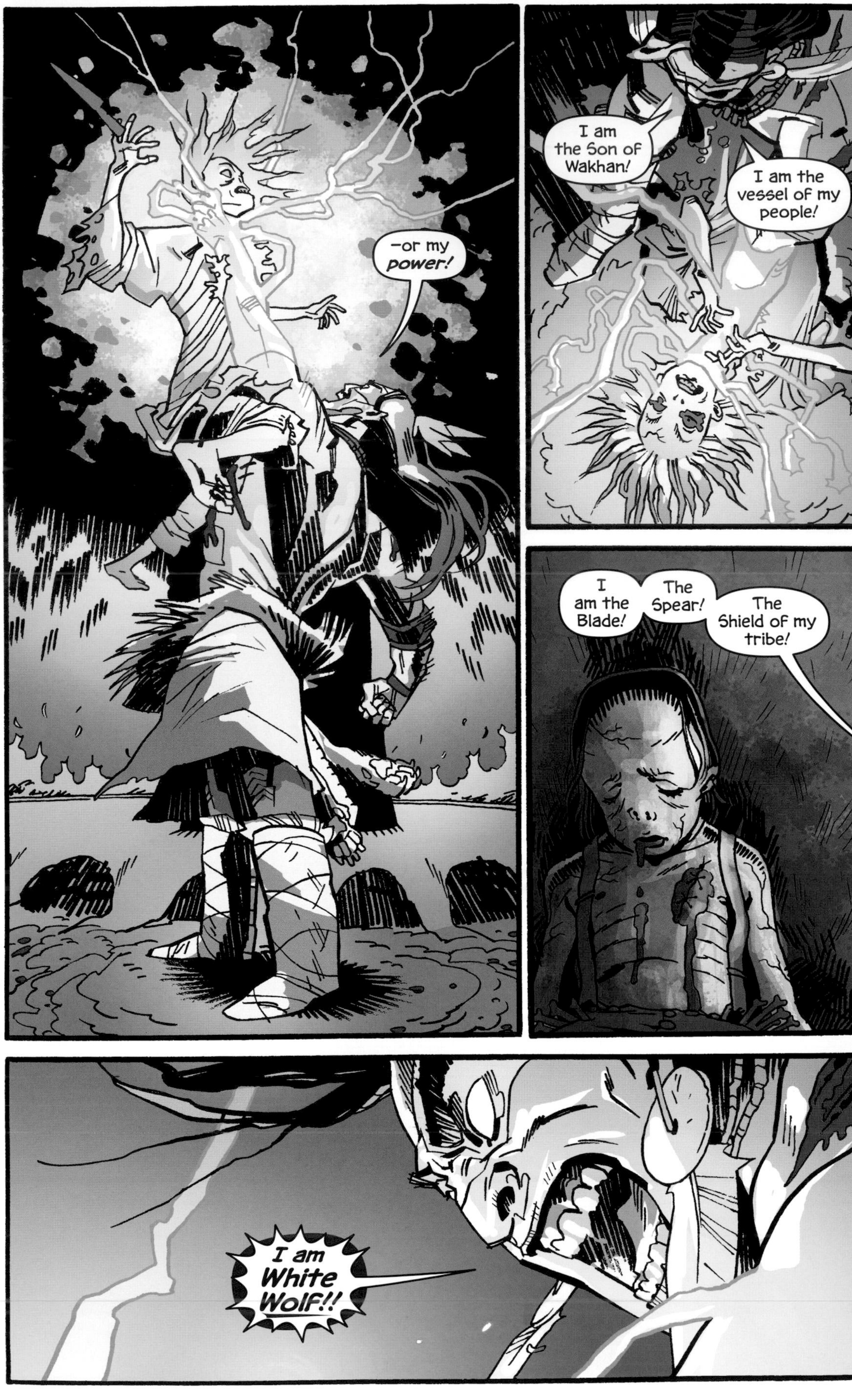

–or my *power!*
I am the Son of Wakhan!
I am the vessel of my people!
I am the Blade!
The Spear!
The Shield of my tribe!
I am White Wolf!!

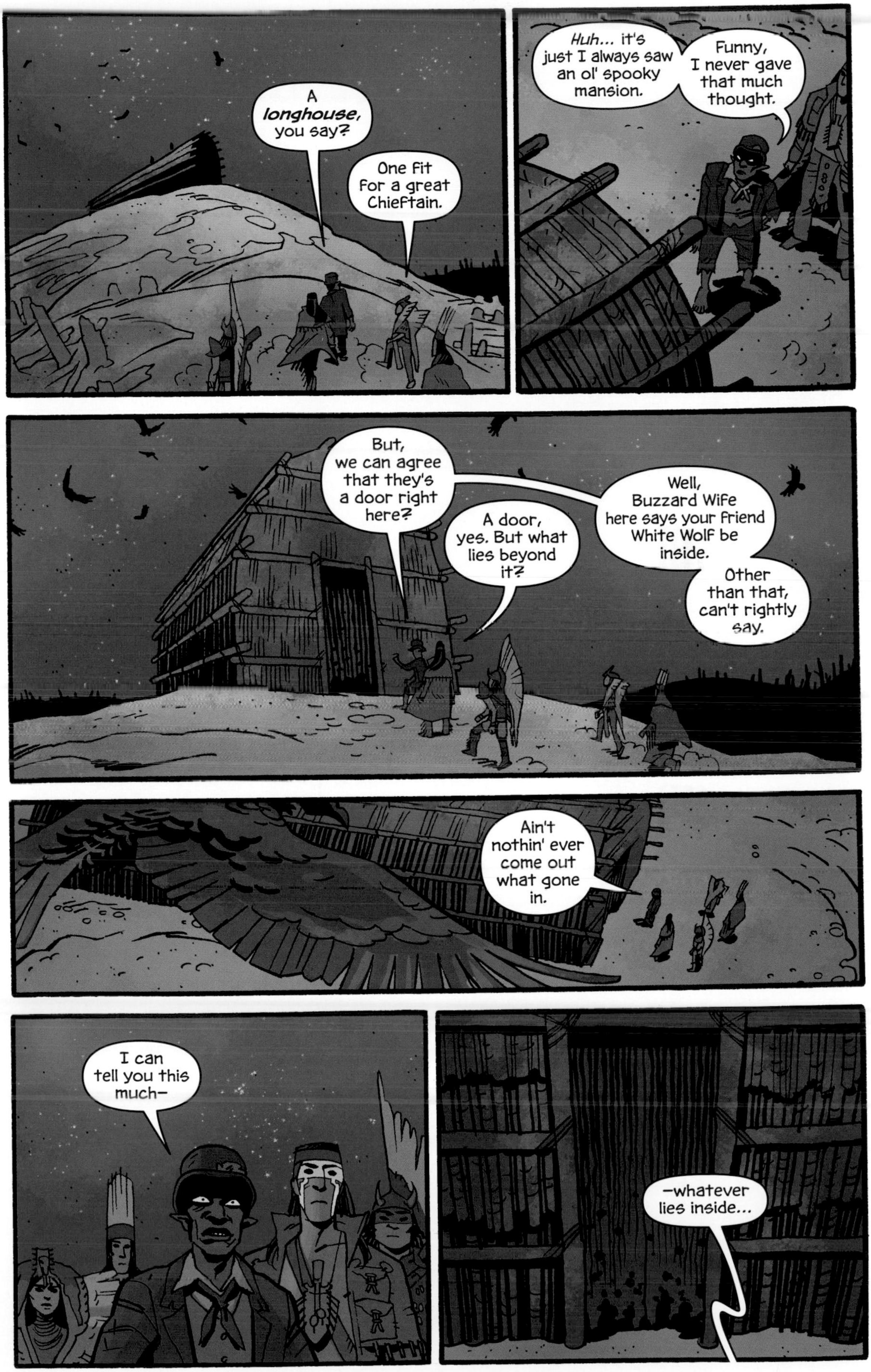
A *longhouse,* you say?
One fit for a great Chieftain.
Huh... it's just I always saw an ol' spooky mansion.
Funny, I never gave that much thought.
But, we can agree that they's a door right here?
A door, yes. But what lies beyond it?
Well, Buzzard Wife here says your friend White Wolf be inside.
Other than that, can't rightly say.
Ain't nothin' ever come out what gone in.
I can tell you this much—
—whatever lies inside...

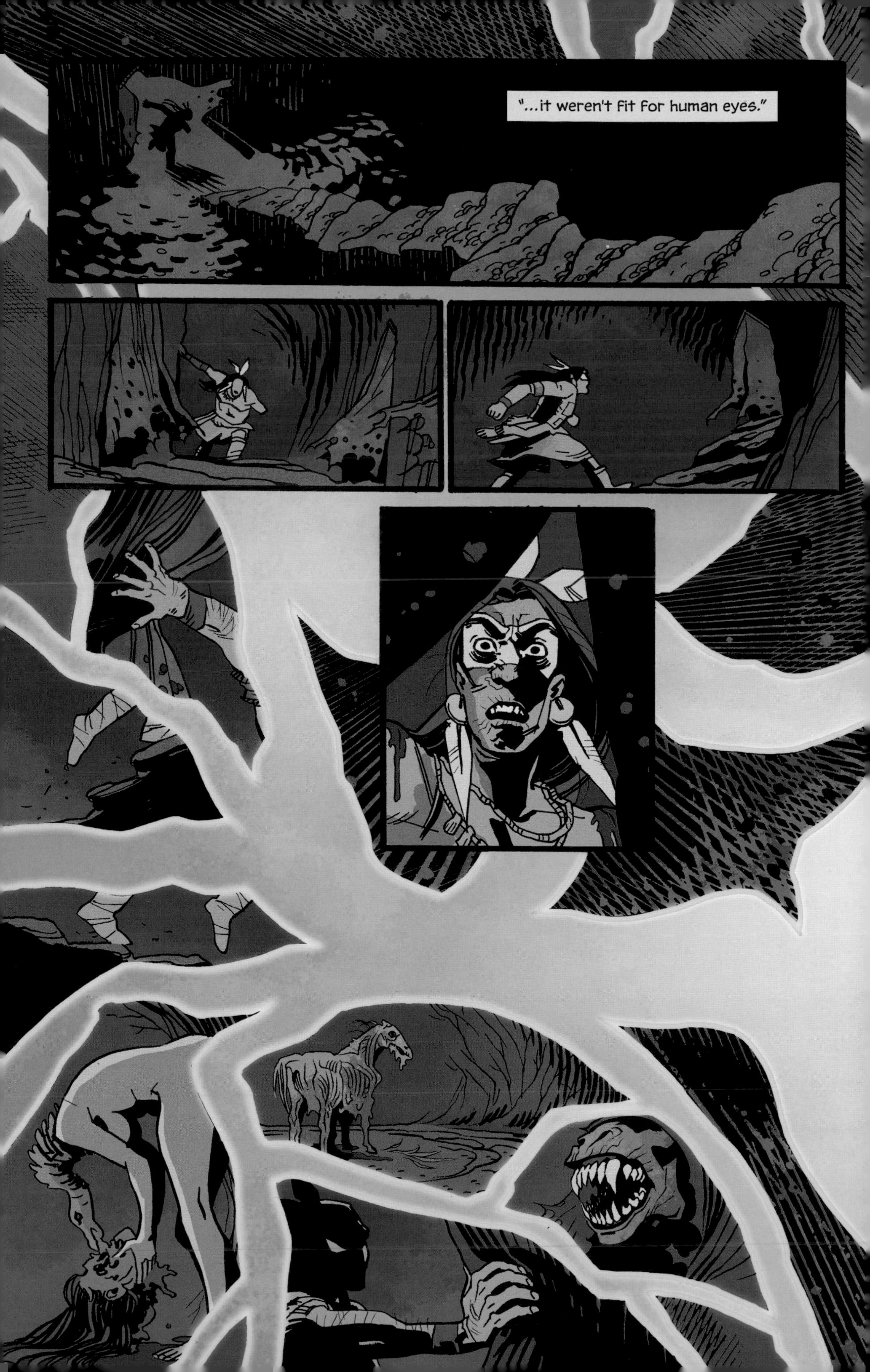
"...it weren't fit for human eyes."

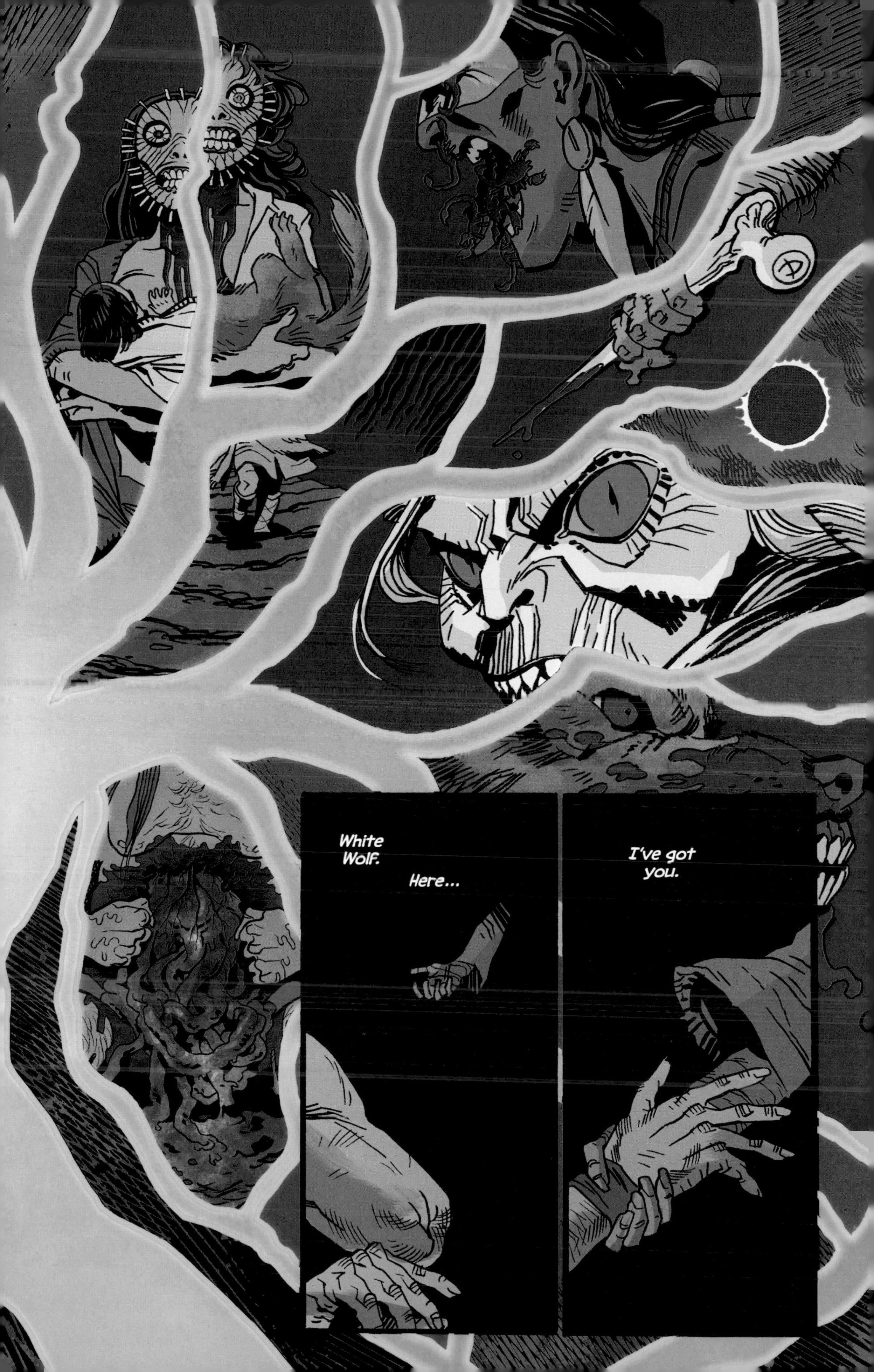
White Wolf.
Here...
I've got you.

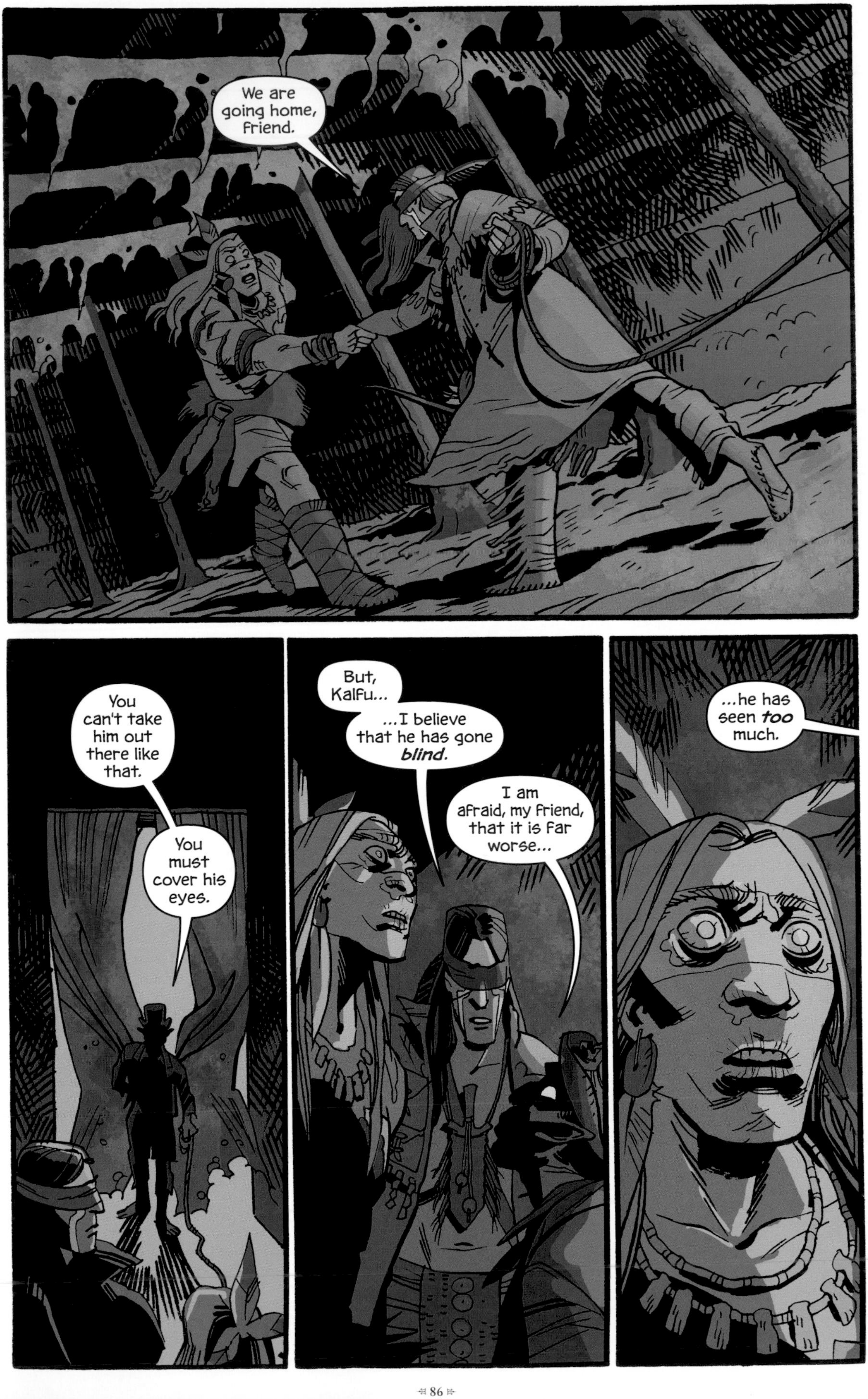
We are going home, friend.
You can't take him out there like that.
You must cover his eyes.
But, Kalfu...
...I believe that he has gone *blind*.
I am afraid, my friend, that it is far worse...
...he has seen *too* much.

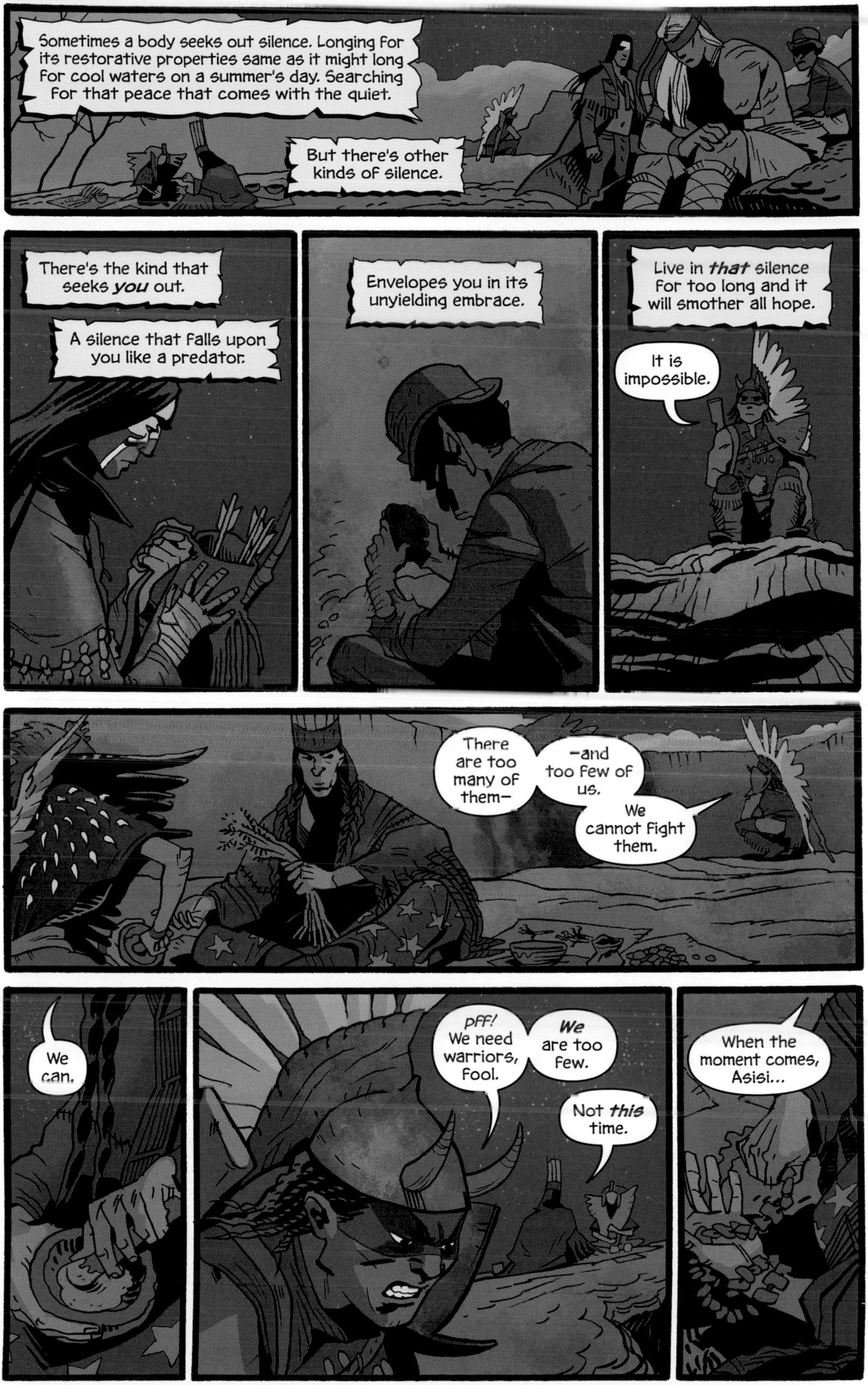

Sometimes a body seeks out silence. Longing for its restorative properties same as it might long for cool waters on a summer's day. Searching for that peace that comes with the quiet.
But there's other kinds of silence.
There's the kind that seeks *you* out.
A silence that falls upon you like a predator.
Envelopes you in its unyielding embrace.
Live in *that* silence for too long and it will smother all hope.
It is impossible.
There are too many of them—
—and too few of us.
We cannot fight them.
We can.
pff! We need warriors, Fool.
We are too few.
Not *this* time.
When the moment comes, Asisi...

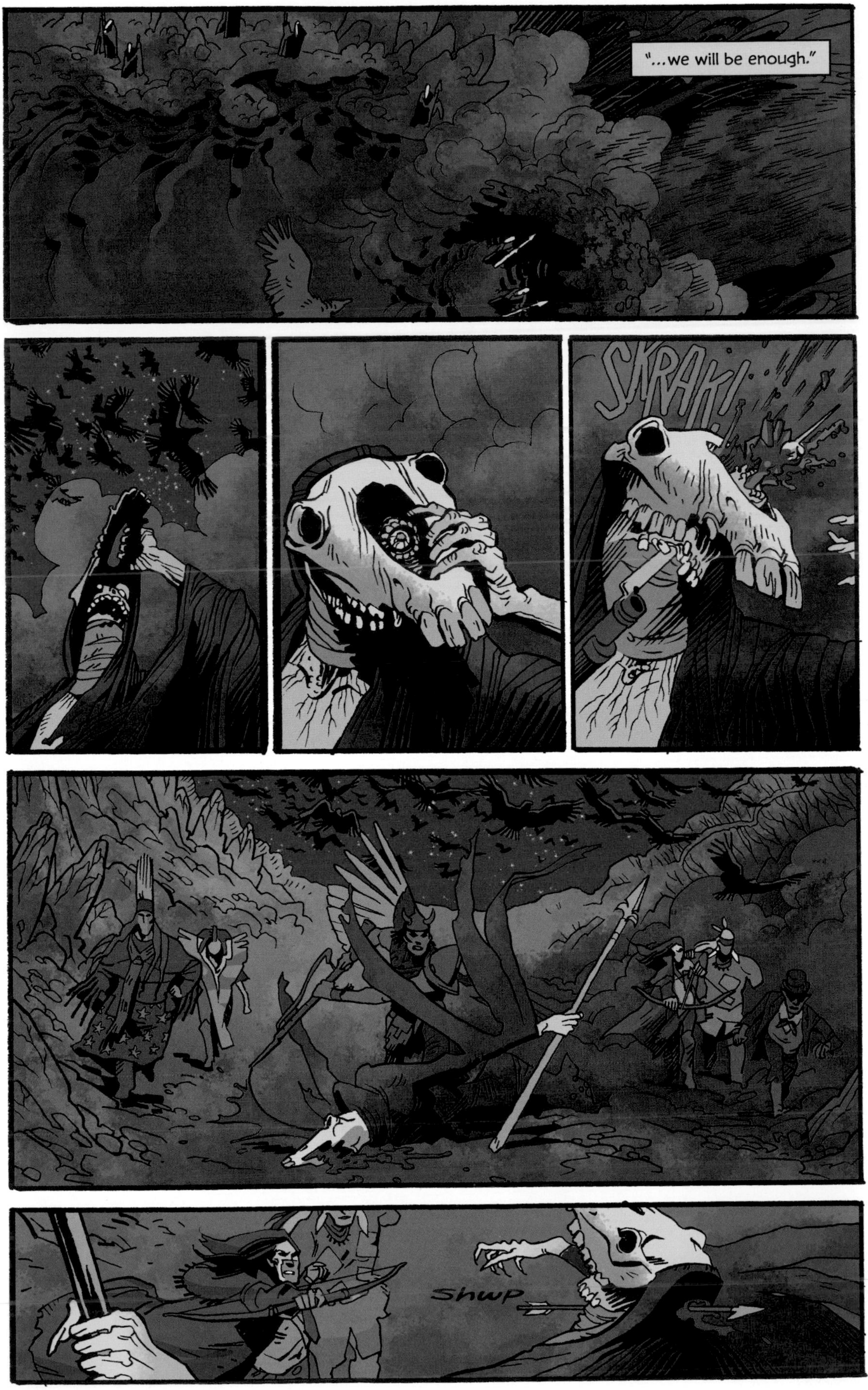
"...we will be enough."
SKRAK!
Shwp

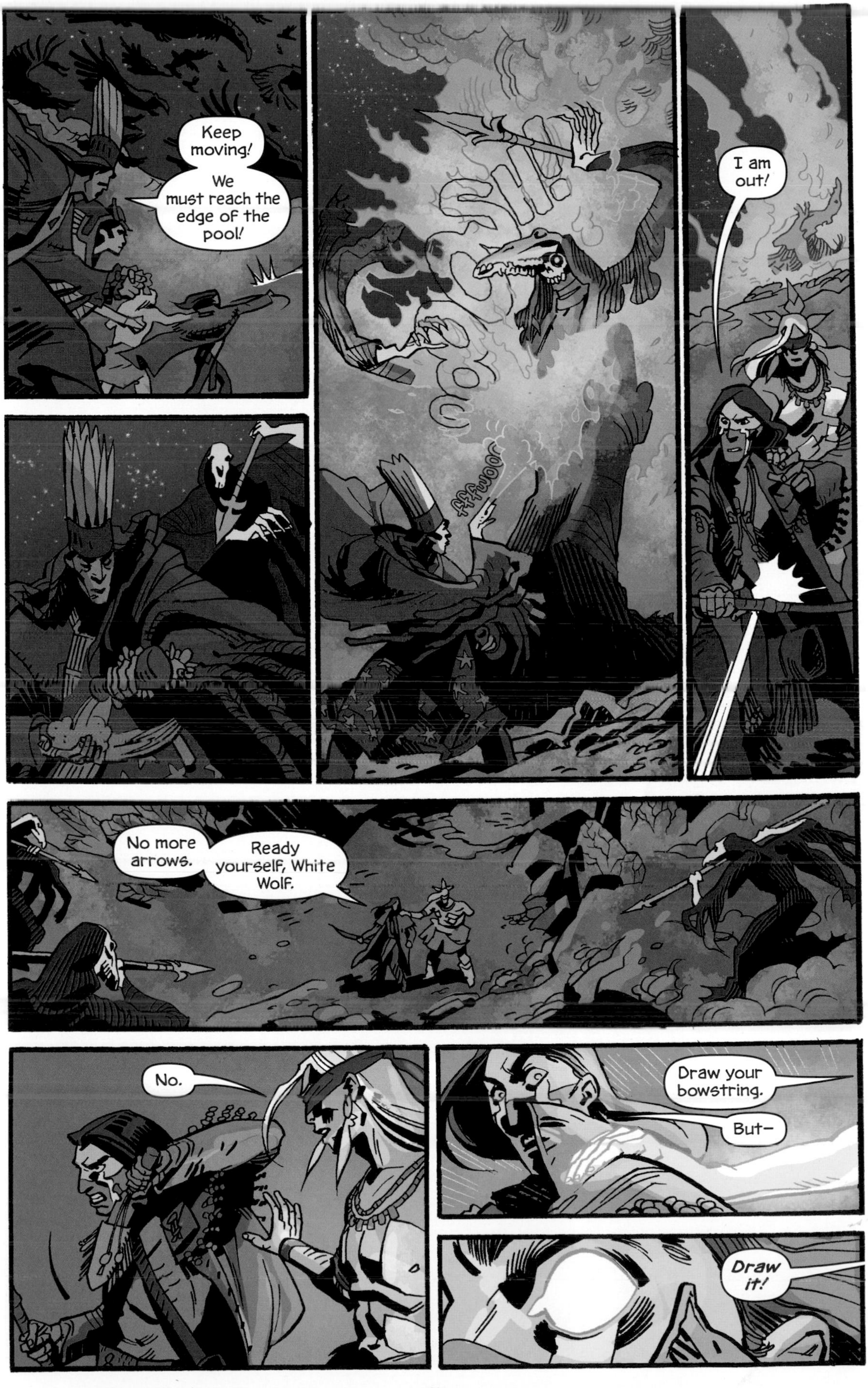
Keep moving!
We must reach the edge of the pool!
I am out!
No more arrows.
Ready yourself, White Wolf.
No.
Draw your bowstring.
But–
Draw it!

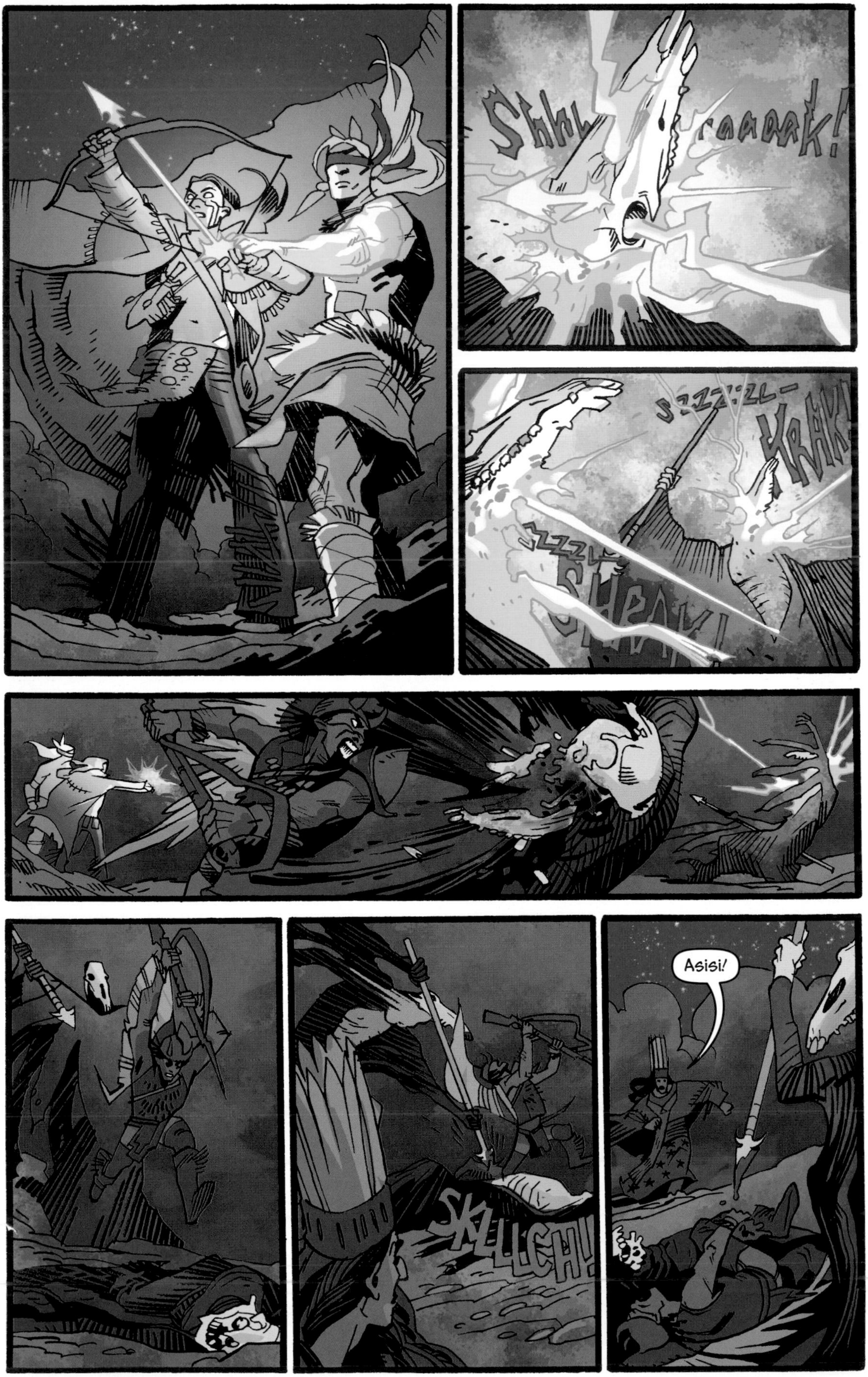
SKLLLCH!
Asisi!

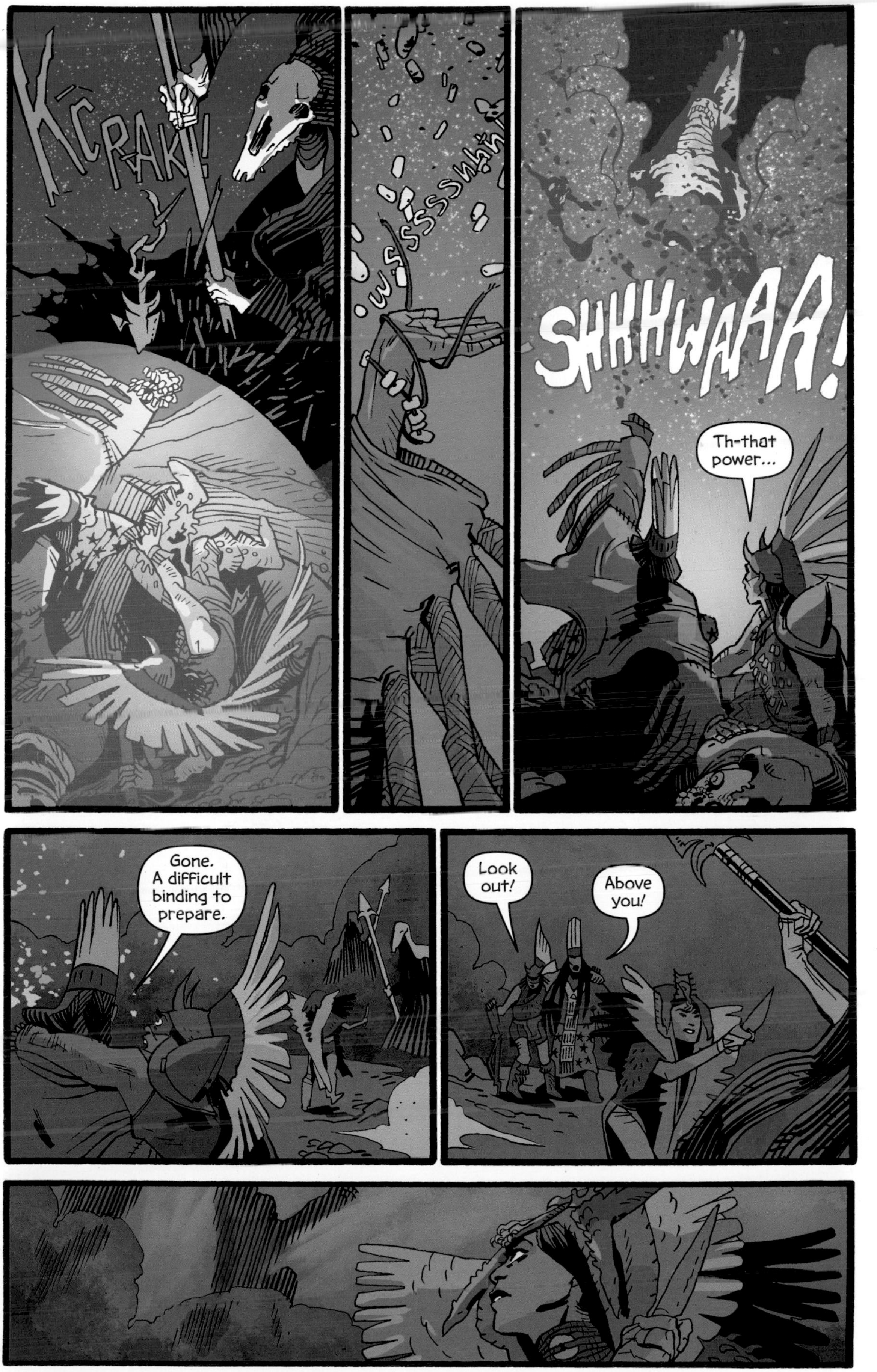
K'CRAK!
WSSSSSHHH
SHHHWAAAR!
Th-that power...
Gone. A difficult binding to prepare.
Look out!
Above you!

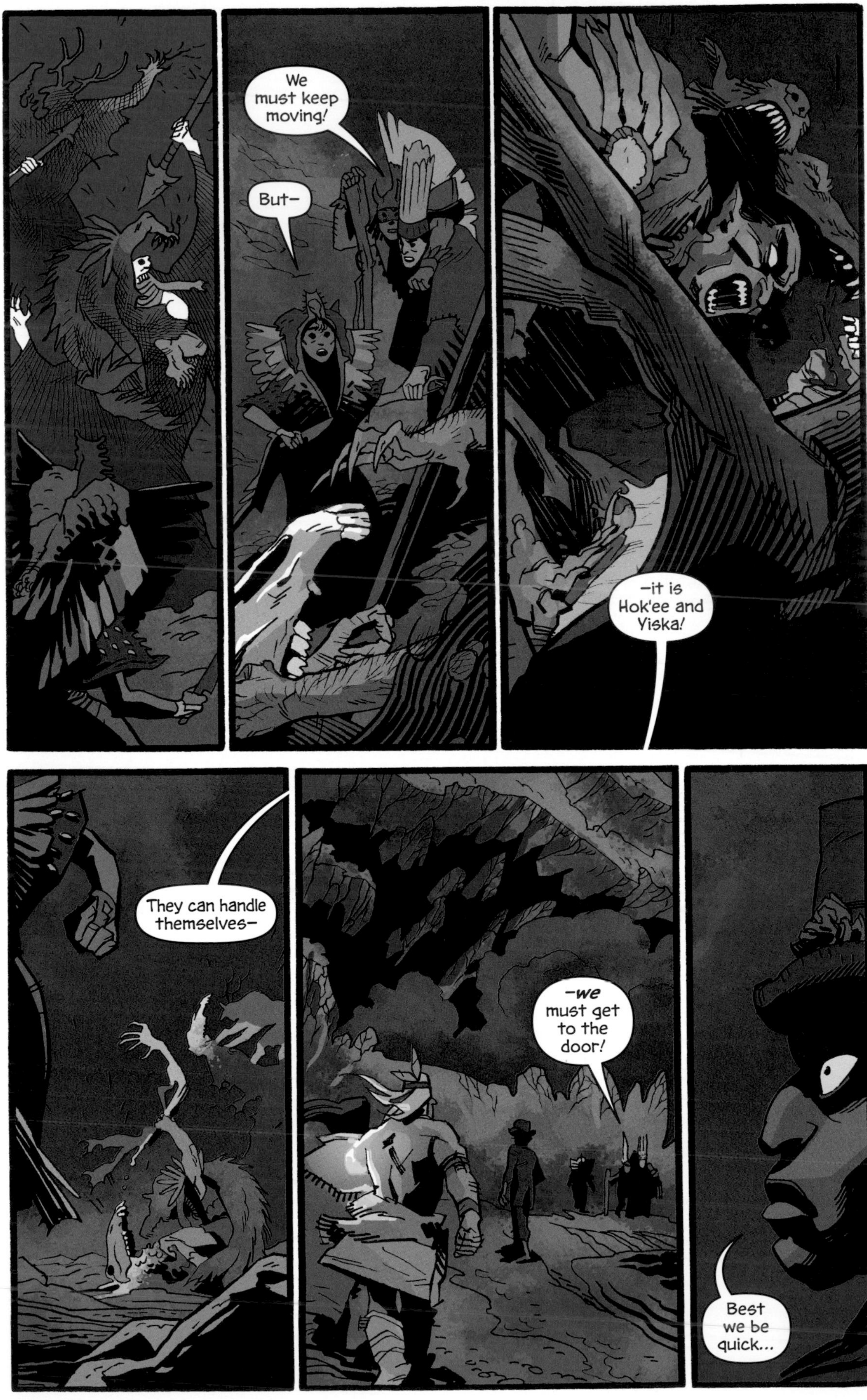
We must keep moving!
But–
–it is Hok'ee and Yiska!
They can handle themselves–
–we must get to the door!
Best we be quick...

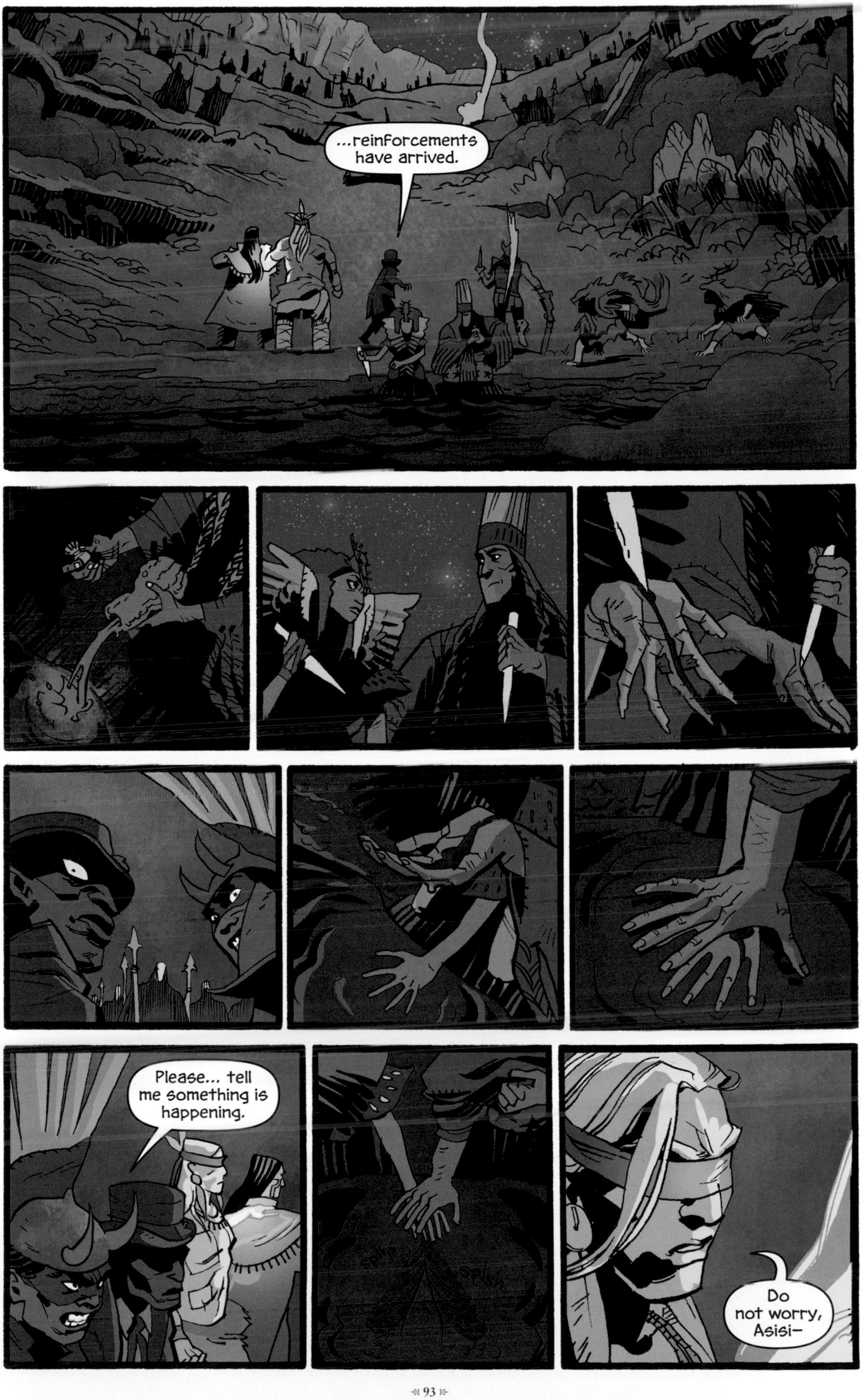
...reinforcements have arrived.
Please... tell me something is happening.
Do not worry, Asisi—

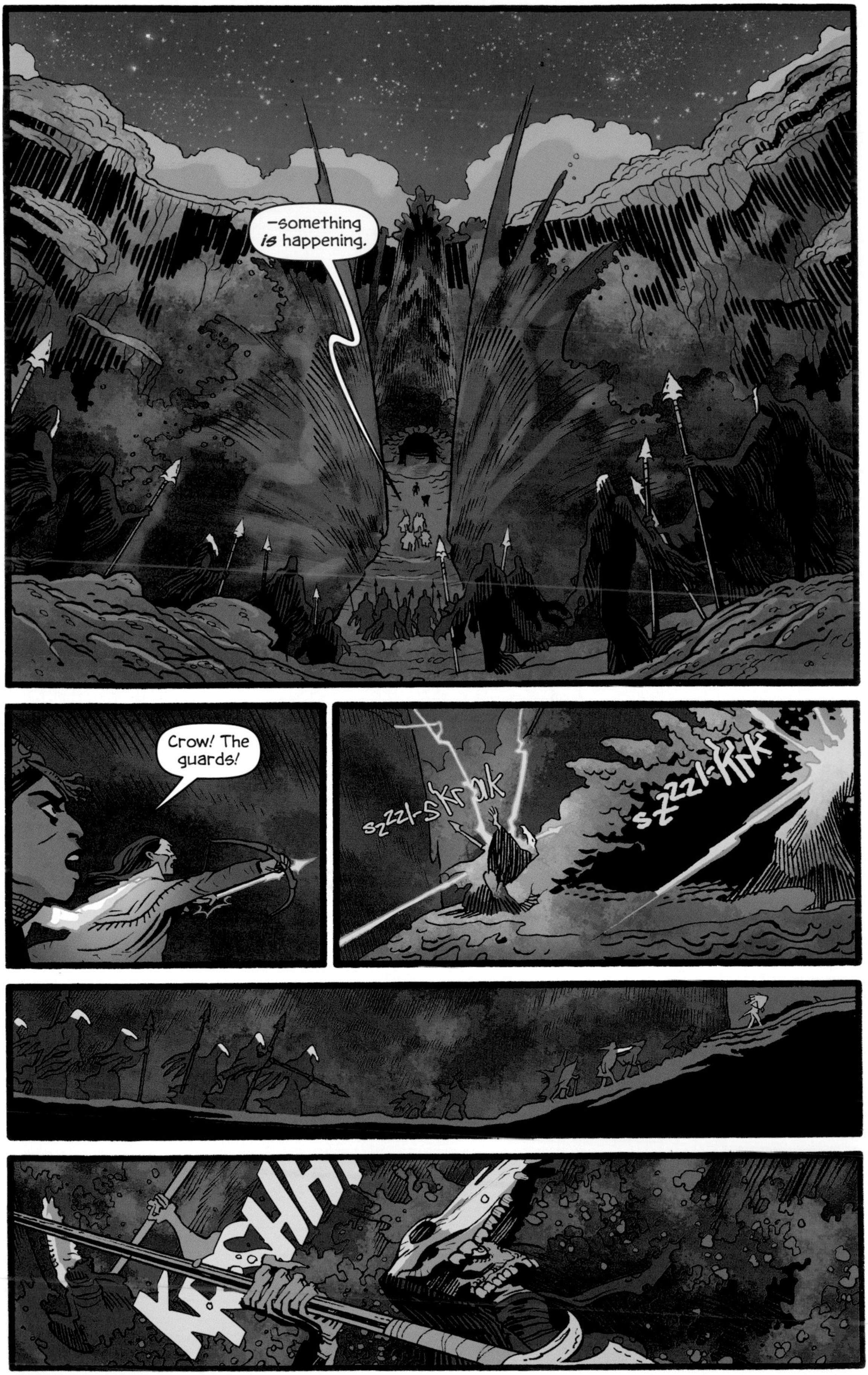
–something *is* happening.
Crow! The guards!
szzzl-sKrak
szzzl-KrK

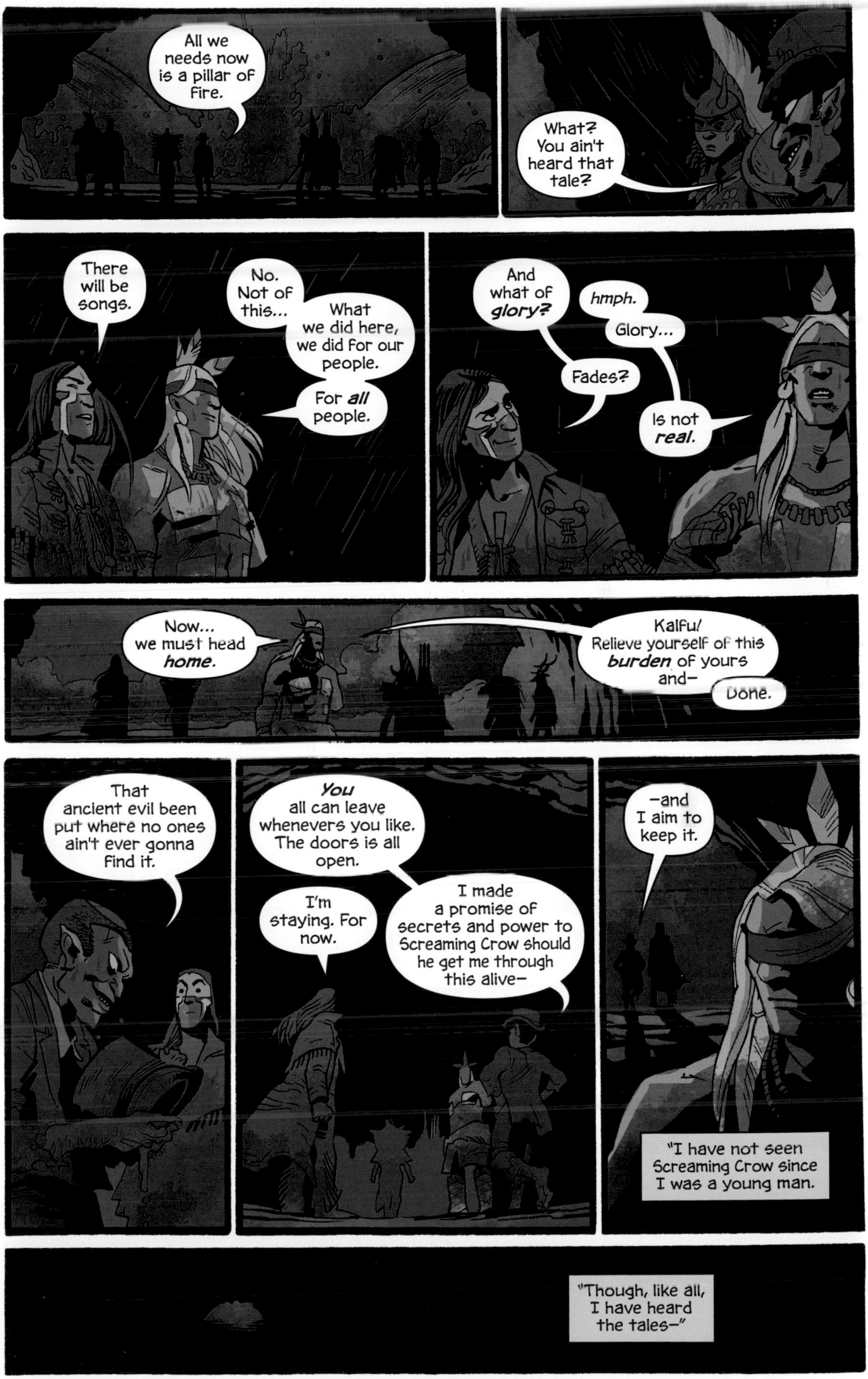

All we needs now is a pillar of fire.
What? You ain't heard that tale?
There will be songs.
No. Not of this...
What we did here, we did for our people.
For *all* people.
And what of *glory?*
hmph.
Glory...
Fades?
Is not *real.*
Now... we must head *home.*
Kalfu! Relieve yourself of this *burden* of yours and—
Done.
That ancient evil been put where no ones ain't ever gonna find it.
You all can leave whenevers you like. The doors is all open.
I'm staying. For now.
I made a promise of secrets and power to Screaming Crow should he get me through this alive—
—and I aim to keep it.
"I have not seen Screaming Crow since I was a young man.
"Though, like all, I have heard the tales—"

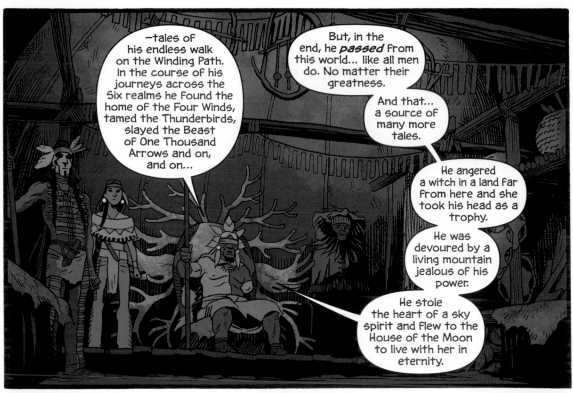

—tales of his endless walk on the Winding Path. In the course of his journeys across the Six realms he found the home of the Four Winds, tamed the Thunderbirds, slayed the Beast of One Thousand Arrows and on, and on...

But, in the end, he *passed* from this world... like all men do. No matter their greatness.

And that... a source of many more tales.

He angered a witch in a land far from here and she took his head as a trophy.

He was devoured by a living mountain jealous of his power.

He stole the heart of a sky spirit and flew to the House of the Moon to live with her in eternity.

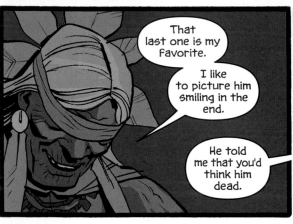

That last one is my favorite.

I like to picture him smiling in the end.

He told me that you'd think him dead.

Apparently, it's a common mistake.

But, I did not come to trade tales, White Wolf. I was *sent* here to deliver a message...

"The very existence of Creation stands on the precipice. The *Six* will soon be united.

"All hope lies with a young girl. A girl who is somewhere between a wish and a promise.

"But, she cannot do it alone. She needs the help of the Four Tribes.

"So speaks the Voice of Thunder."

CHAPTER ONE

Dust to Dust

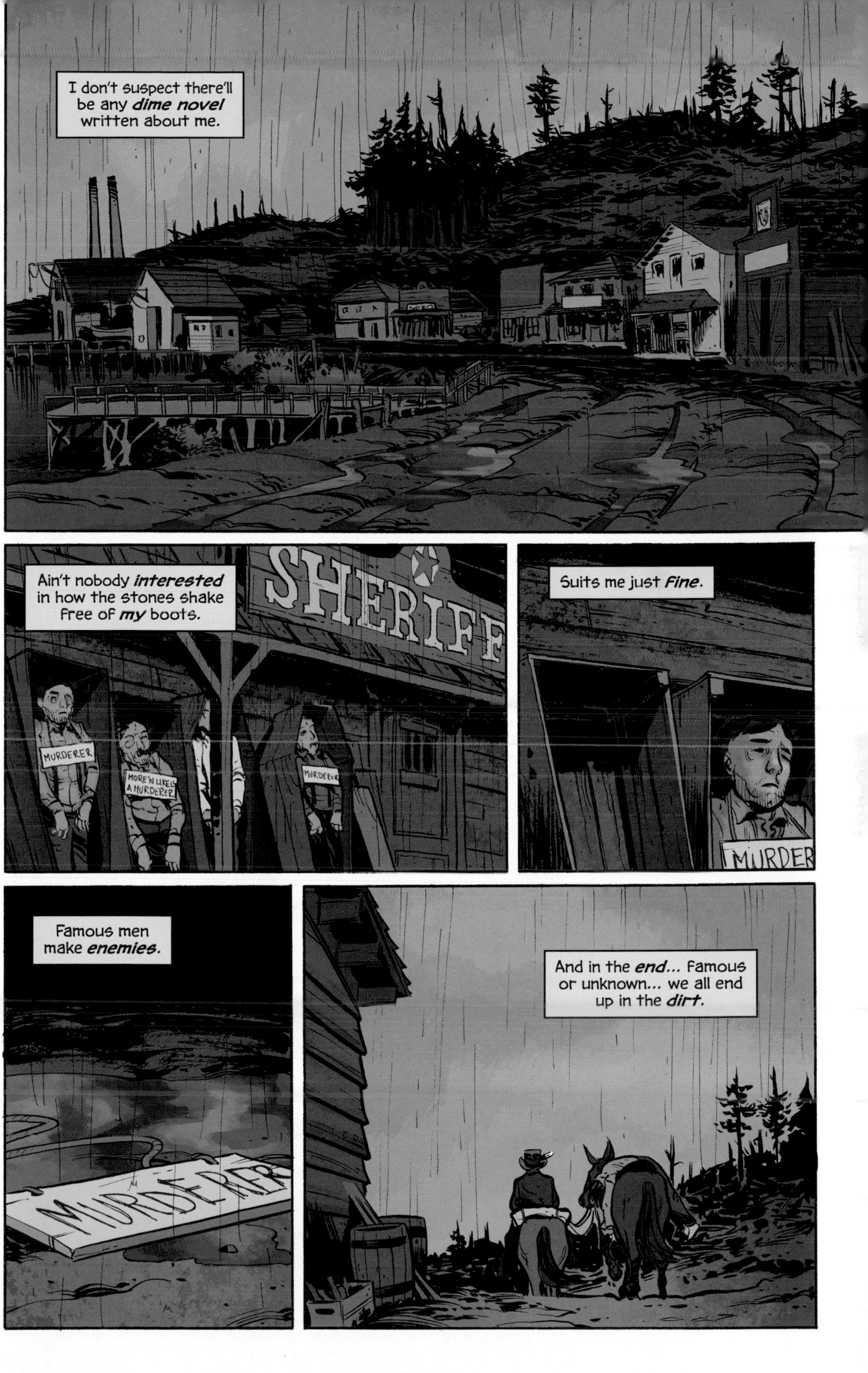
I don't suspect there'll be any *dime novel* written about me.
SHERIFF
Ain't nobody *interested* in how the stones shake free of *my* boots.
MURDERER
MORE'N LIKELY A MURDERER
MURDERER
Suits me just *fine*.
MURDER
Famous men make *enemies*.
MURDERER
And in the *end*... Famous or unknown... we all end up in the *dirt*.

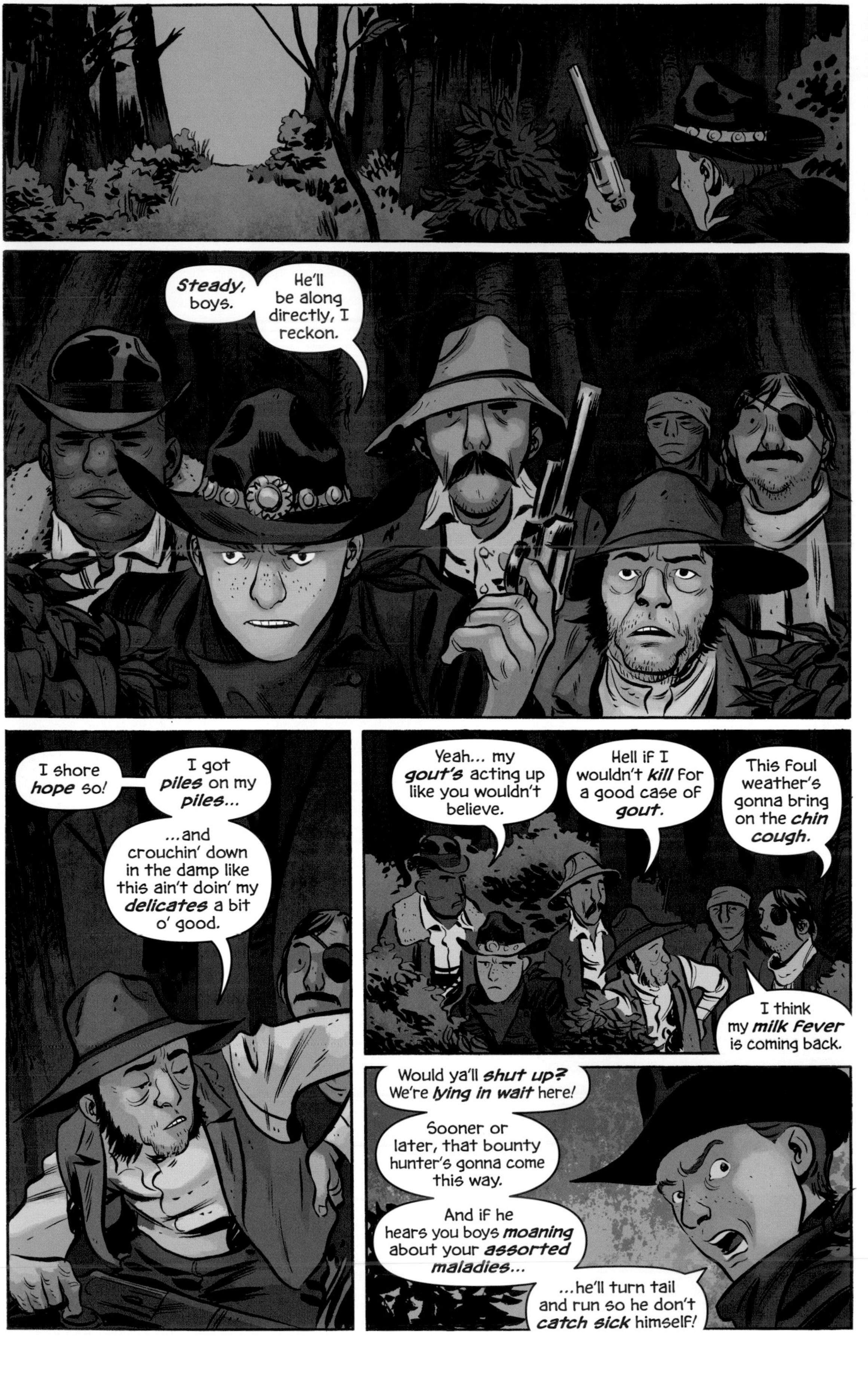
Steady, boys.
He'll be along directly, I reckon.
I shore hope so!
I got piles on my piles...
...and crouchin' down in the damp like this ain't doin' my delicates a bit o' good.
Yeah... my gout's acting up like you wouldn't believe.
Hell if I wouldn't kill for a good case of gout.
This foul weather's gonna bring on the chin cough.
I think my milk fever is coming back.
Would ya'll shut up? We're lying in wait here!
Sooner or later, that bounty hunter's gonna come this way.
And if he hears you boys moaning about your assorted maladies...
...he'll turn tail and run so he don't catch sick himself!

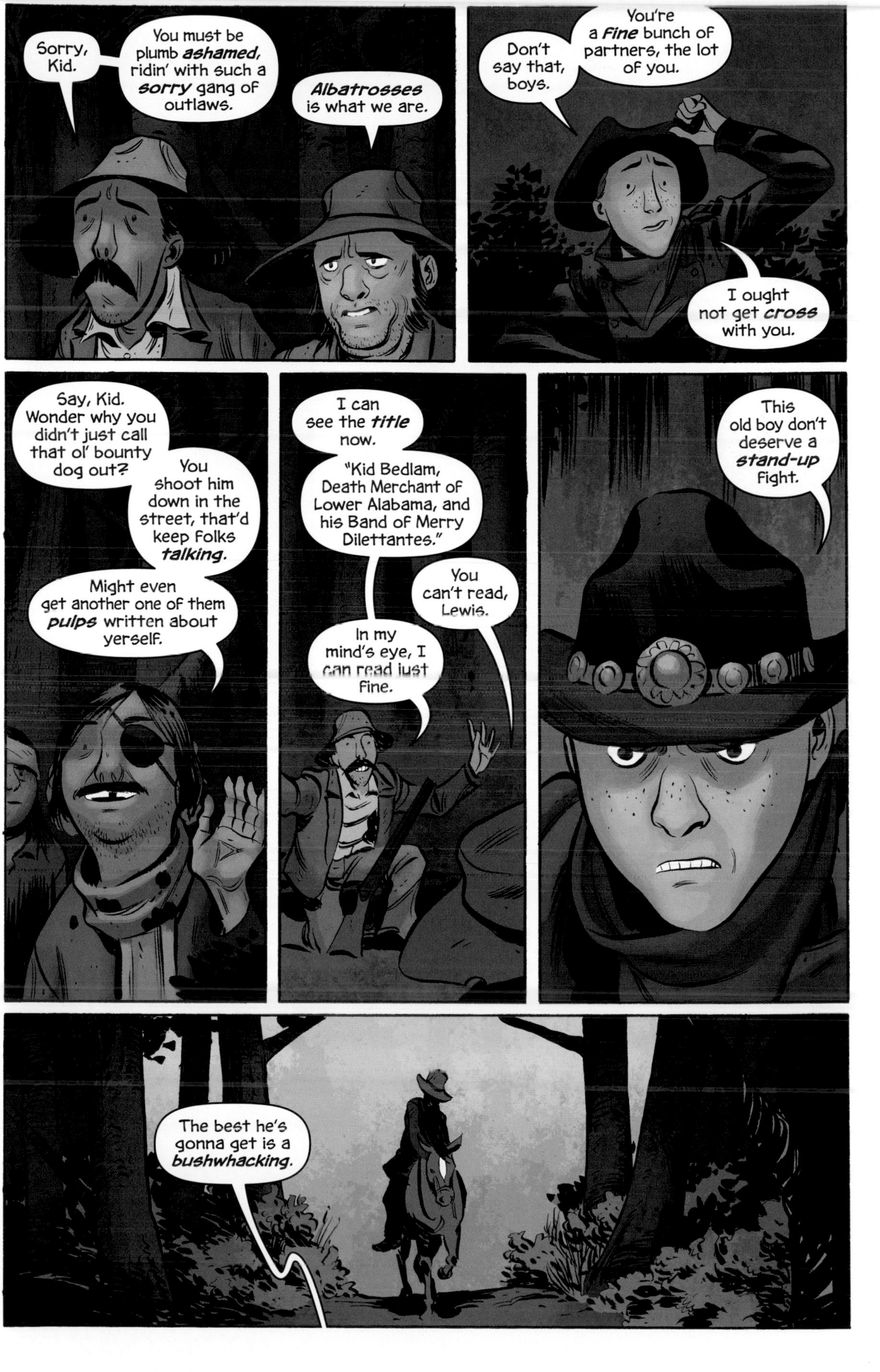
Sorry, Kid.
You must be plumb *ashamed*, ridin' with such a *sorry* gang of outlaws.
Albatrosses is what we are.
Don't say that, boys.
You're a *fine* bunch of partners, the lot of you.
I ought not get *cross* with you.
Say, Kid. Wonder why you didn't just call that ol' bounty dog out?
You shoot him down in the street, that'd keep folks *talking*.
Might even get another one of them *pulps* written about yerself.
I can see the *title* now.
"Kid Bedlam, Death Merchant of Lower Alabama, and his Band of Merry Dilettantes."
You can't read, Lewis.
In my mind's eye, I can read just fine.
This old boy don't deserve a *stand-up* fight.
The best he's gonna get is a *bushwhacking*.

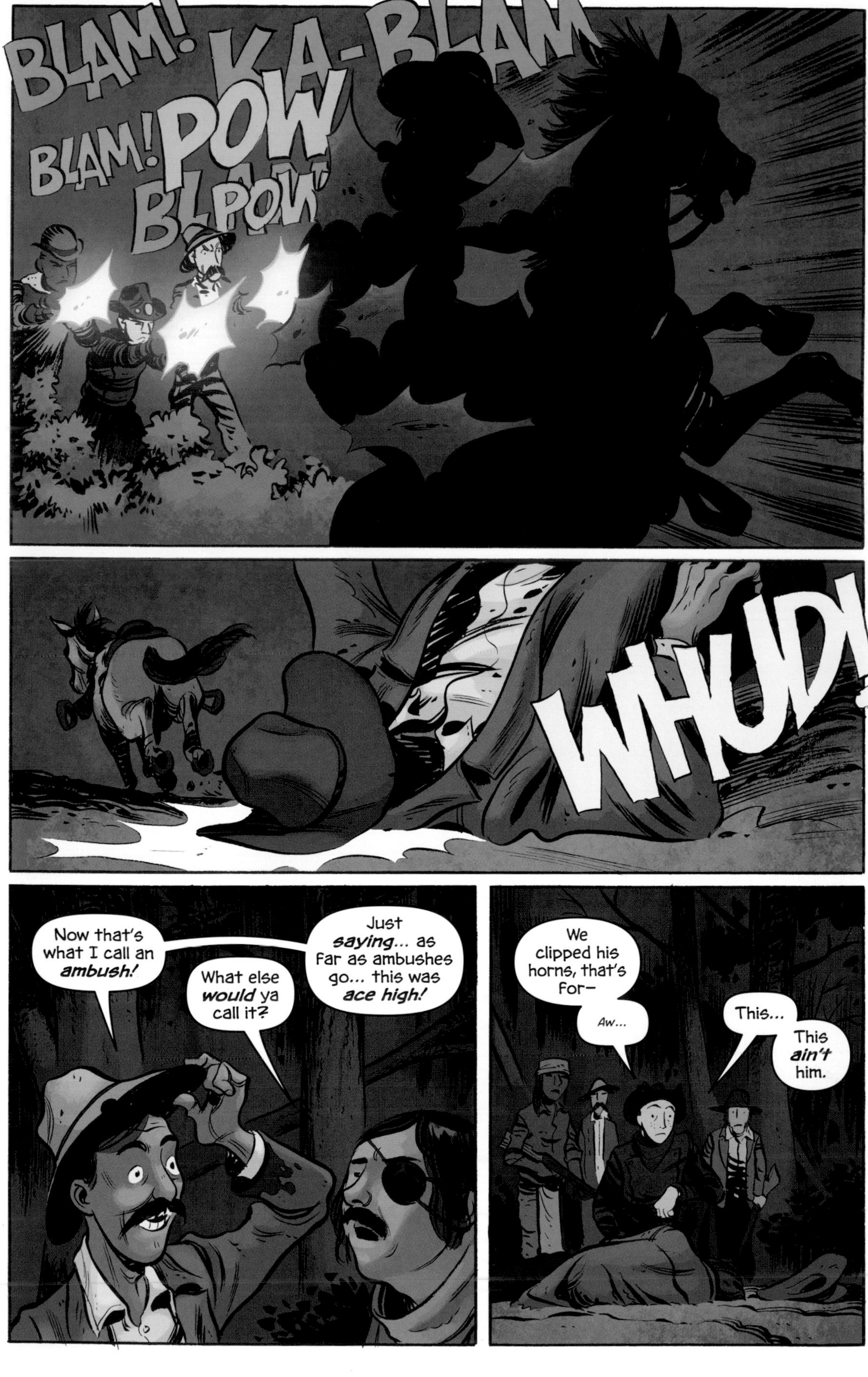
BLAM! KA-BLAM
BLAM! POW
BLPOW
WHUD!
Now that's what I call an ambush!
What else would ya call it?
Just saying... as far as ambushes go... this was ace high!
We clipped his horns, that's for–
Aw...
This... This ain't him.

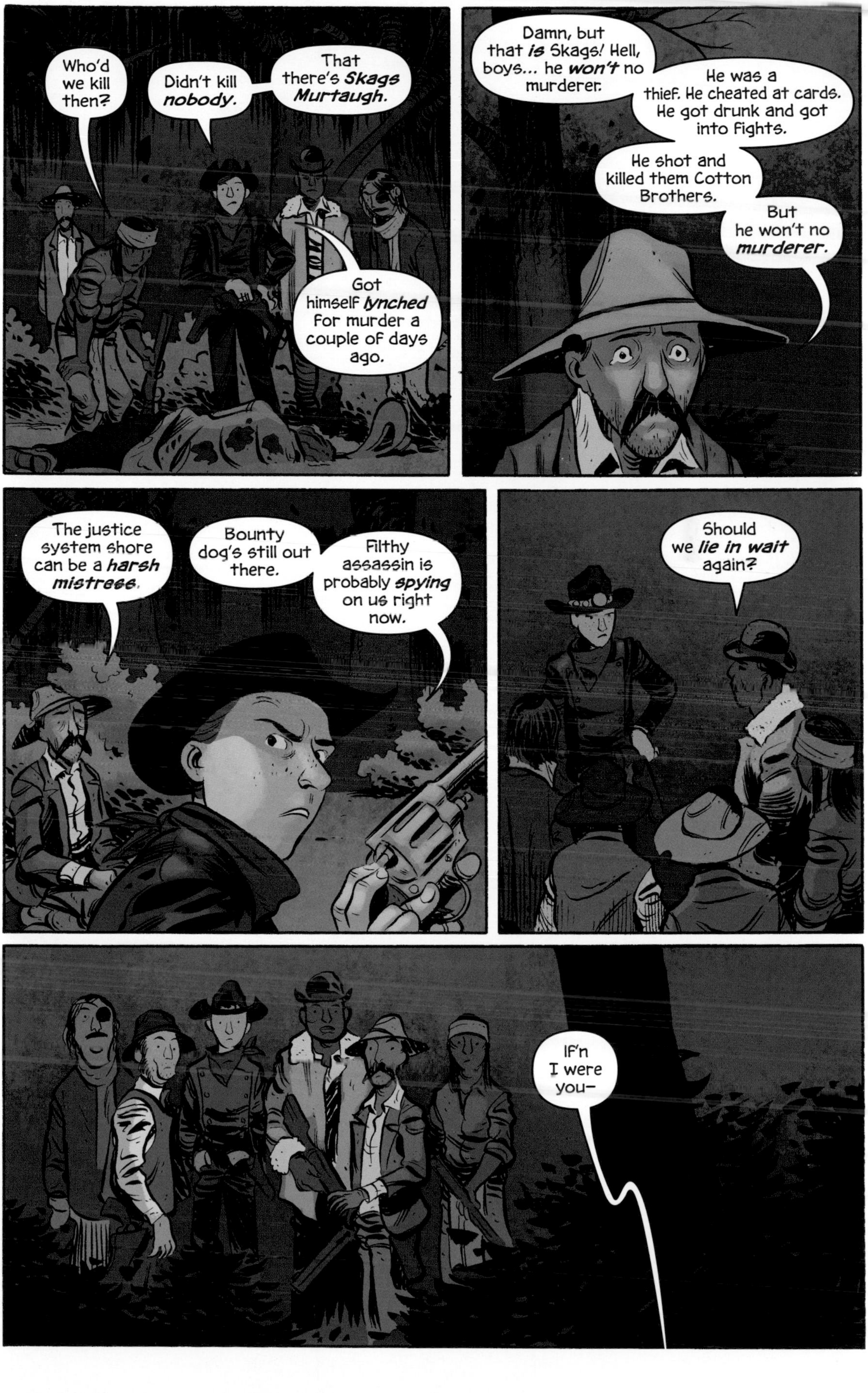

Who'd we kill then?
Didn't kill *nobody*.
That there's *Skags Murtaugh*.
Got himself *lynched* for murder a couple of days ago.
Damn, but that *is* Skags! Hell, boys... he *won't* no murderer.
He was a thief. He cheated at cards. He got drunk and got into fights.
He shot and killed them Cotton Brothers.
But he won't no *murderer*.
The justice system shore can be a *harsh mistress*.
Bounty dog's still out there.
Filthy assassin is probably *spying* on us right now.
Should we *lie in wait* again?
If'n I were you—

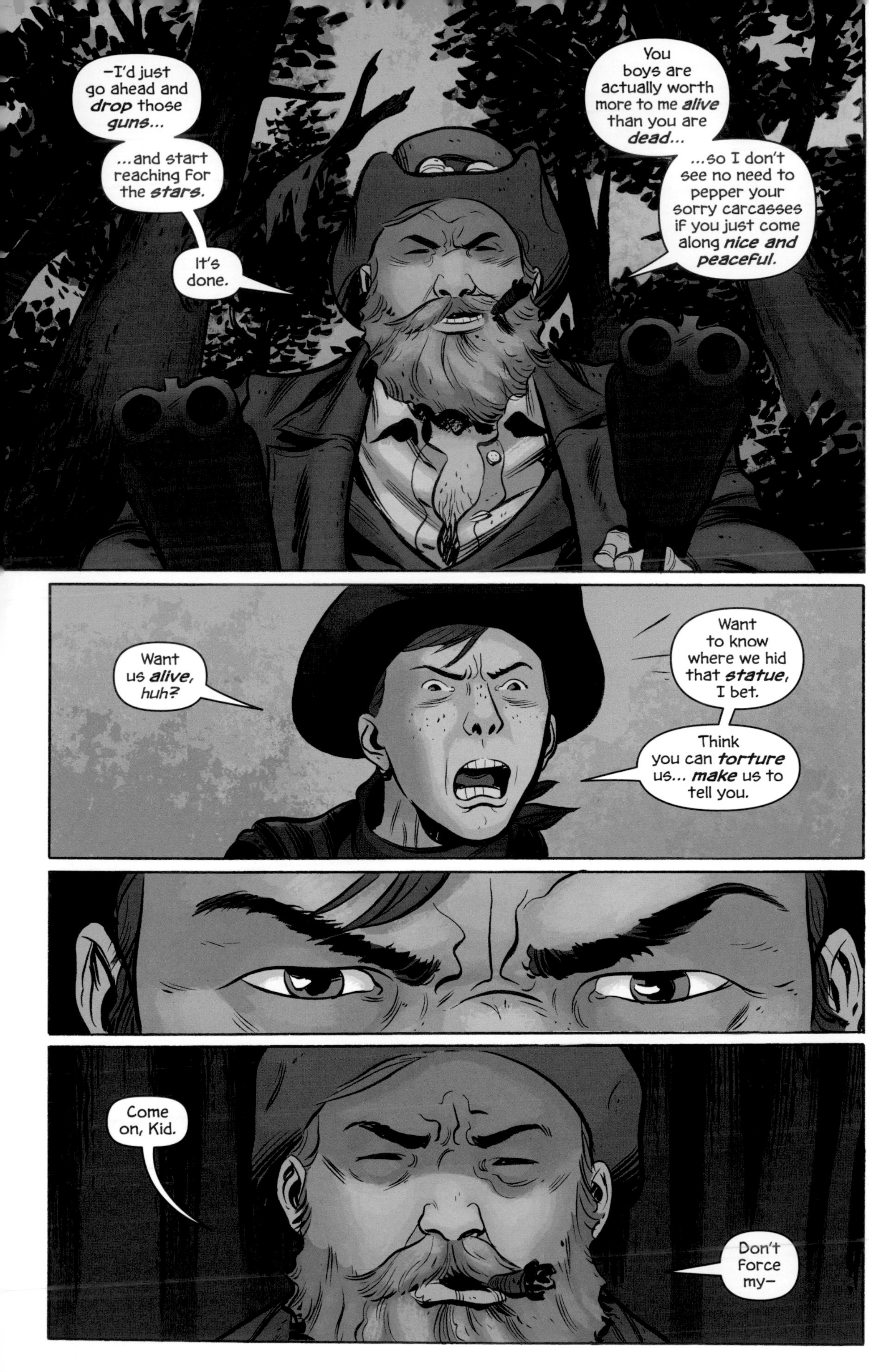

–I'd just go ahead and drop those guns...
...and start reaching for the stars.
It's done.
You boys are actually worth more to me alive than you are dead...
...so I don't see no need to pepper your sorry carcasses if you just come along nice and peaceful.
Want us alive, huh?
Want to know where we hid that statue, I bet.
Think you can torture us... make us to tell you.
Come on, Kid.
Don't force my–

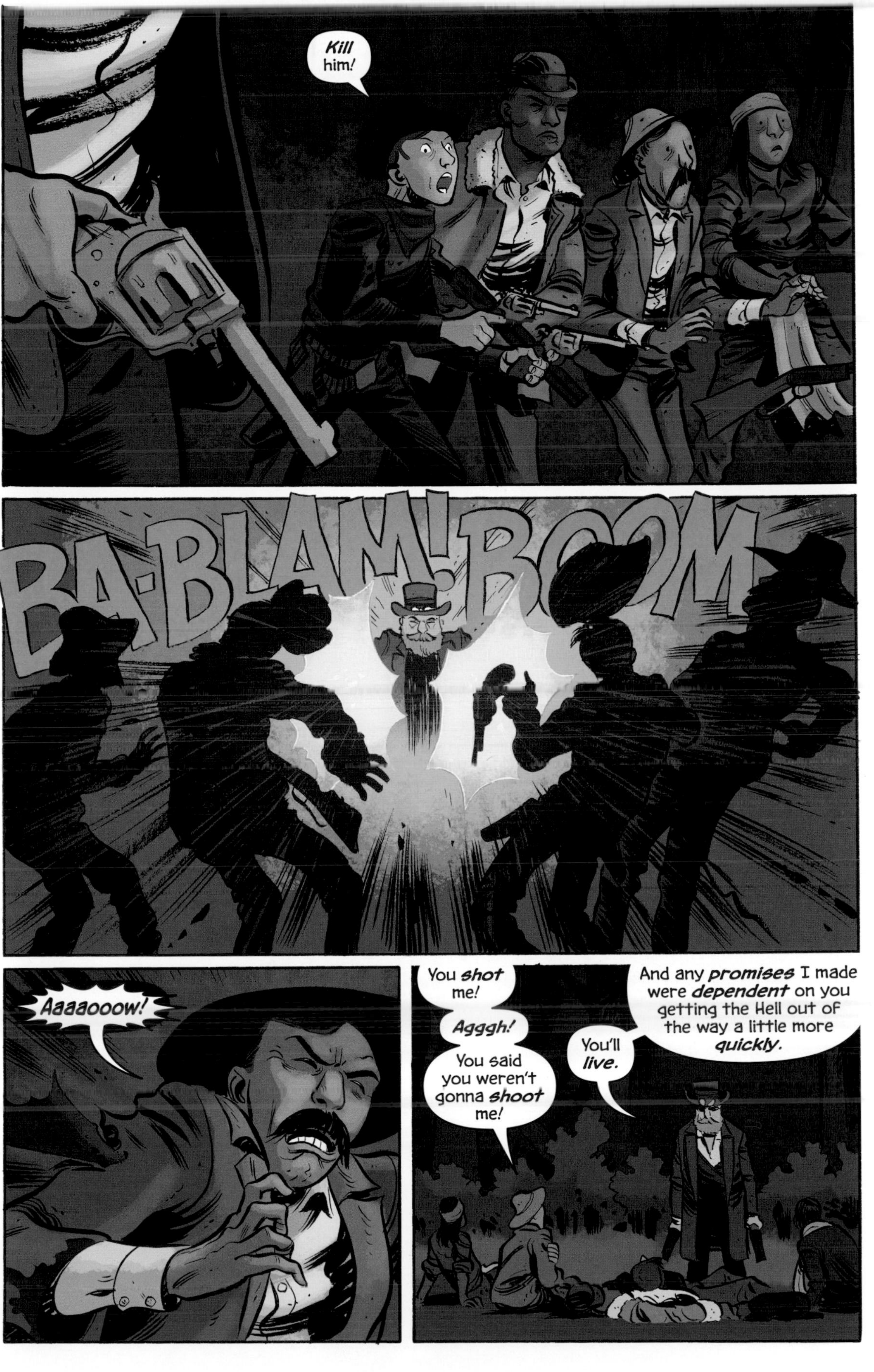
Kill him!
BA-BLAM! BOOM
Aaaaooow!
You shot me!
Agggh!
You said you weren't gonna shoot me!
You'll live.
And any promises I made were dependent on you getting the Hell out of the way a little more quickly.

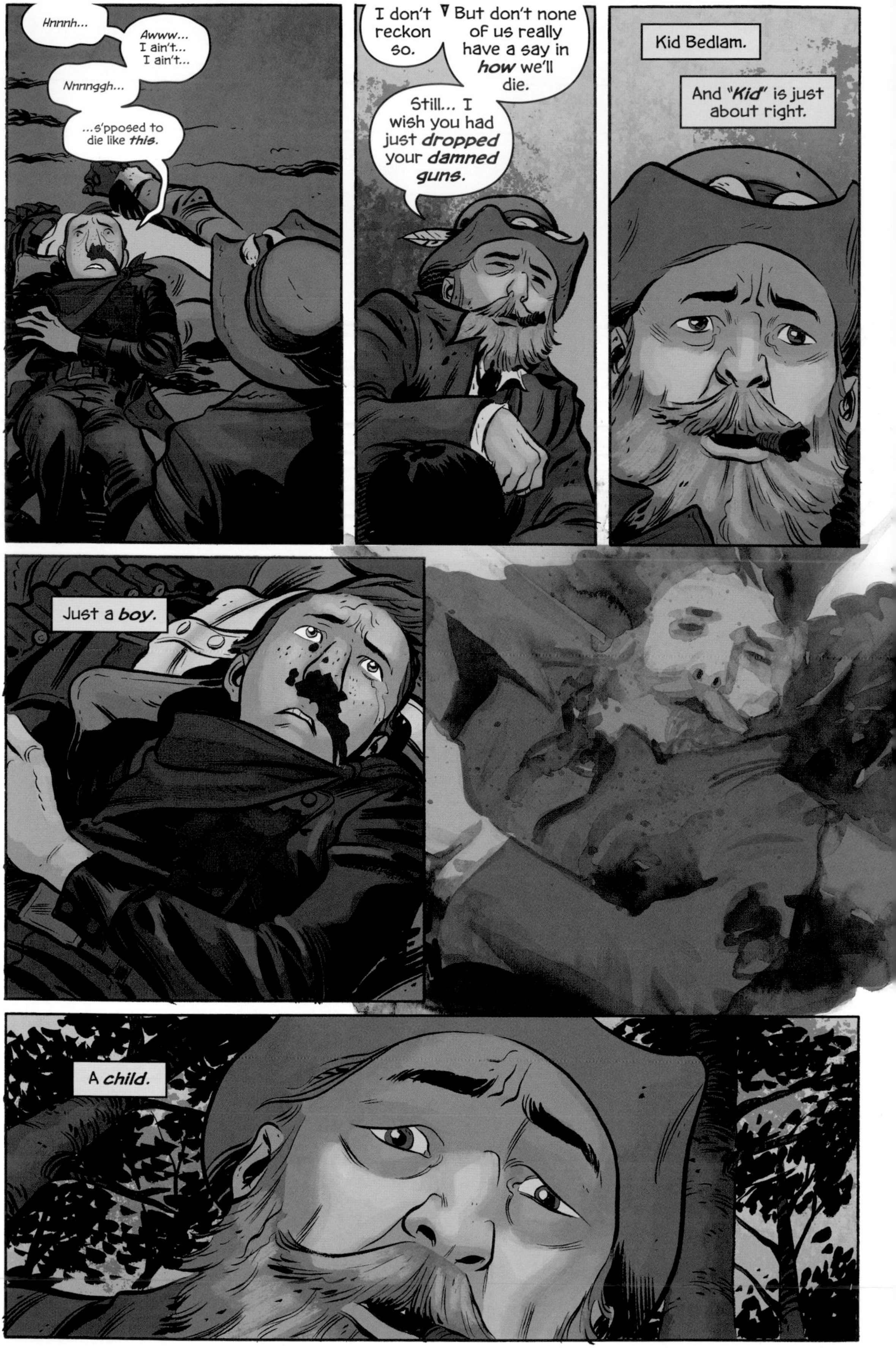

Hnnnh...
Awww... I ain't... I ain't...
Nnnngh...
...s'pposed to die like *this*.
I don't reckon so.
But don't none of us really have a say in *how* we'll die.
Still... I wish you had just *dropped* your *damned guns*.
Kid Bedlam.
And "*Kid*" is just about right.
Just a *boy*.
A *child*.

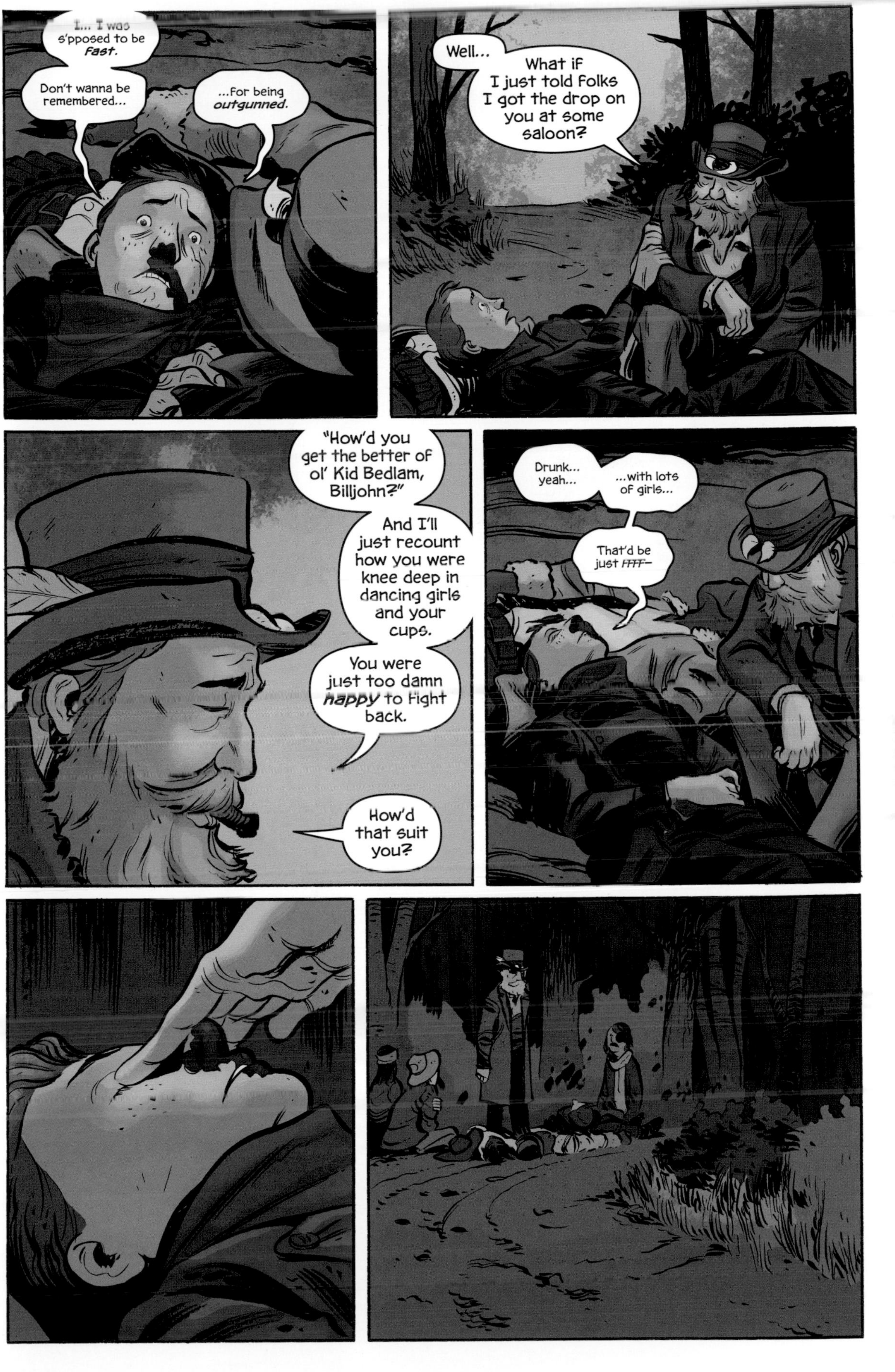
I... I was s'pposed to be *fast.*
Don't wanna be remembered...
...for being *outgunned.*
Well...
What if I just told folks I got the drop on you at some saloon?
"How'd you get the better of ol' Kid Bedlam, Billjohn?"
And I'll just recount how you were knee deep in dancing girls and your cups.
You were just too damn *happy* to fight back.
How'd that suit you?
Drunk... yeah...
...with lots of girls...
That'd be just FFFF–

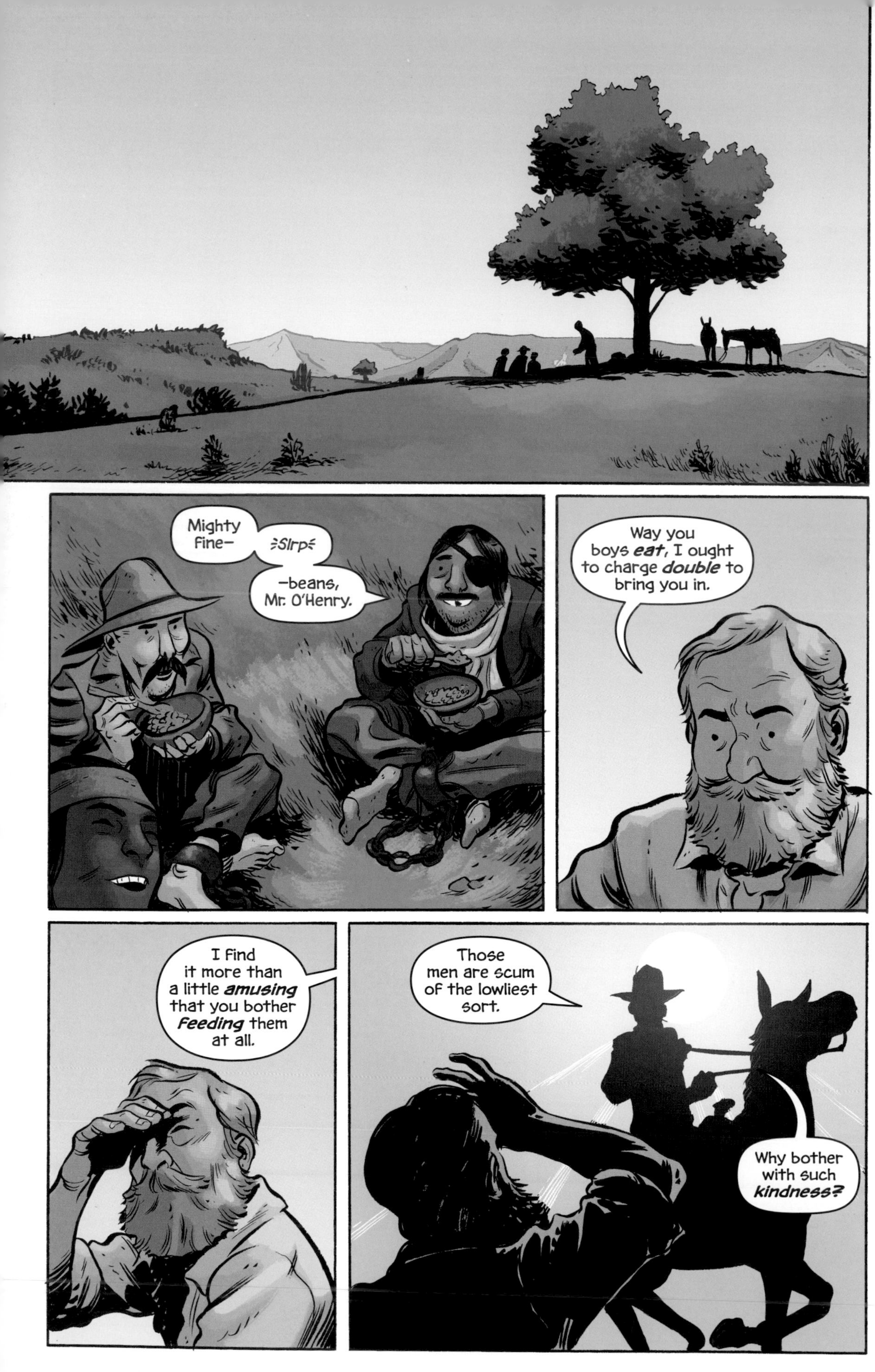
Mighty fine—
≈Slrp≈
—beans, Mr. O'Henry.
Way you boys *eat*, I ought to charge *double* to bring you in.
I find it more than a little *amusing* that you bother *feeding* them at all.
Those men are scum of the lowliest sort.
Why bother with such *kindness?*

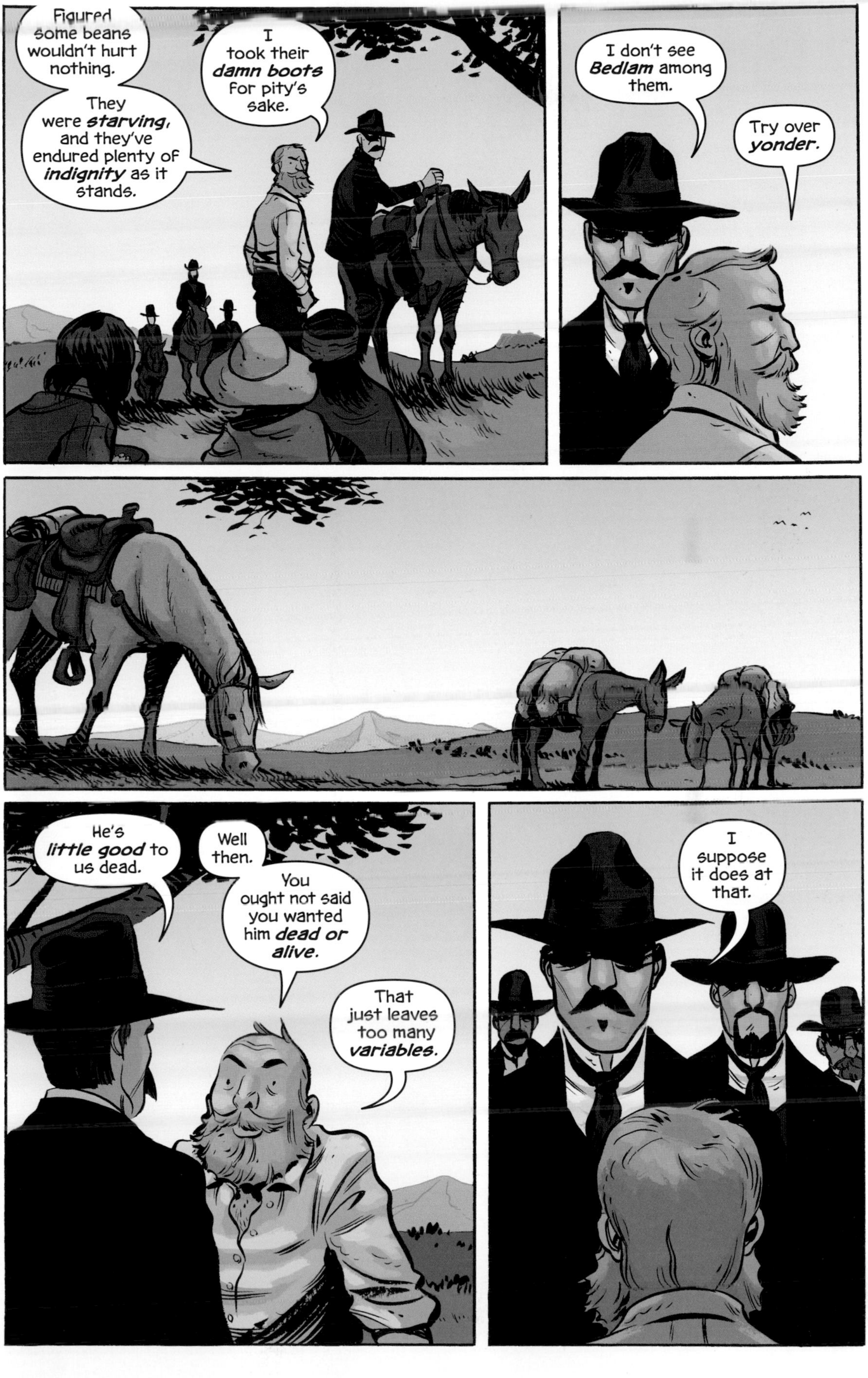
Figured some beans wouldn't hurt nothing.
They were *starving*, and they've endured plenty of *indignity* as it stands.
I took their *damn boots* for pity's sake.
I don't see *Bedlam* among them.
Try over *yonder*.
He's *little good* to us dead.
Well then.
You ought not said you wanted him *dead or alive*.
That just leaves too many *variables*.
I suppose it does at that.

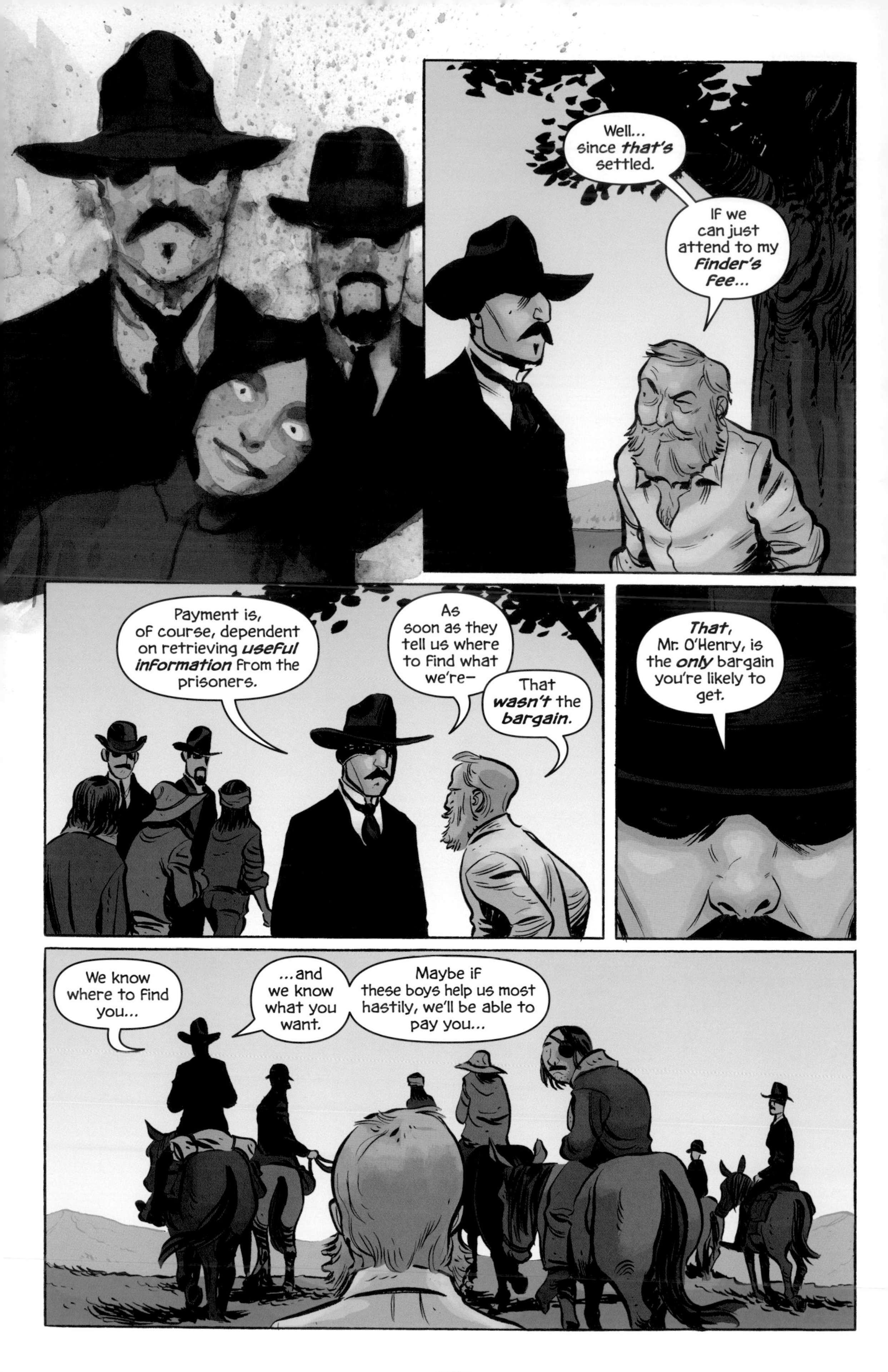

Well... since *that's* settled.
If we can just attend to my *Finder's Fee...*
Payment is, of course, dependent on retrieving *useful information* from the prisoners.
As soon as they tell us where to find what we're–
That *wasn't* the *bargain.*
That, Mr. O'Henry, is the *only* bargain you're likely to get.
We know where to find you...
...and we know what you want.
Maybe if these boys help us most hastily, we'll be able to pay you...

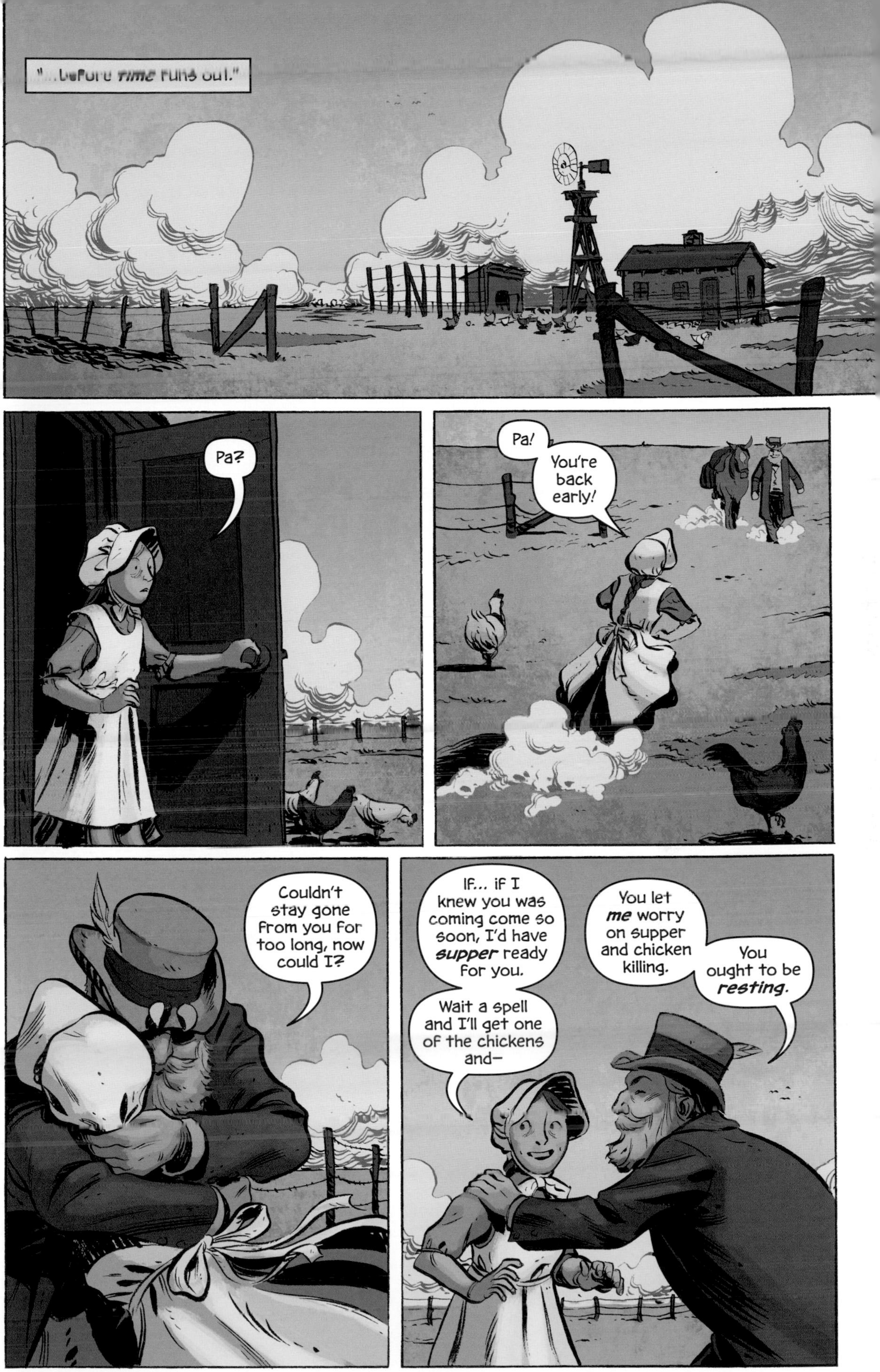
"...before time runs out."
Pa?
Pa!
You're back early!
Couldn't stay gone from you for too long, now could I?
If... if I knew you was coming come so soon, I'd have supper ready for you.
Wait a spell and I'll get one of the chickens and–
You let me worry on supper and chicken killing.
You ought to be resting.

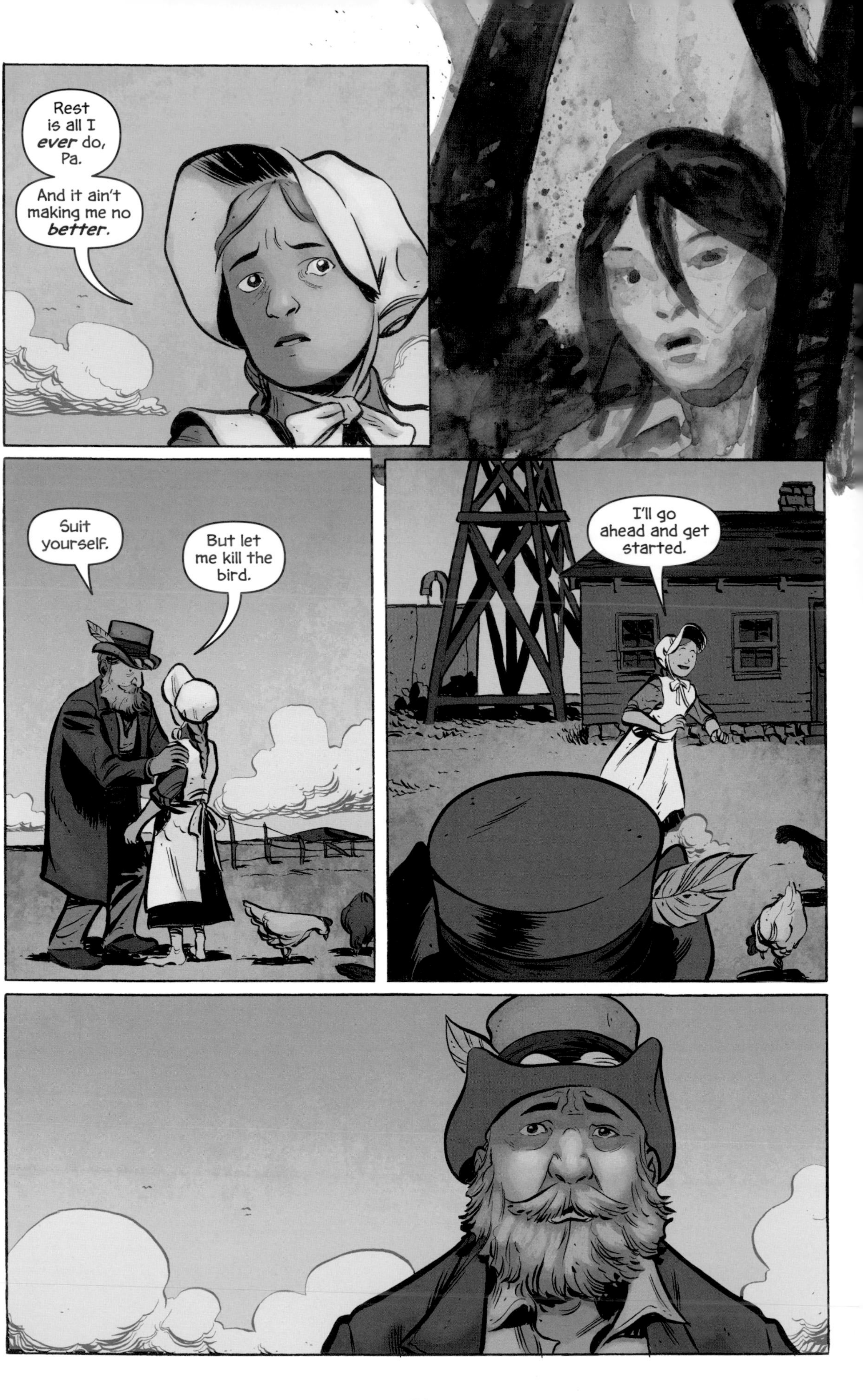
Rest is all I *ever* do, Pa.
And it ain't making me no *better*.
Suit yourself.
But let me kill the bird.
I'll go ahead and get started.

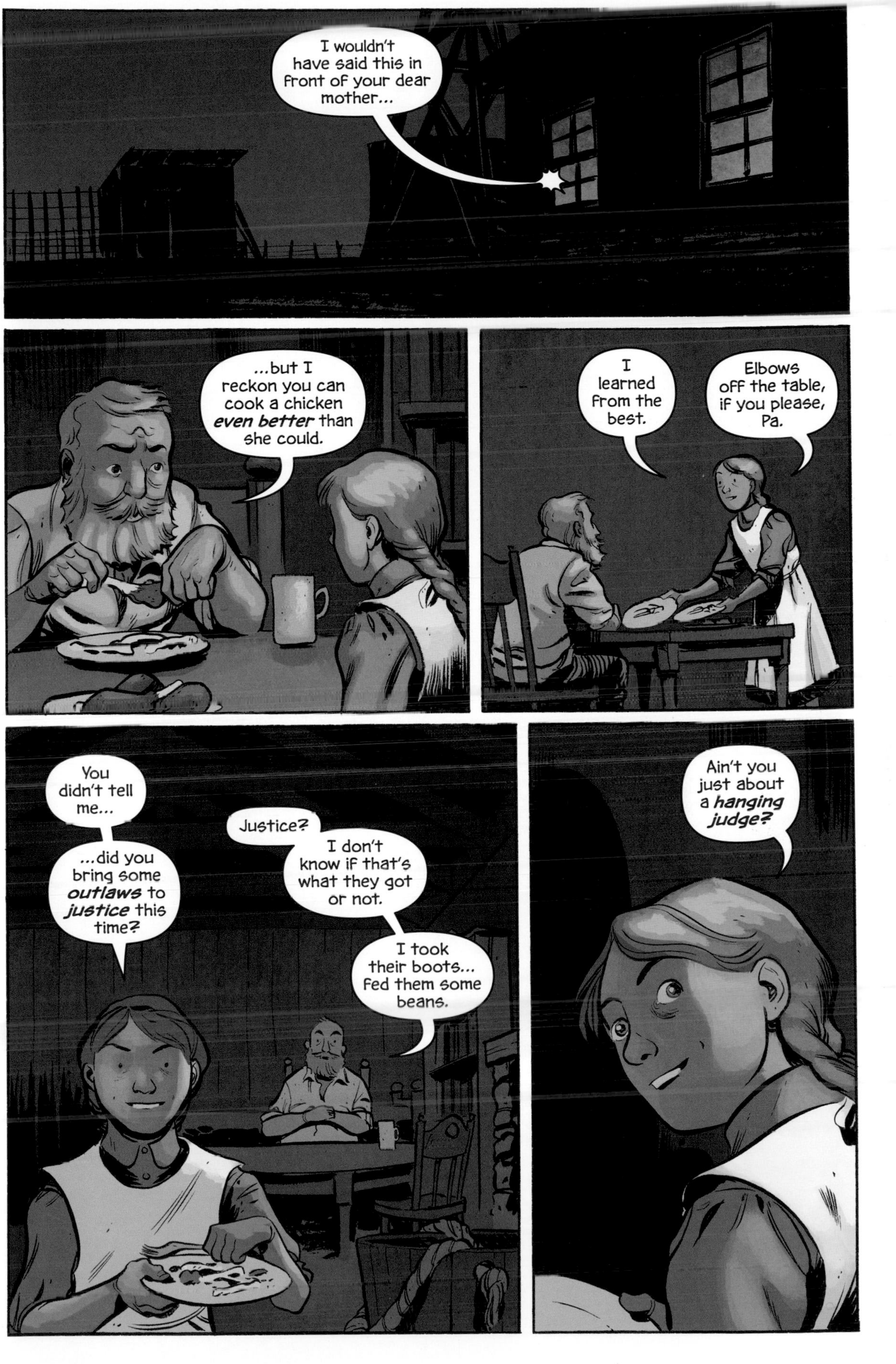
I wouldn't have said this in front of your dear mother...
...but I reckon you can cook a chicken *even better* than she could.
I learned from the best.
Elbows off the table, if you please, Pa.
You didn't tell me...
...did you bring some *outlaws* to *justice* this time?
Justice?
I don't know if that's what they got or not.
I took their boots... Fed them some beans.
Ain't you just about a *hanging judge?*

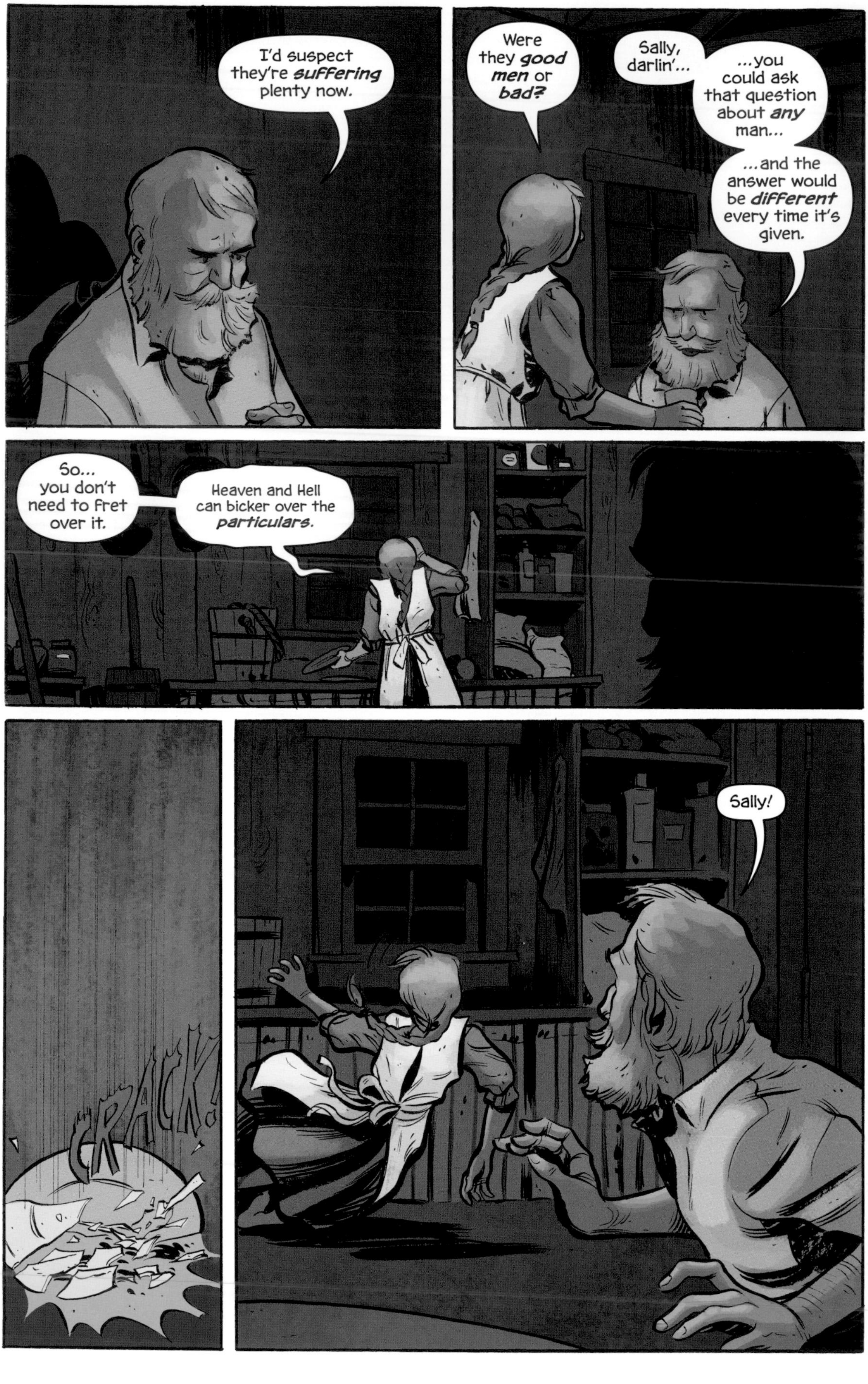
I'd suspect they're *suffering* plenty now.
Were they ***good men*** or ***bad?***
Sally, darlin'...
...you could ask that question about ***any*** man...
...and the answer would be ***different*** every time it's given.
So... you don't need to fret over it.
Heaven and Hell can bicker over the ***particulars***.
CRACK!
Sally!

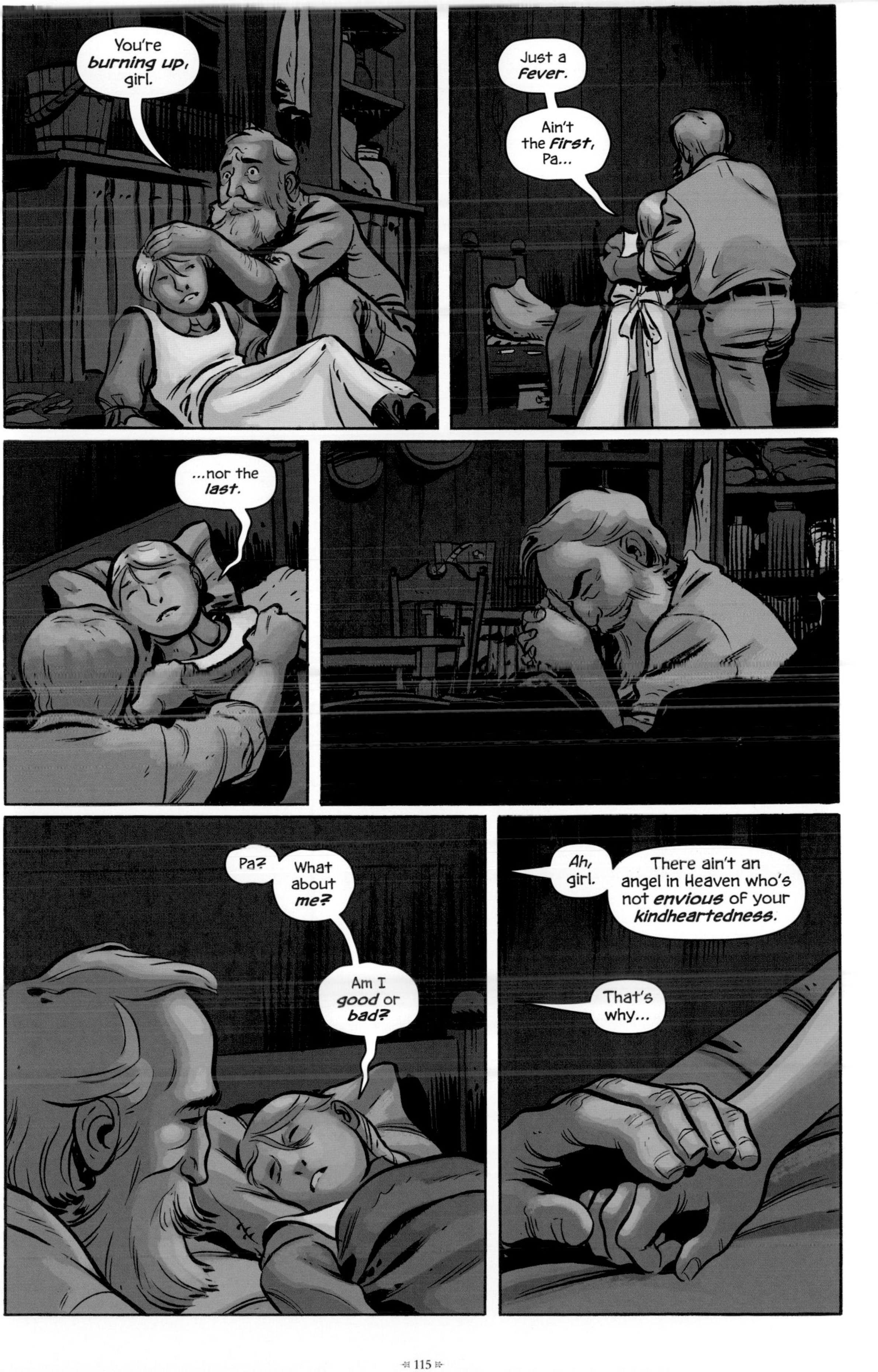
You're burning up, girl.
Just a fever.
Ain't the first, Pa...
...nor the last.
Pa?
What about me?
Am I good or bad?
Ah, girl.
There ain't an angel in Heaven who's not envious of your kindheartedness.
That's why...

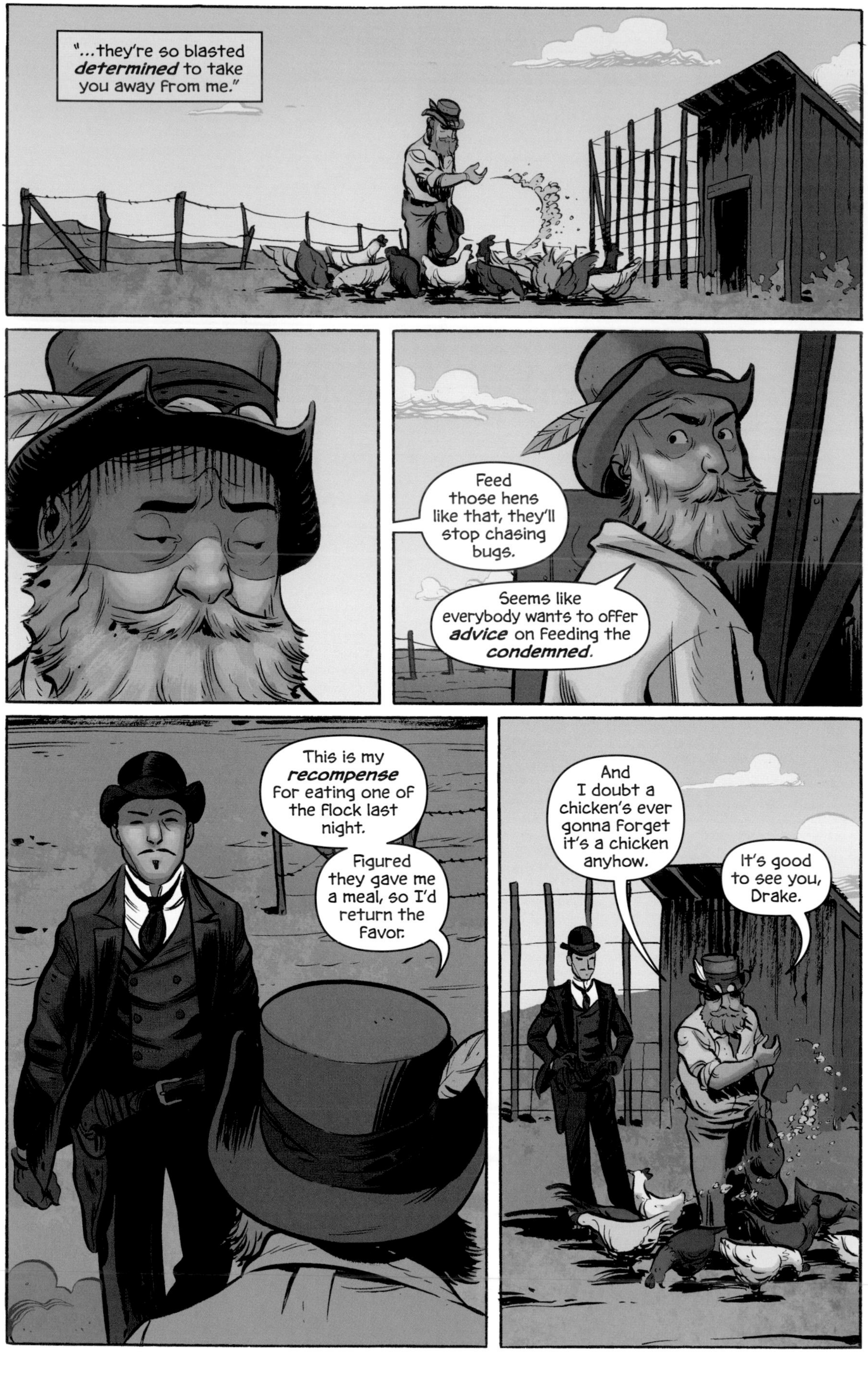
"...they're so blasted *determined* to take you away from me."
Feed those hens like that, they'll stop chasing bugs.
Seems like everybody wants to offer *advice* on feeding the *condemned*.
This is my *recompense* for eating one of the flock last night.
Figured they gave me a meal, so I'd return the favor.
And I doubt a chicken's ever gonna forget it's a chicken anyhow.
It's good to see you, Drake.

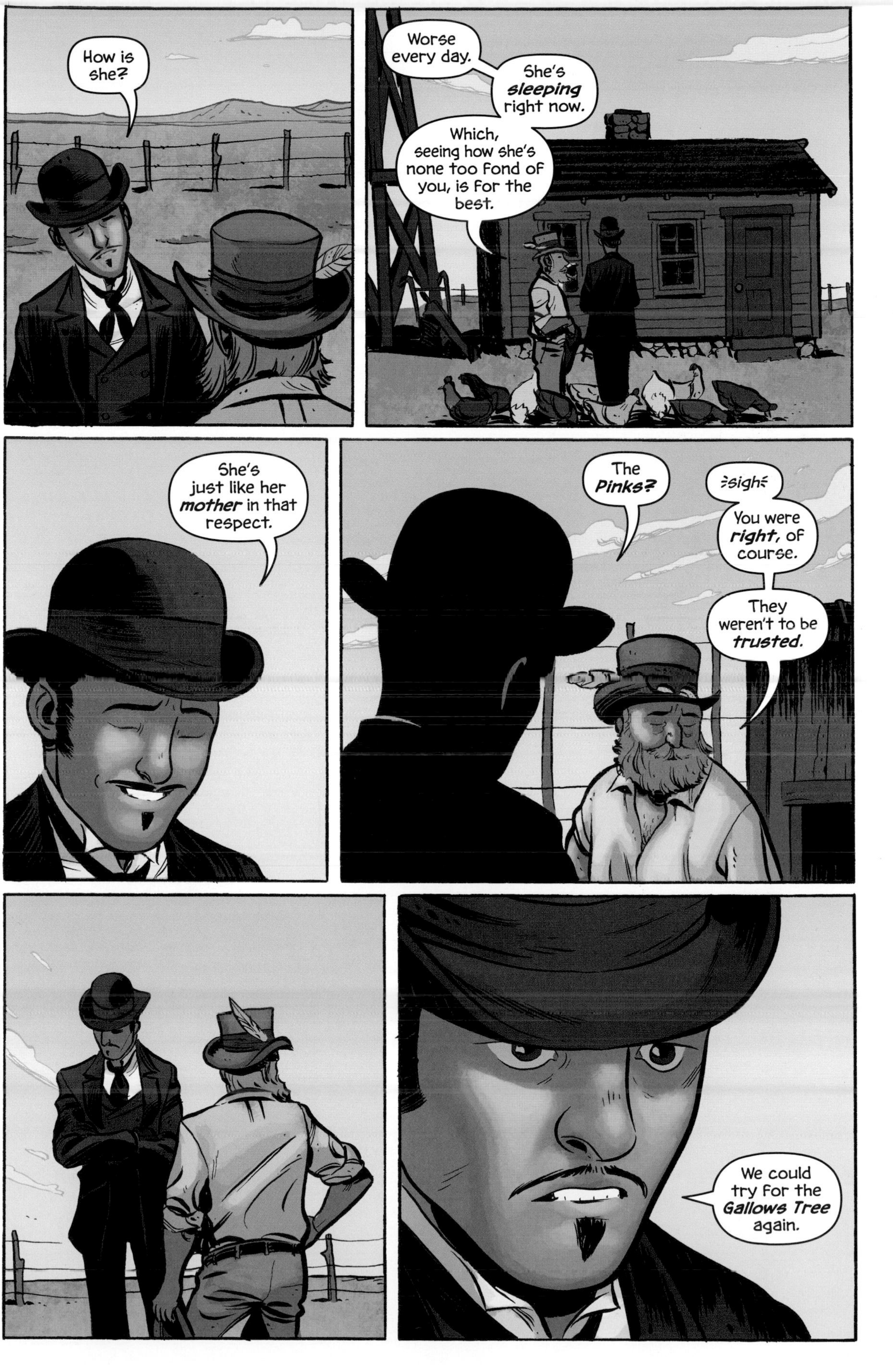
How is she?
Worse every day.
She's *sleeping* right now.
Which, seeing how she's none too fond of you, is for the best.
She's just like her *mother* in that respect.
The *Pinks?*
sigh
You were *right,* of course.
They weren't to be *trusted.*
We could try for the *Gallows Tree* again.

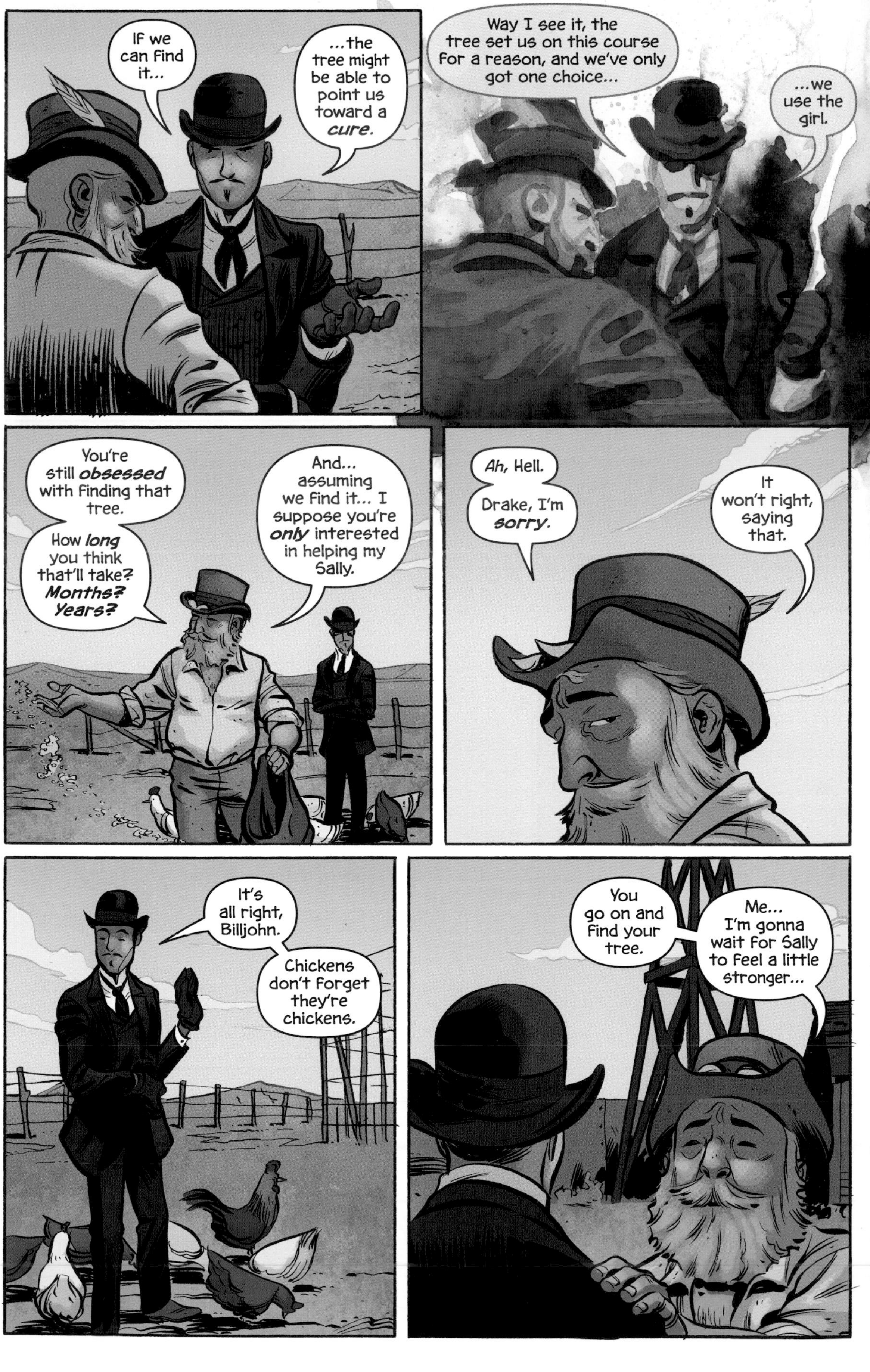
If we can find it...
...the tree might be able to point us toward a *cure*.
Way I see it, the tree set us on this course for a reason, and we've only got one choice...
...we use the girl.
You're still *obsessed* with finding that tree.
How *long* you think that'll take? *Months? Years?*
And... assuming we find it... I suppose you're *only* interested in helping my Sally.
Ah, Hell.
Drake, I'm *sorry*.
It won't right, saying that.
It's all right, Billjohn.
Chickens don't forget they're chickens.
You go on and find your tree.
Me... I'm gonna wait for Sally to feel a little stronger...

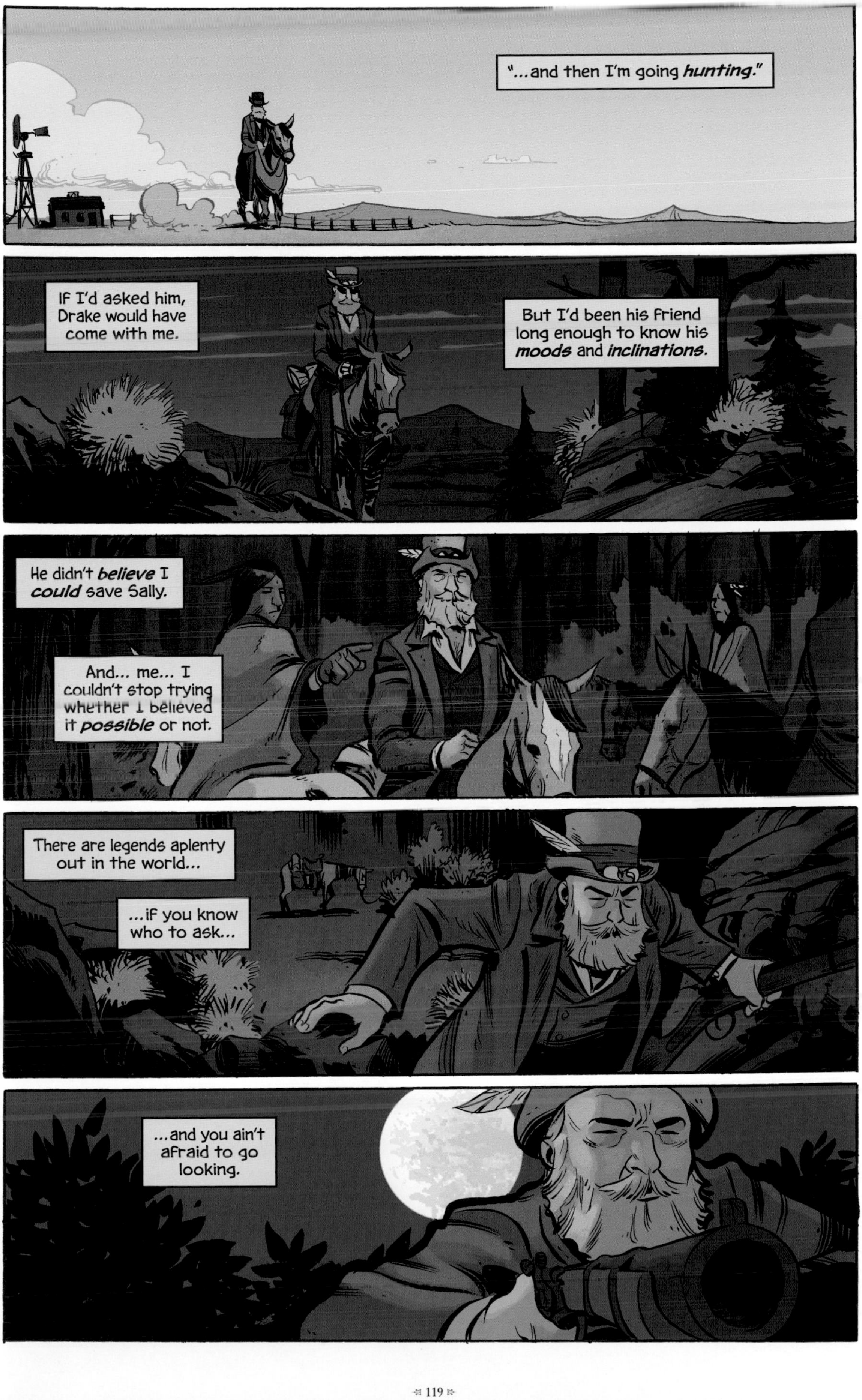
"...and then I'm going *hunting*."
If I'd asked him, Drake would have come with me.
But I'd been his friend long enough to know his *moods* and *inclinations*.
He didn't *believe* I *could* save Sally.
And... me... I couldn't stop trying whether I believed it *possible* or not.
There are legends aplenty out in the world...
...if you know who to ask...
...and you ain't afraid to go looking.

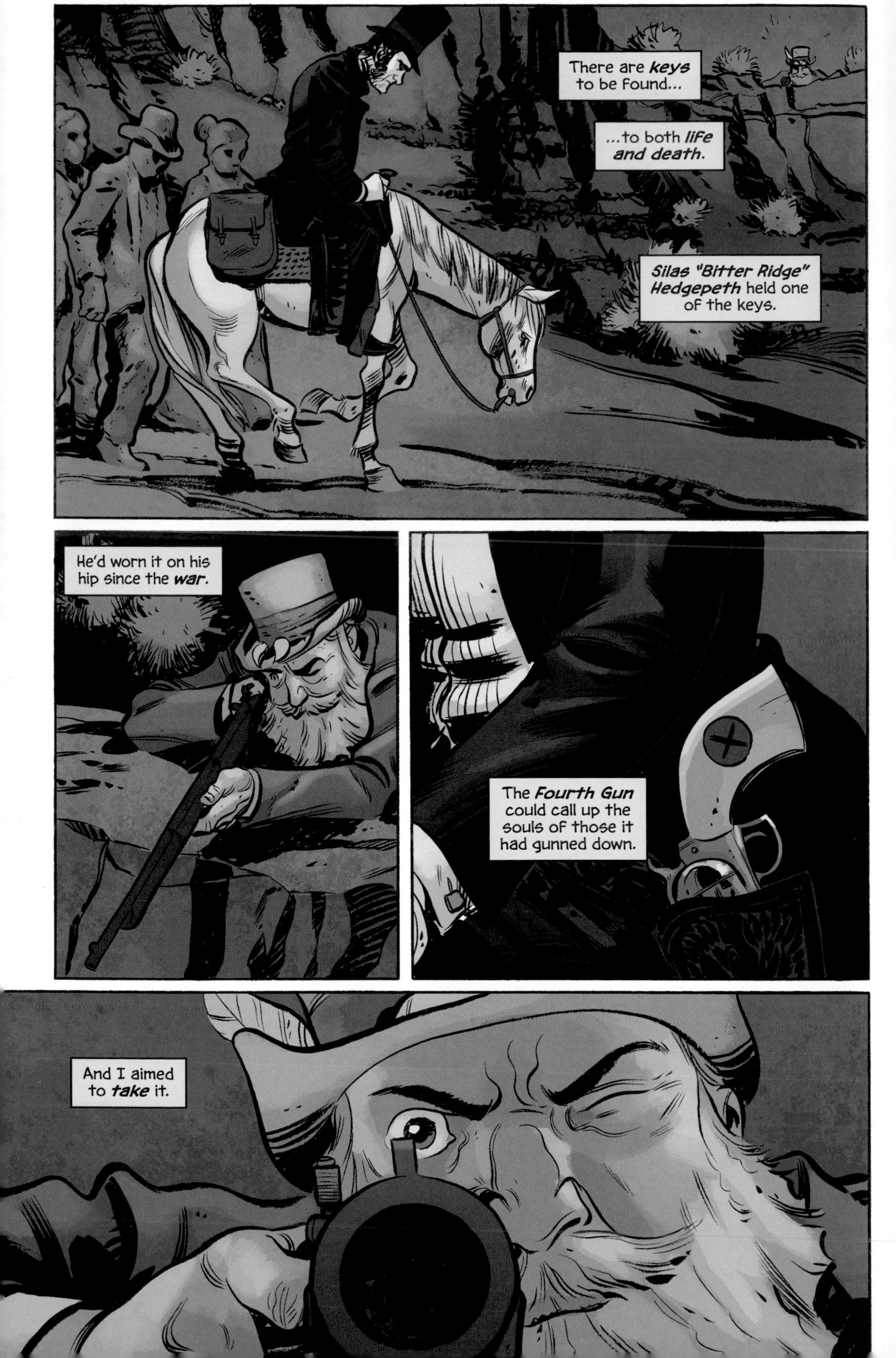
There are *keys* to be found...
...to both *life and death*.
Silas "Bitter Ridge" Hedgepeth held one of the keys.
He'd worn it on his hip since the *war*.
The *Fourth Gun* could call up the souls of those it had gunned down.
And I aimed to *take* it.

Dust to Dust

CHAPTER
TWO

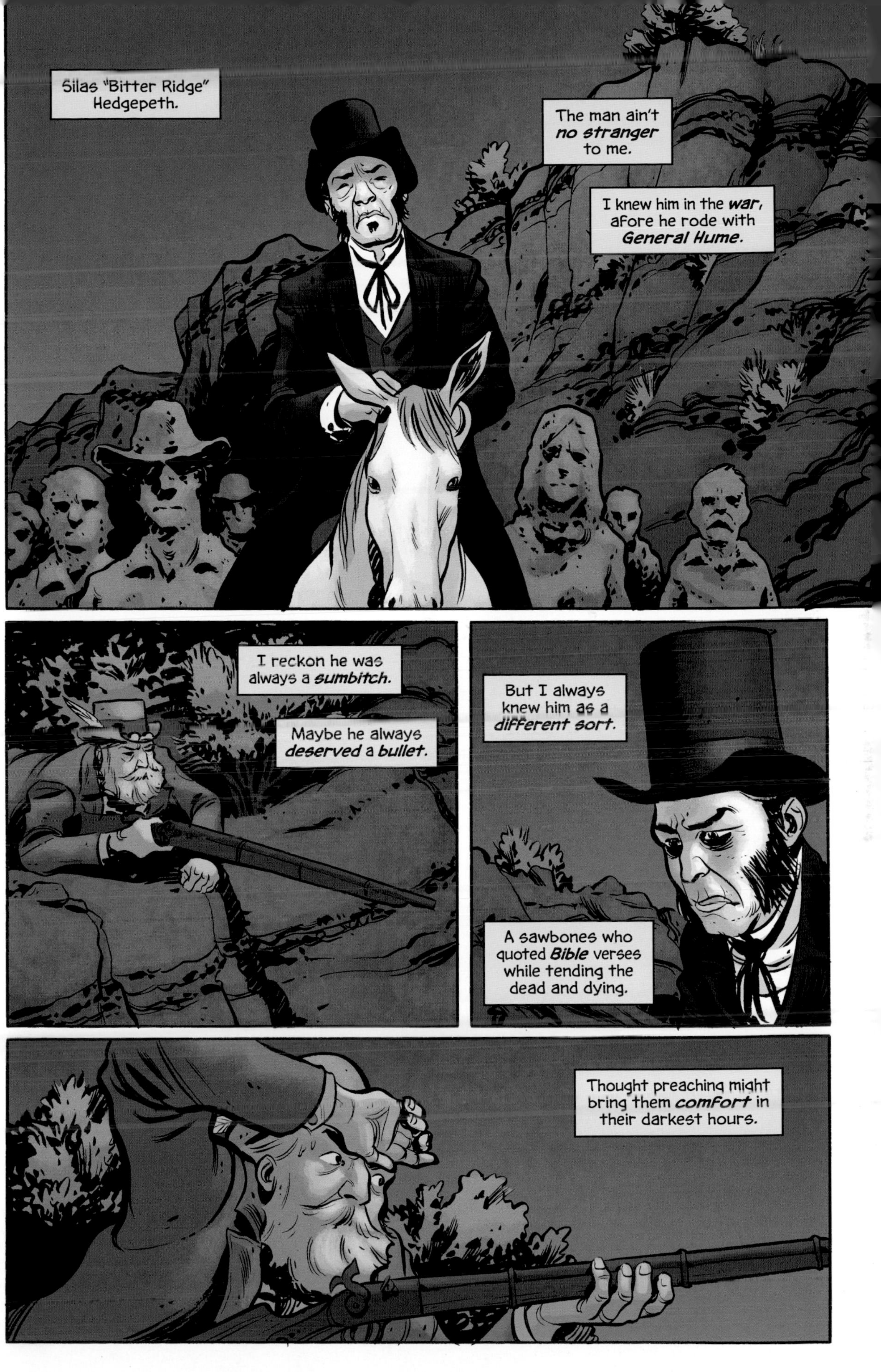

Silas "Bitter Ridge" Hedgepeth.
The man ain't *no stranger* to me.
I knew him in the *war*, afore he rode with *General Hume*.
I reckon he was always a *sumbitch*.
Maybe he always *deserved* a *bullet*.
But I always knew him as a *different sort*.
A sawbones who quoted *Bible* verses while tending the dead and dying.
Thought preaching might bring them *comfort* in their darkest hours.

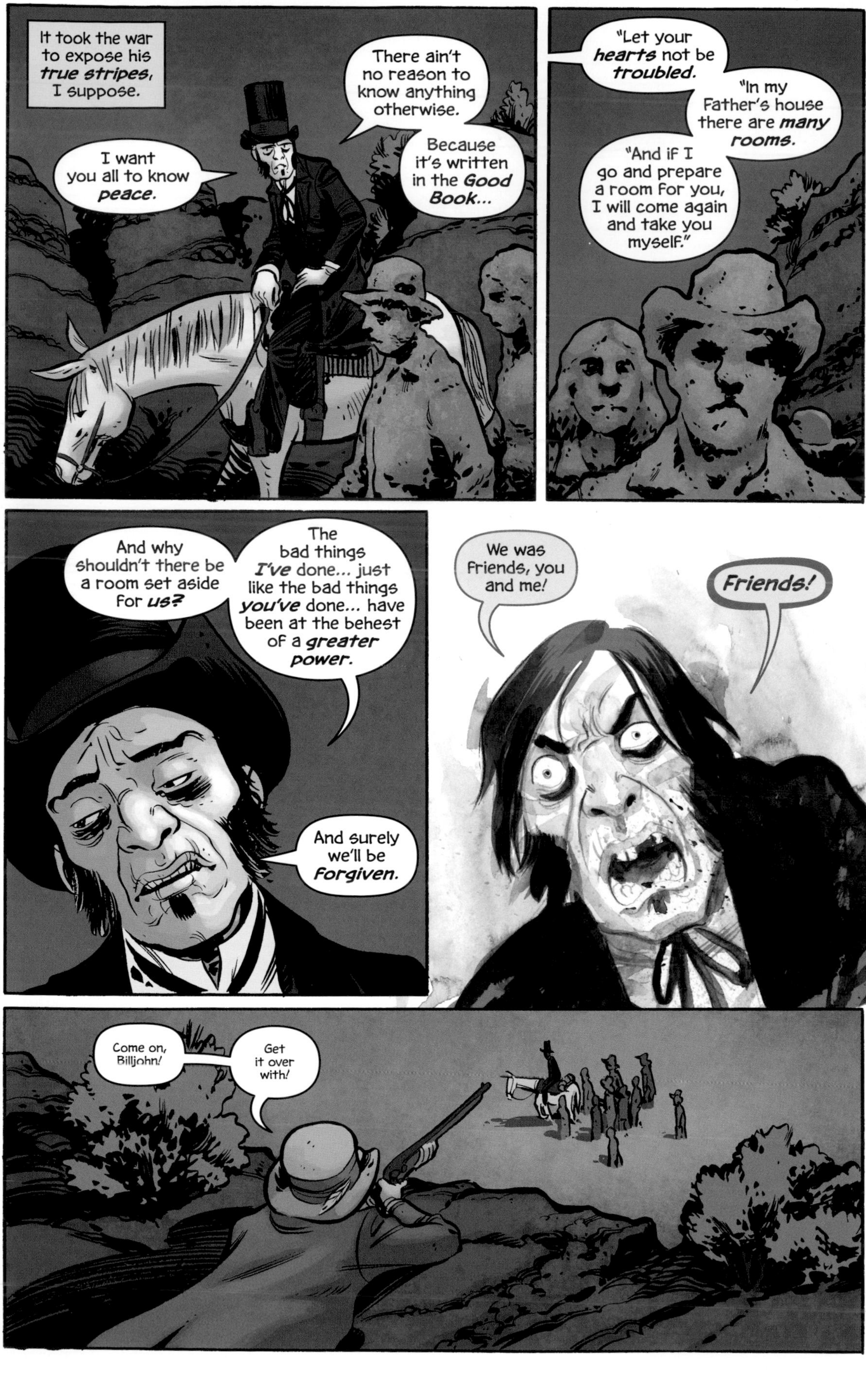
It took the war to expose his *true stripes*, I suppose.
I want you all to know *peace*.
There ain't no reason to know anything otherwise.
Because it's written in the *Good Book*...
"Let your *hearts* not be *troubled*.
"In my Father's house there are *many rooms*.
"And if I go and prepare a room for you, I will come again and take you myself."
And why shouldn't there be a room set aside for *us?*
The bad things *I've* done... just like the bad things *you've* done... have been at the behest of a *greater power*.
And surely we'll be *forgiven*.
We was friends, you and me!
Friends!
Come on, Billjohn!
Get it over with!

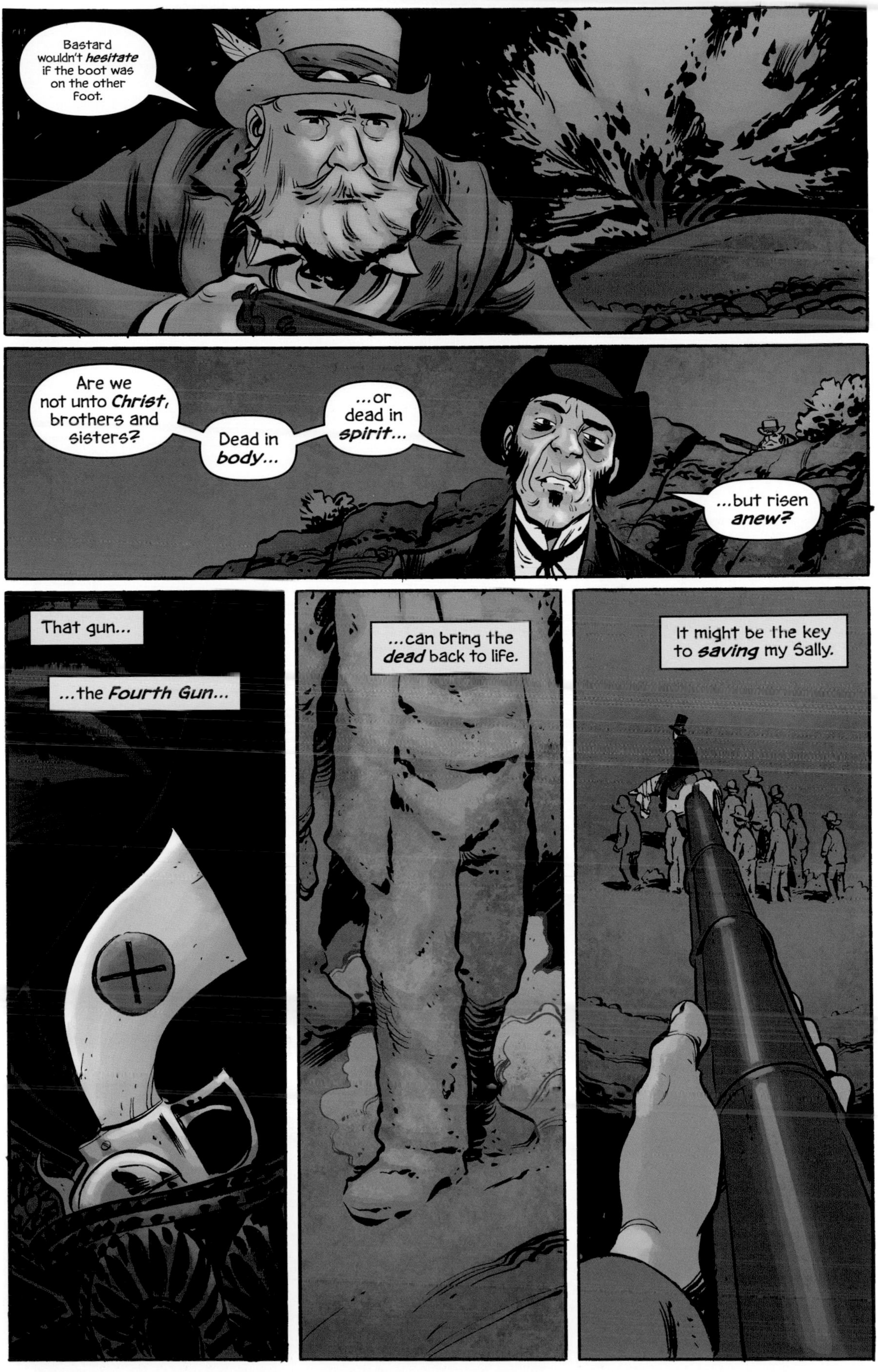
Bastard wouldn't *hesitate* if the boot was on the other foot.
Are we not unto *Christ*, brothers and sisters?
Dead in *body*...
...or dead in *spirit*...
...but risen *anew?*
That gun...
...the *Fourth Gun*...
...can bring the *dead* back to life.
It might be the key to *saving* my Sally.

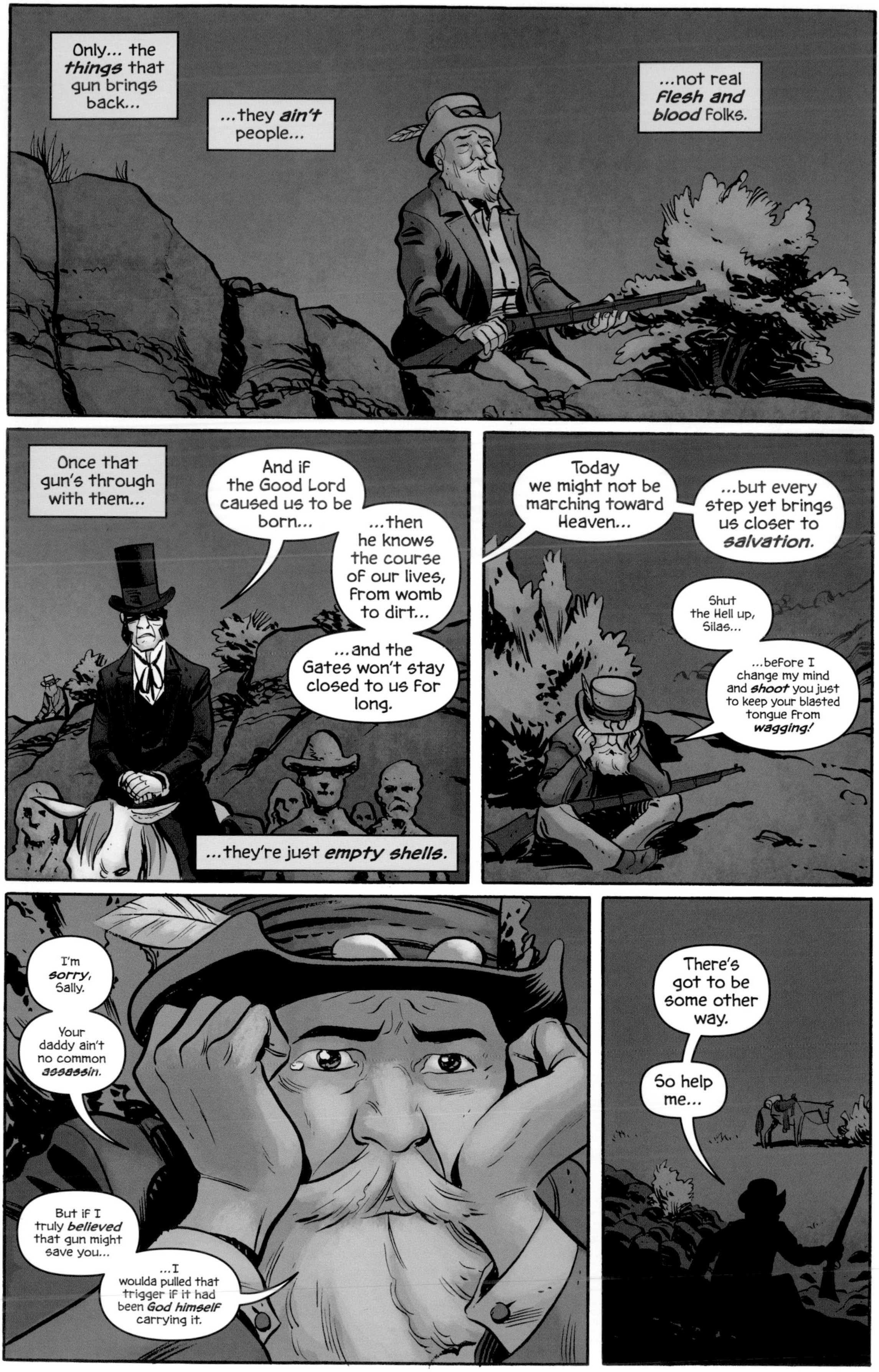

Only... the *things* that gun brings back...
...they *ain't* people...
...not real *flesh and blood* folks.
Once that gun's through with them...
And if the Good Lord caused us to be born...
...then he knows the course of our lives, from womb to dirt...
...and the Gates won't stay closed to us for long.
...they're just *empty shells.*
Today we might not be marching toward Heaven...
...but every step yet brings us closer to *salvation.*
Shut the Hell up, Silas...
...before I change my mind and *shoot* you just to keep your blasted tongue from *wagging!*
I'm *sorry,* Sally.
Your daddy ain't no common *assassin.*
But if I truly *believed* that gun might save you...
...I woulda pulled that trigger if it had been *God himself* carrying it.
There's got to be some other way.
So help me...

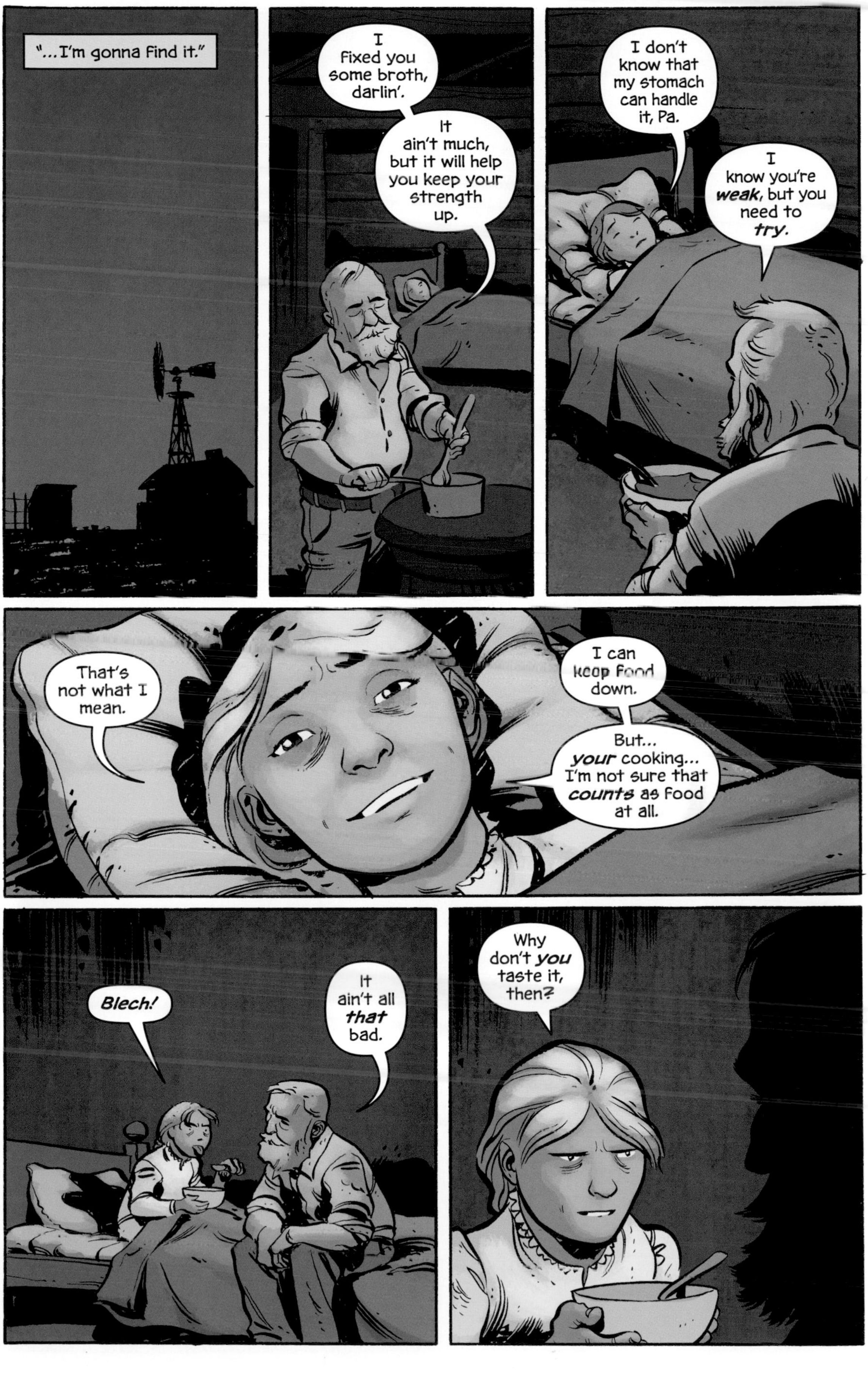
"...I'm gonna find it."
I fixed you some broth, darlin'.
It ain't much, but it will help you keep your strength up.
I don't know that my stomach can handle it, Pa.
I know you're *weak*, but you need to *try*.
That's not what I mean.
I can keep food down.
But... *your* cooking... I'm not sure that *counts* as food at all.
Blech!
It ain't all *that* bad.
Why don't *you* taste it, then?

Well, now...

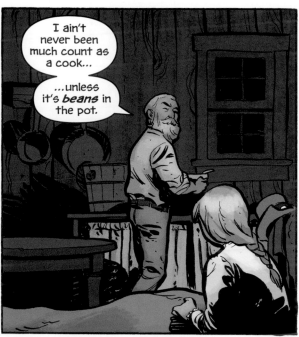

I ain't never been much count as a cook...

...unless it's *beans* in the pot.

It's all right, Pa.

I'm sure I'll be *myself* again soon.

Tomorrow.

Maybe the next day.

I sure hope so, darlin'.

I *hope* so.

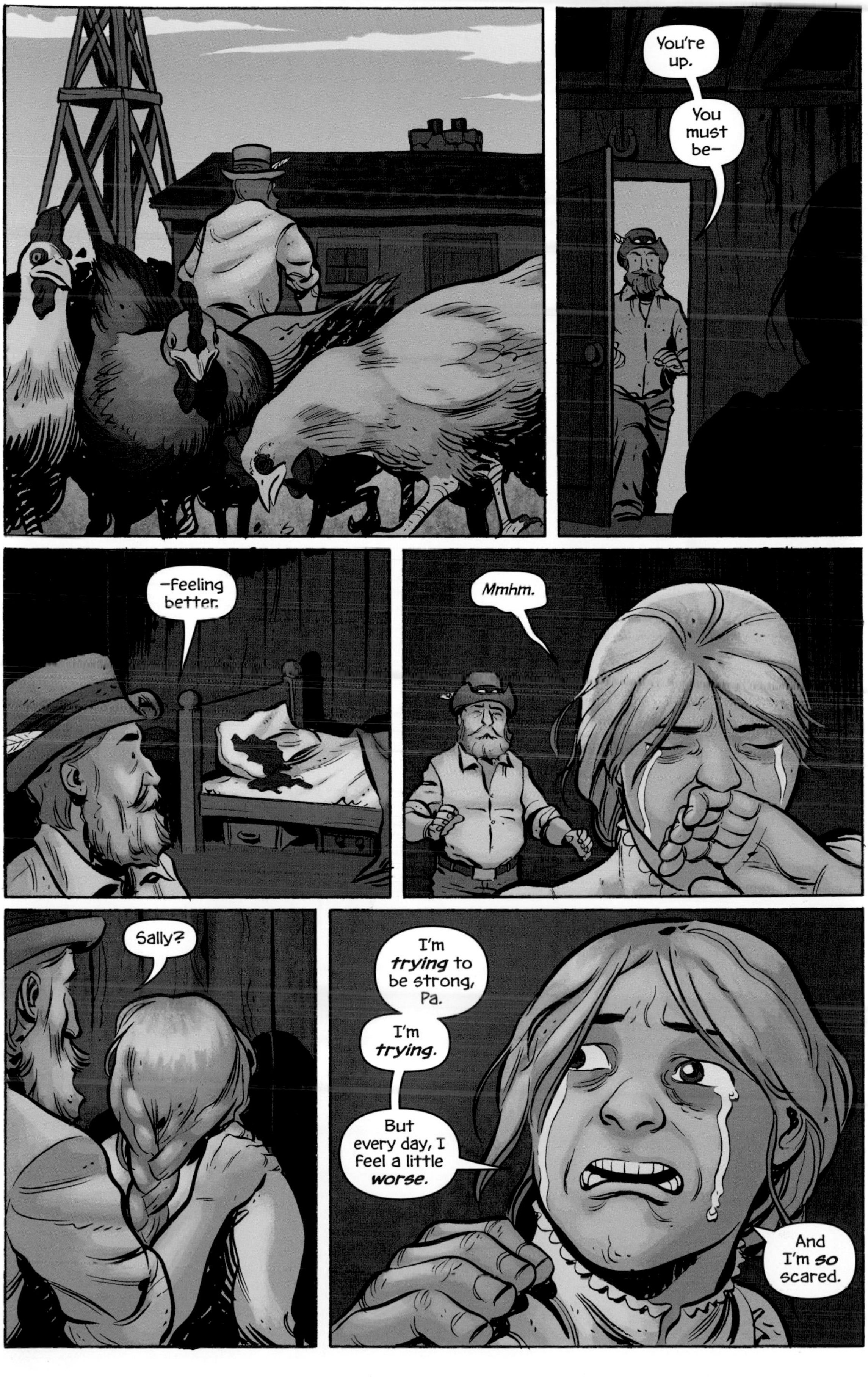

You're up.
You must be—
—Feeling better.
Mmhm.
Sally?
I'm *trying* to be strong, Pa.
I'm *trying*.
But every day, I feel a little *worse*.
And I'm *so* scared.

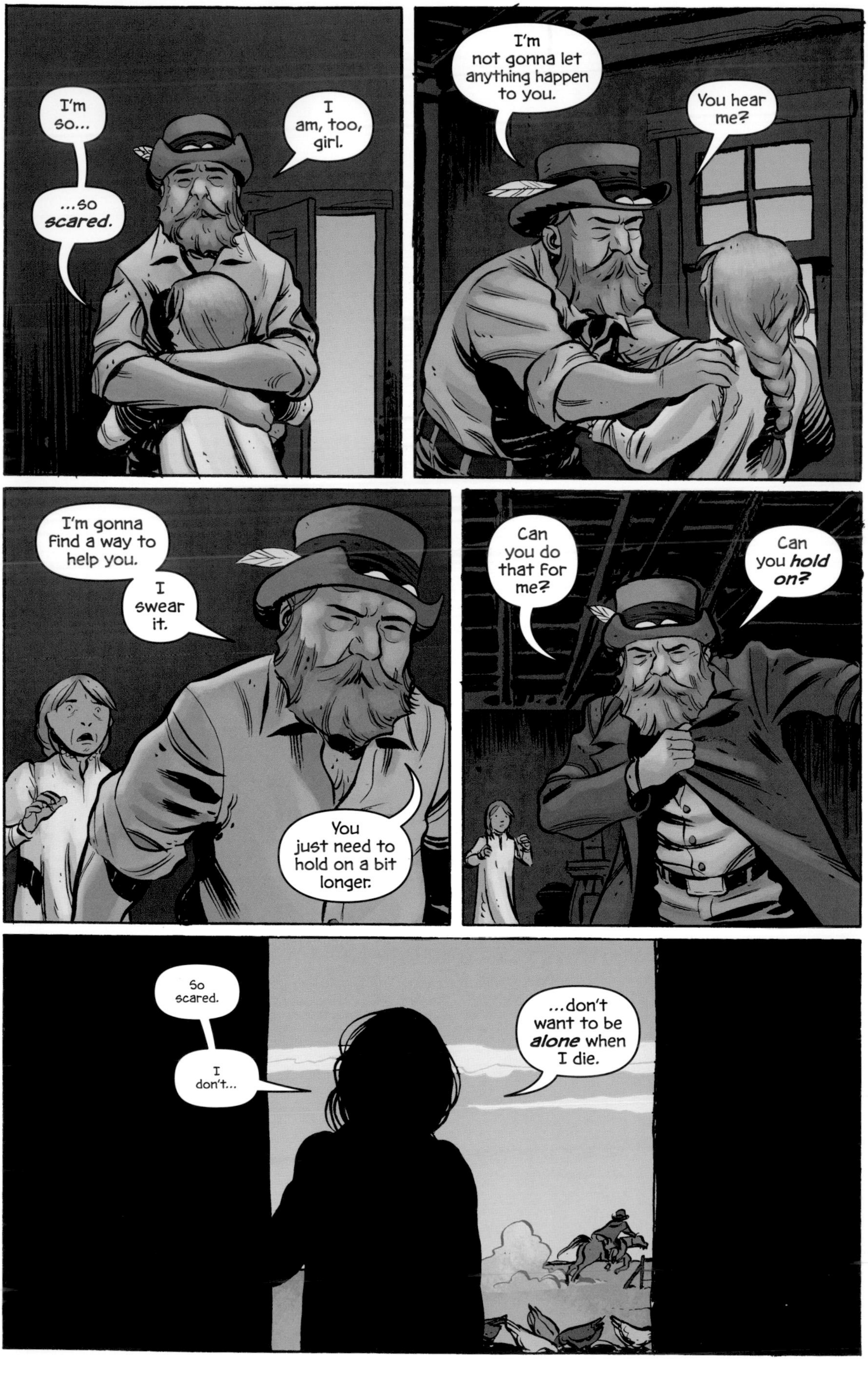
I'm so...
I am, too, girl.
...so *scared.*
I'm not gonna let anything happen to you.
You hear me?
I'm gonna find a way to help you.
I swear it.
You just need to hold on a bit longer.
Can you do that for me?
Can you ***hold on?***
So scared.
I don't...
...don't want to be ***alone*** when I die.

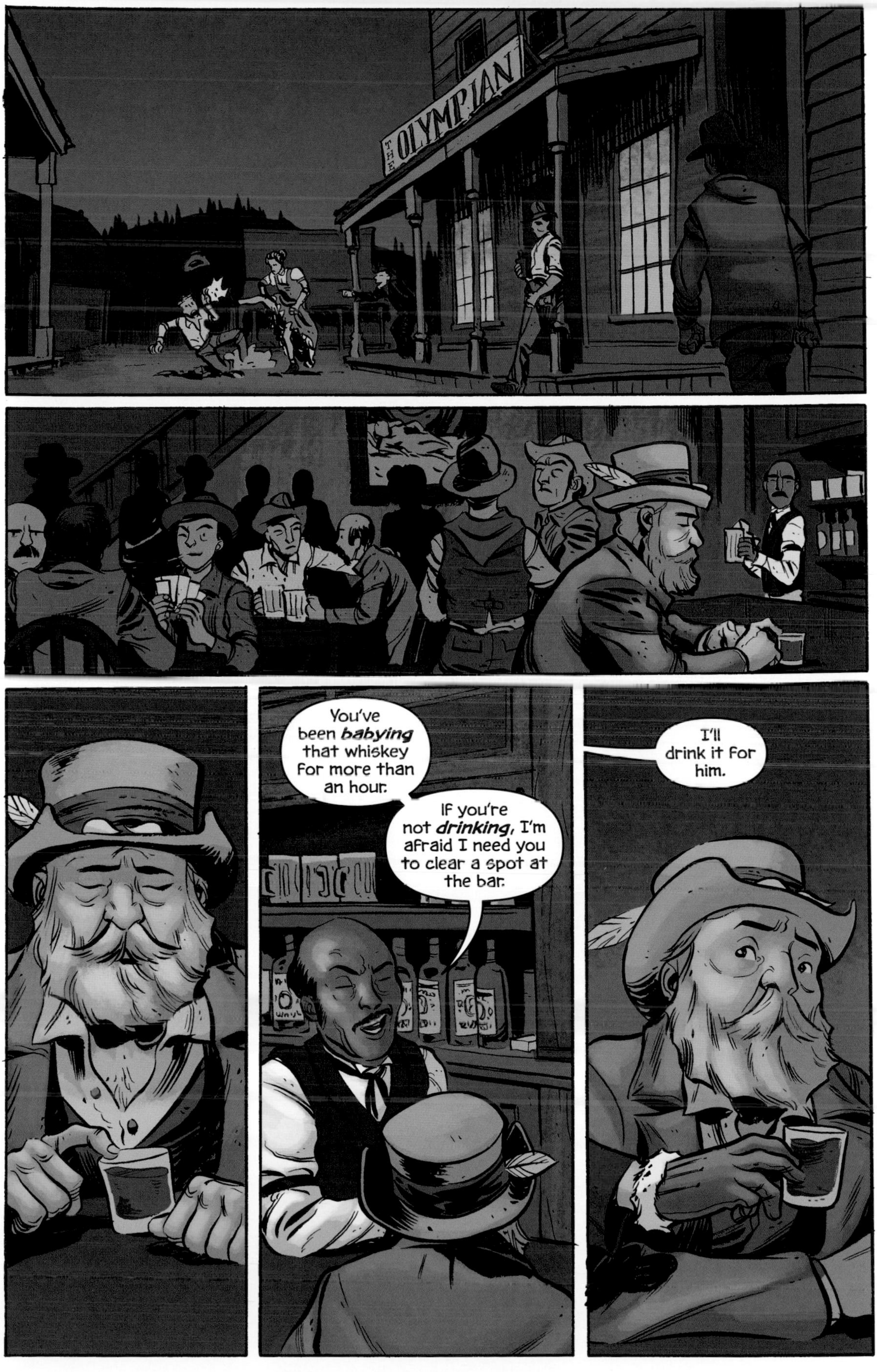

THE OLYMPIAN
You've been babying that whiskey for more than an hour.
If you're not drinking, I'm afraid I need you to clear a spot at the bar.
I'll drink it for him.

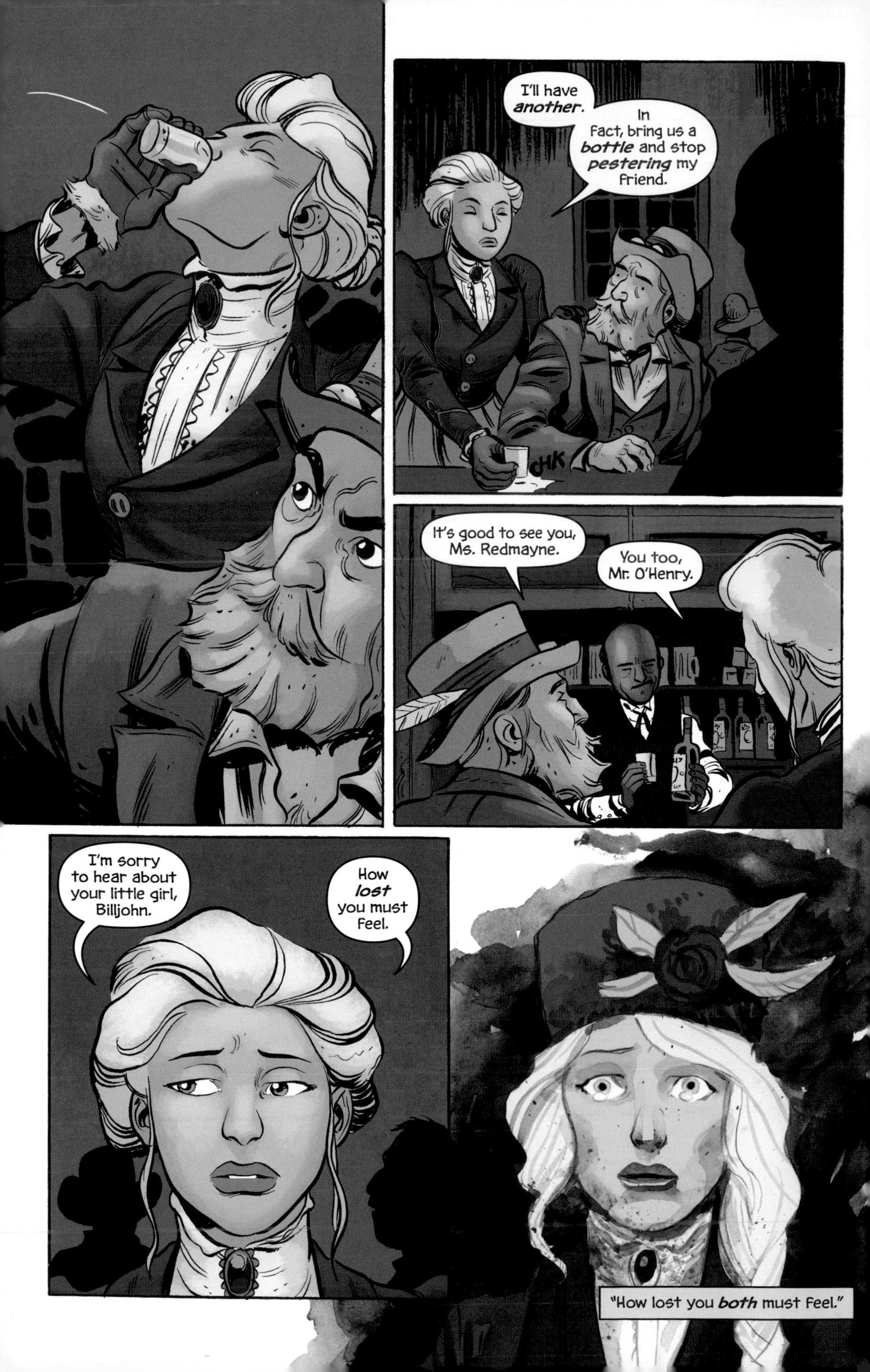
I'll have *another*.
In Fact, bring us a *bottle* and stop *pestering* my friend.
CHK
It's good to see you, Ms. Redmayne.
You too, Mr. O'Henry.
I'm sorry to hear about your little girl, Billjohn.
How *lost* you must feel.
"How lost you *both* must feel."

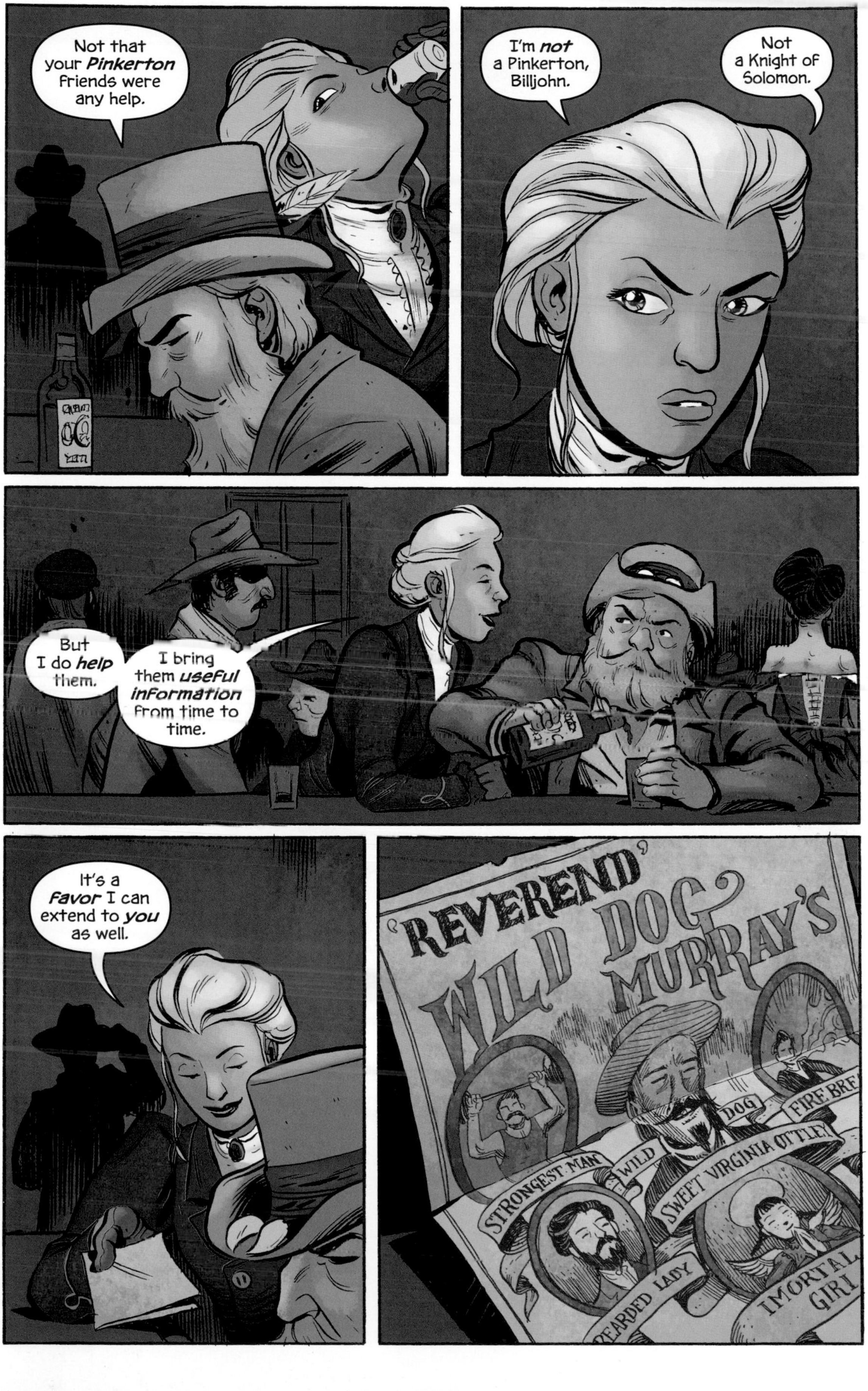
Not that your *Pinkerton* friends were any help.
I'm *not* a Pinkerton, Billjohn.
Not a Knight of Solomon.
But I do *help* them.
I bring them *useful information* from time to time.
It's a *favor* I can extend to *you* as well.
'REVEREND' WILD DOG MURRAY'S
STRONGEST MAN
WILD DOG
SWEET VIRGINIA OTTLEY
BEARDED LADY
IMORTAL GIRL

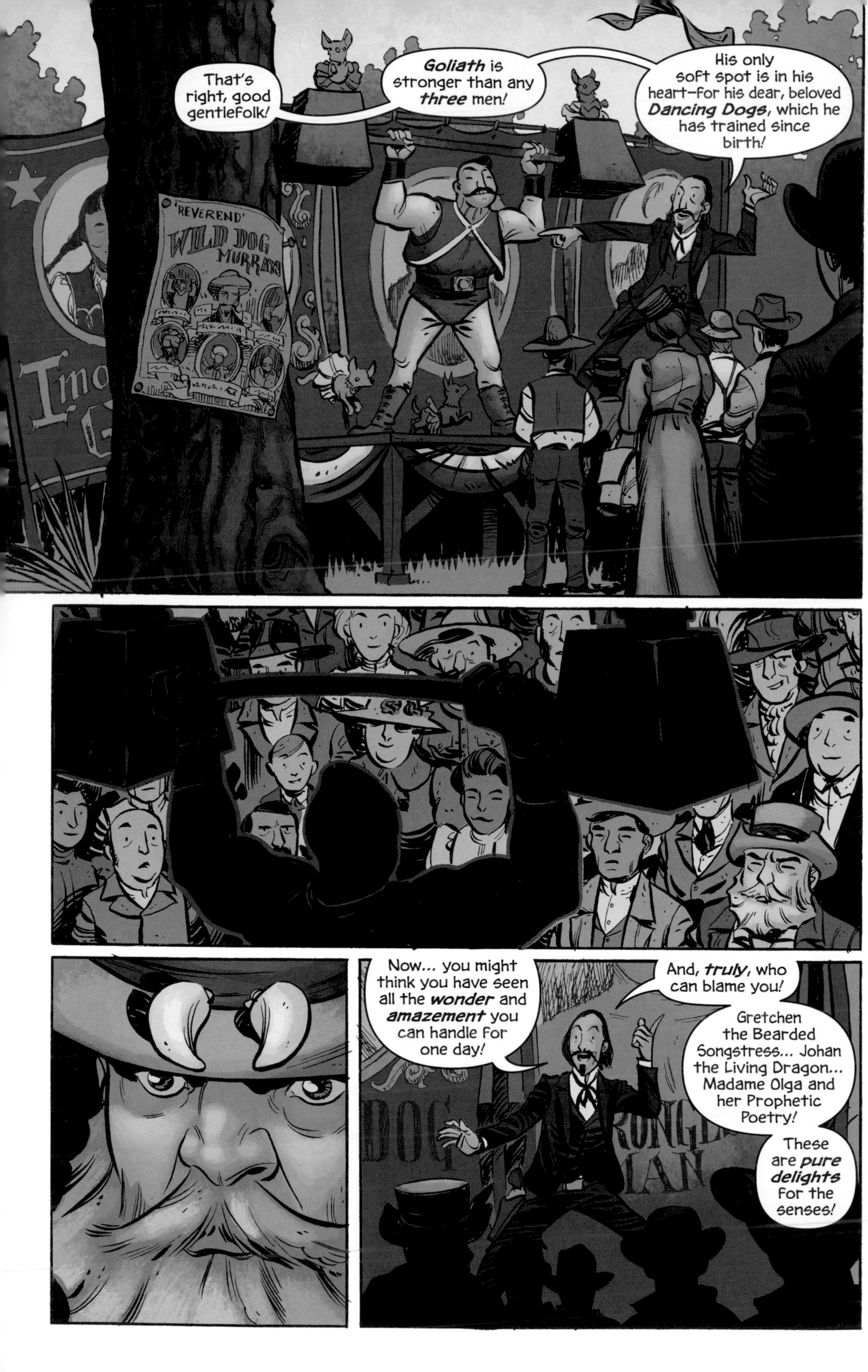
That's right, good gentlefolk!
Goliath is stronger than any three men!
His only soft spot is in his heart—for his dear, beloved Dancing Dogs, which he has trained since birth!
'REVEREND' WILD DOG MURRAYS
Now... you might think you have seen all the wonder and amazement you can handle for one day!
And, truly, who can blame you!
Gretchen the Bearded Songstress... Johan the Living Dragon... Madame Olga and her Prophetic Poetry!
These are pure delights for the senses!

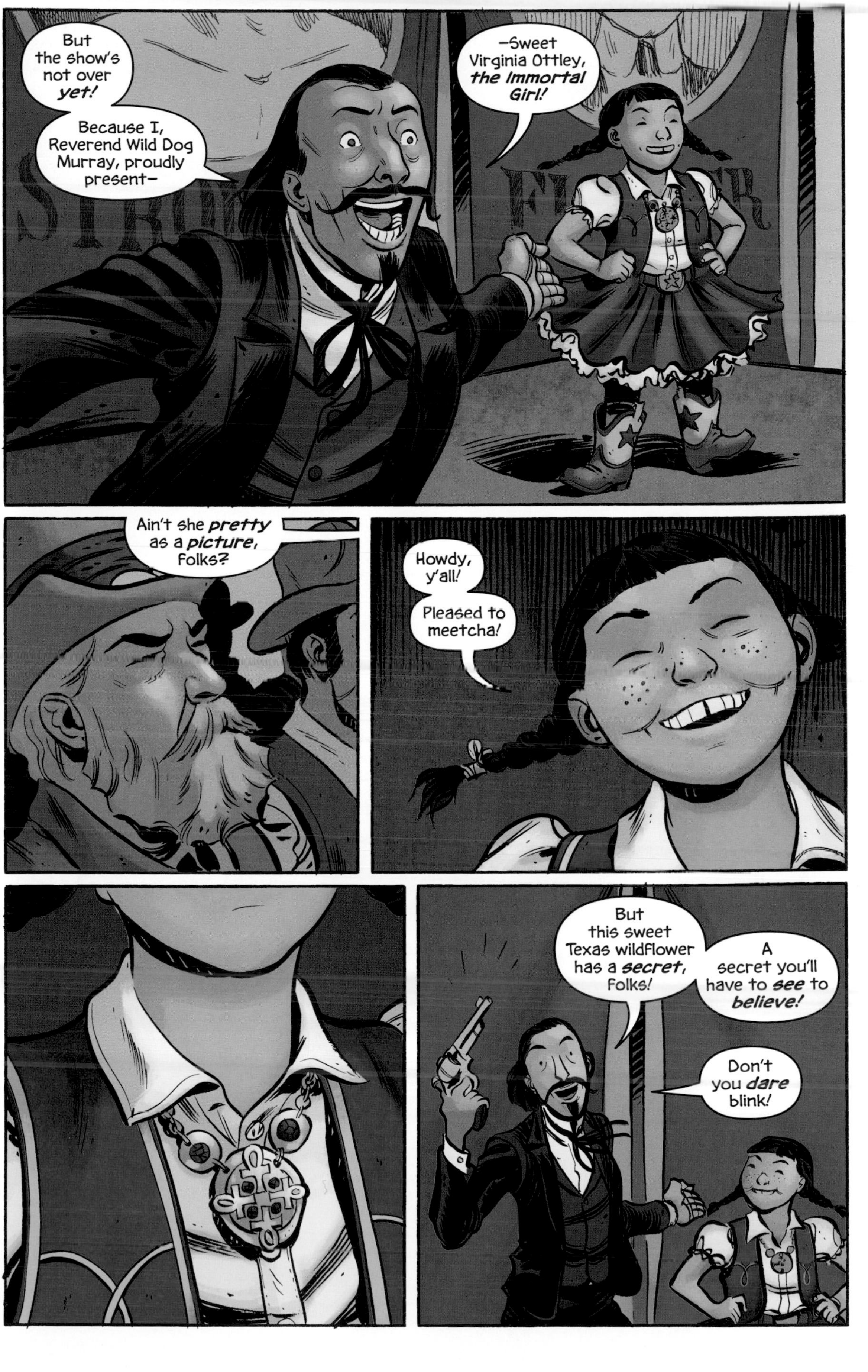
But the show's not over *yet!*
Because I, Reverend Wild Dog Murray, proudly present–
–Sweet Virginia Ottley, ***the Immortal Girl!***
Ain't she ***pretty*** as a ***picture***, Folks?
Howdy, y'all!
Pleased to meetcha!
But this sweet Texas wildflower has a ***secret***, Folks!
A secret you'll have to ***see*** to ***believe!***
Don't you ***dare*** blink!

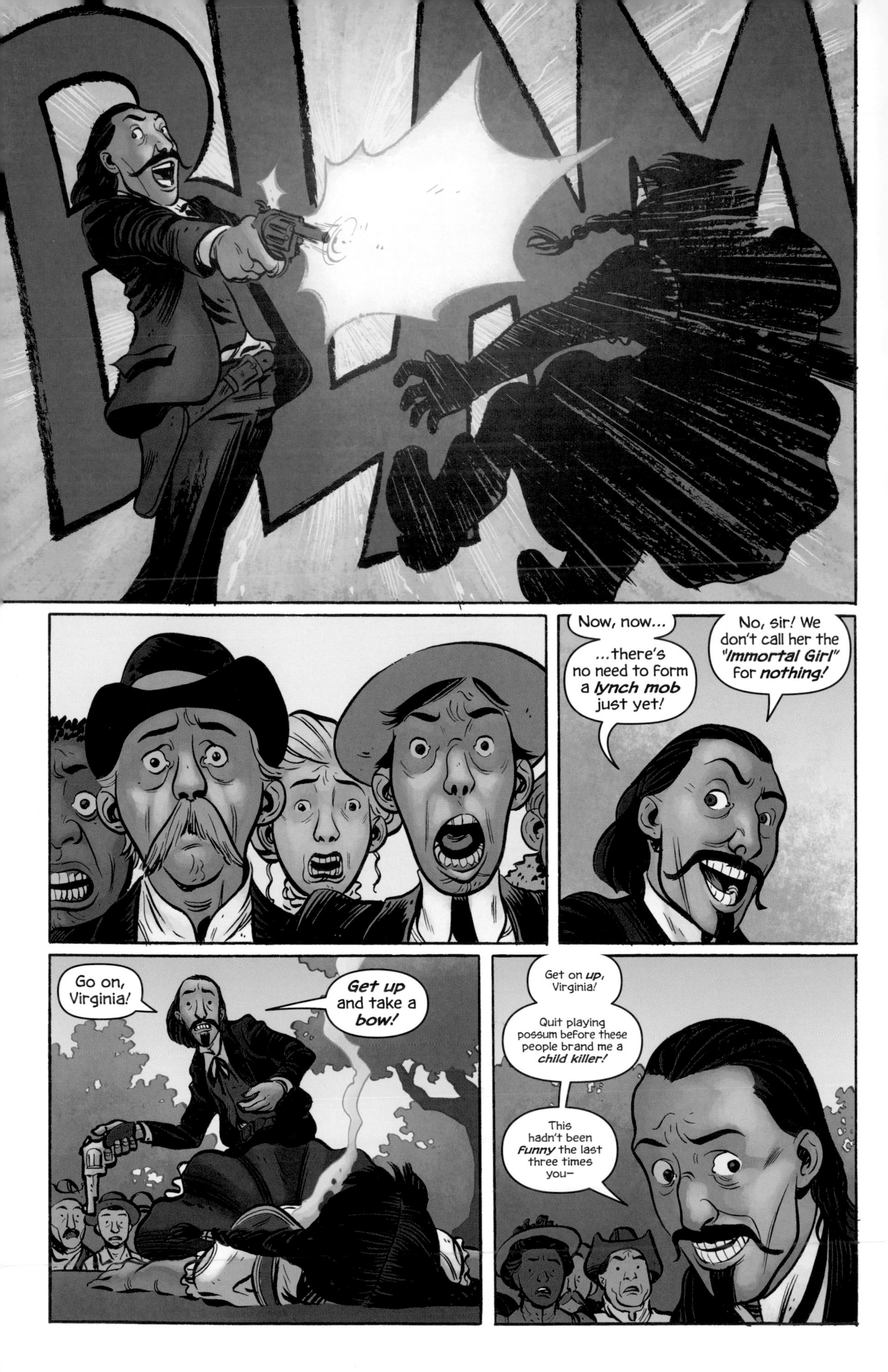
Now, now...
...there's no need to form a lynch mob just yet!
No, sir! We don't call her the "Immortal Girl" for nothing!
Go on, Virginia!
Get up and take a bow!
Get on up, Virginia!
Quit playing possum before these people brand me a child killer!
This hadn't been funny the last three times you–

No need to *fret!*

I was just *Funnin'* with ya!

There ain't a bullet in all the land that can lay me low!

CLAP CLAP AP CLAP CLA CLAP CLAP CLAP CL CLAP CLAP CIAP

Now, gentlefolk, I know what you're saying.

You sure would like to feel *immortal*, just like *Virginia*.

While that might not be in the cards, I've got the *next best thing* right here!

Reverend Wild Dog Murray's Vitality Formula!

It cures *all* your ills... both those you *know* about and those you *don't!*

And you can buy your very own bottle for less than the cost of shot of a Firewater at your local saloon!

※ 137 ※

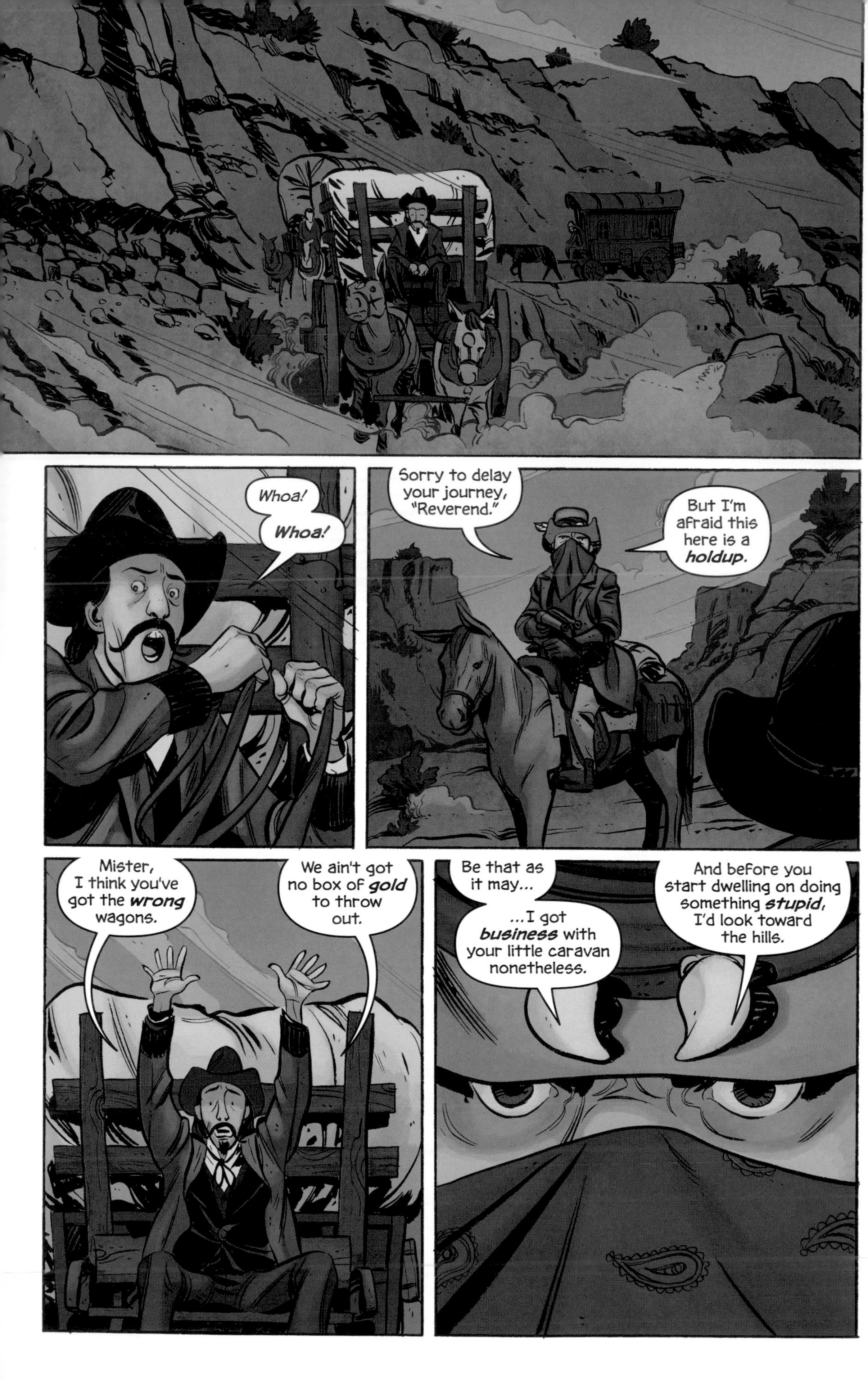
Whoa!
Whoa!
Sorry to delay your journey, "Reverend."
But I'm afraid this here is a holdup.
Mister, I think you've got the wrong wagons.
We ain't got no box of gold to throw out.
Be that as it may...
...I got business with your little caravan nonetheless.
And before you start dwelling on doing something stupid, I'd look toward the hills.

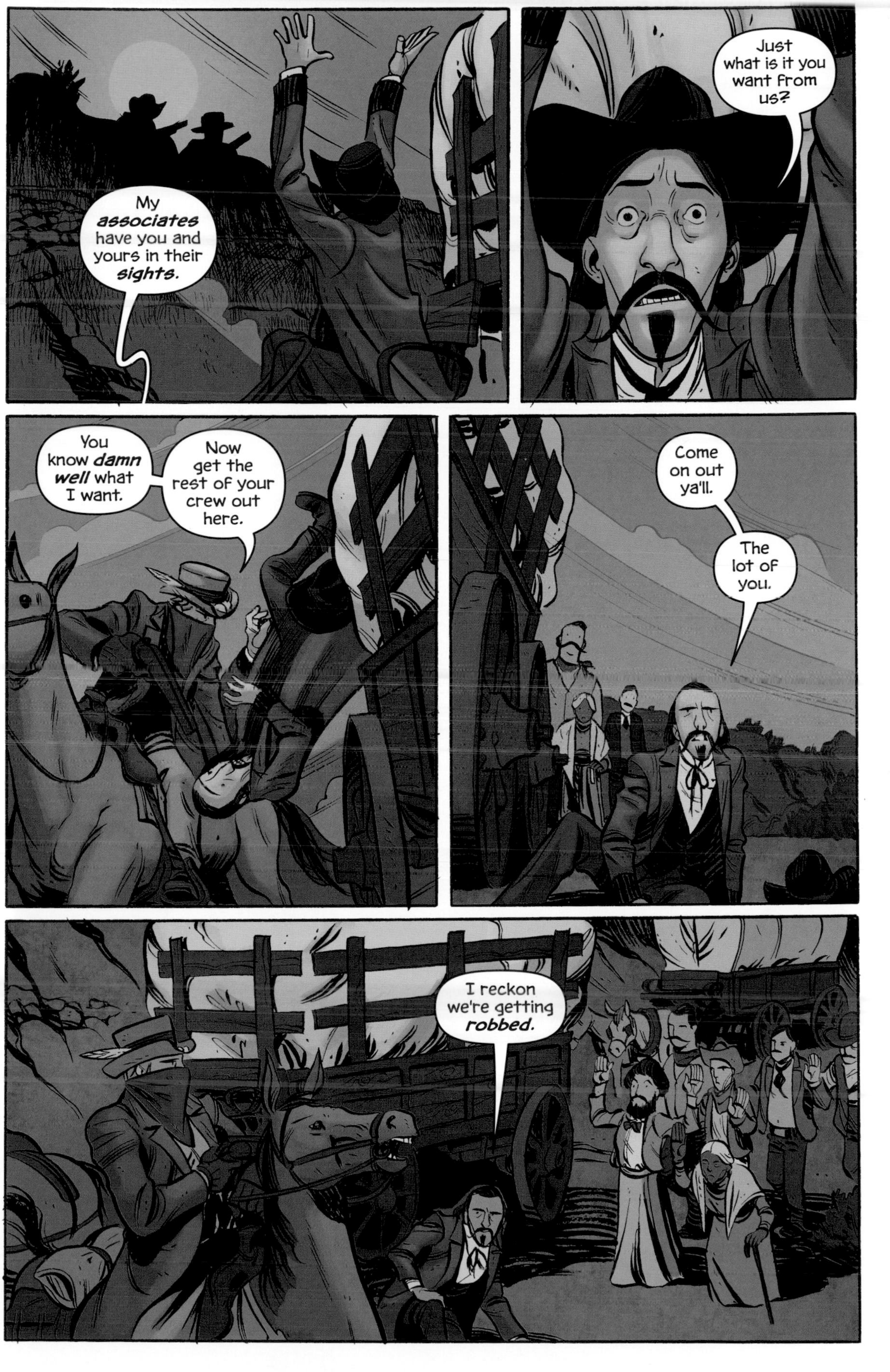
My associates have you and yours in their sights.
Just what is it you want from us?
You know damn well what I want.
Now get the rest of your crew out here.
Come on out ya'll.
The lot of you.
I reckon we're getting robbed.

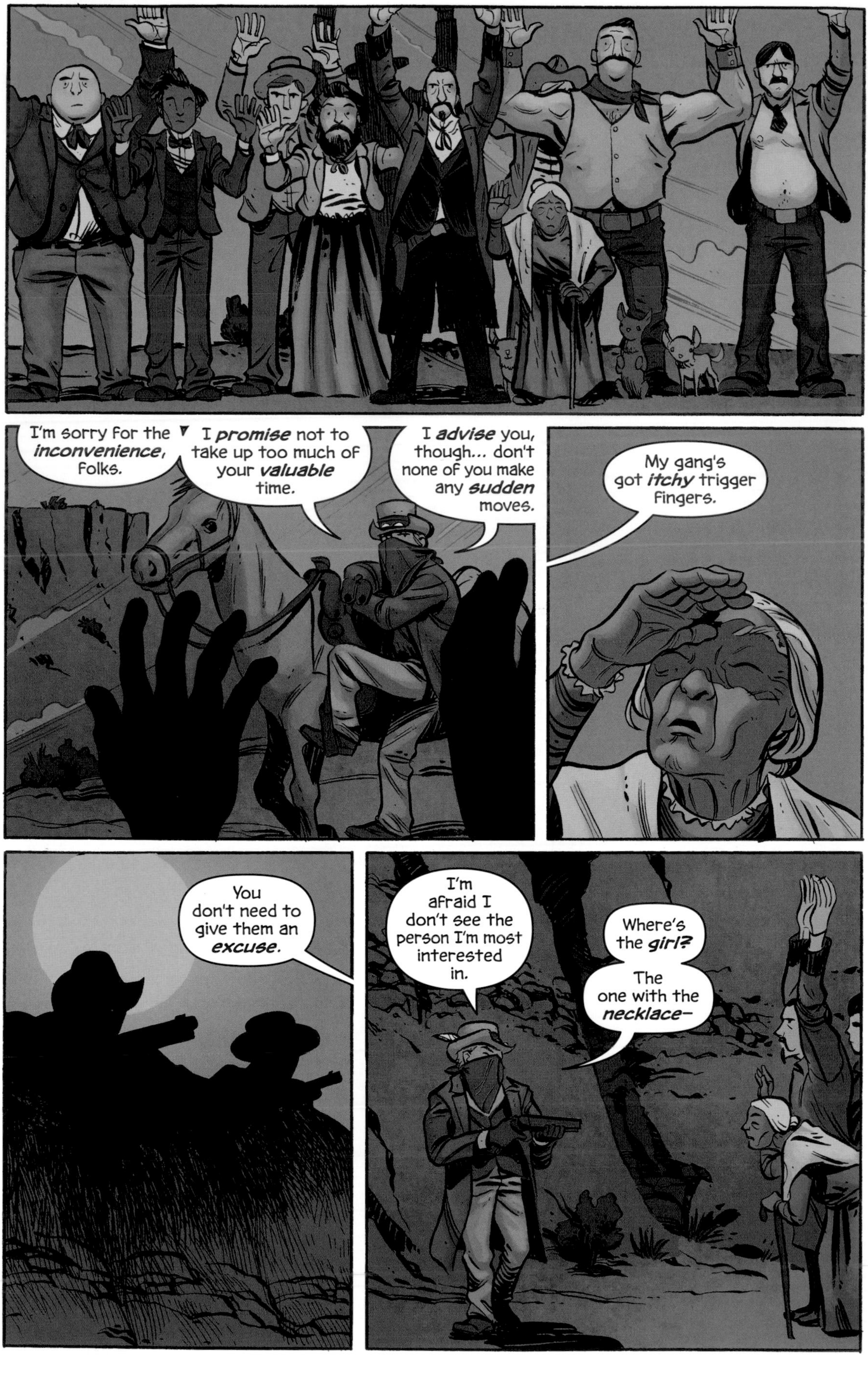
I'm sorry for the *inconvenience*, folks.
I *promise* not to take up too much of your *valuable* time.
I *advise* you, though... don't none of you make any *sudden* moves.
My gang's got *itchy* trigger fingers.
You don't need to give them an *excuse*.
I'm afraid I don't see the person I'm most interested in.
Where's the *girl?*
The one with the *necklace*—

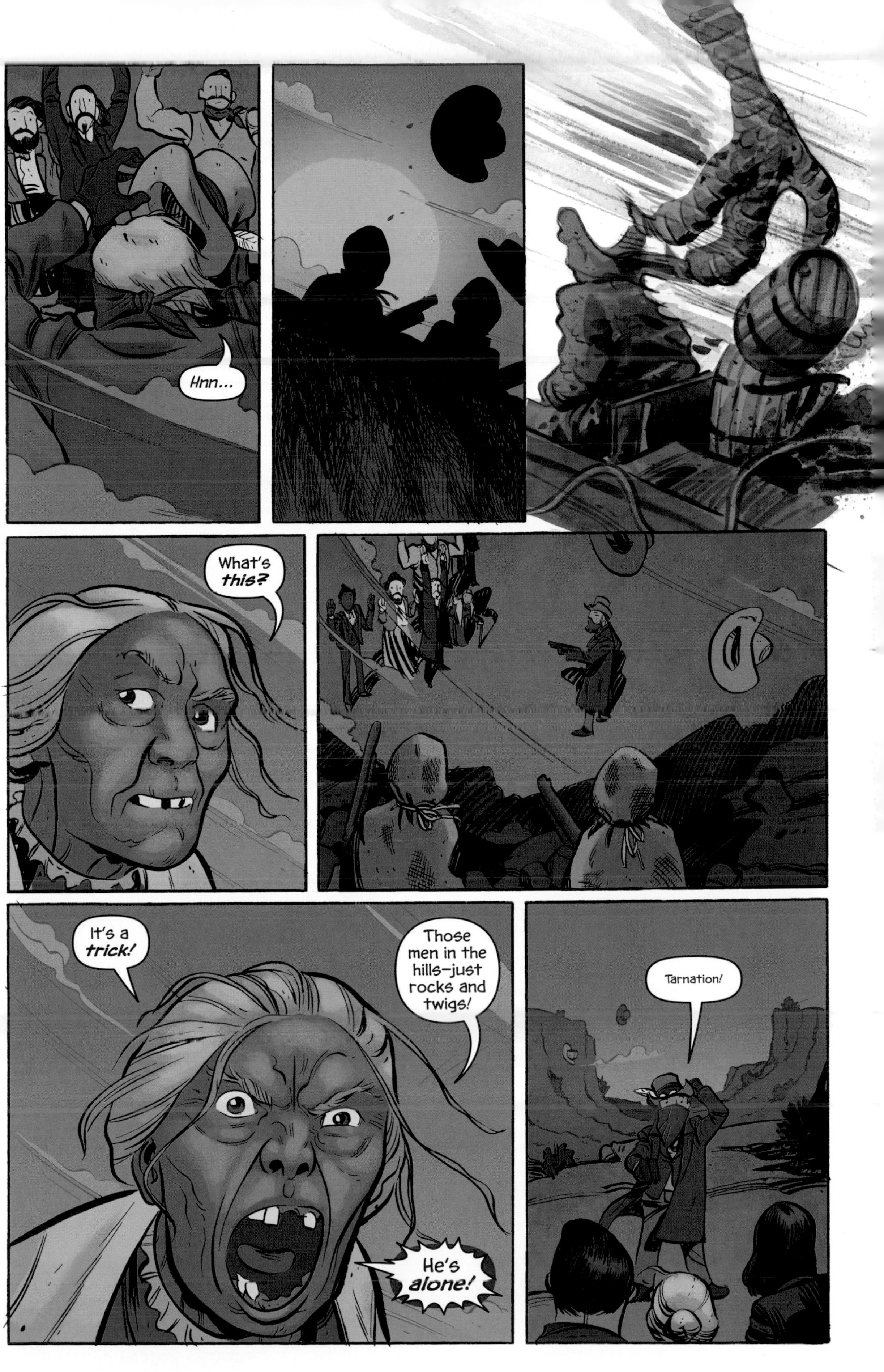
Hnn...
What's this?
It's a trick!
Those men in the hills—just rocks and twigs!
He's alone!
Tarnation!

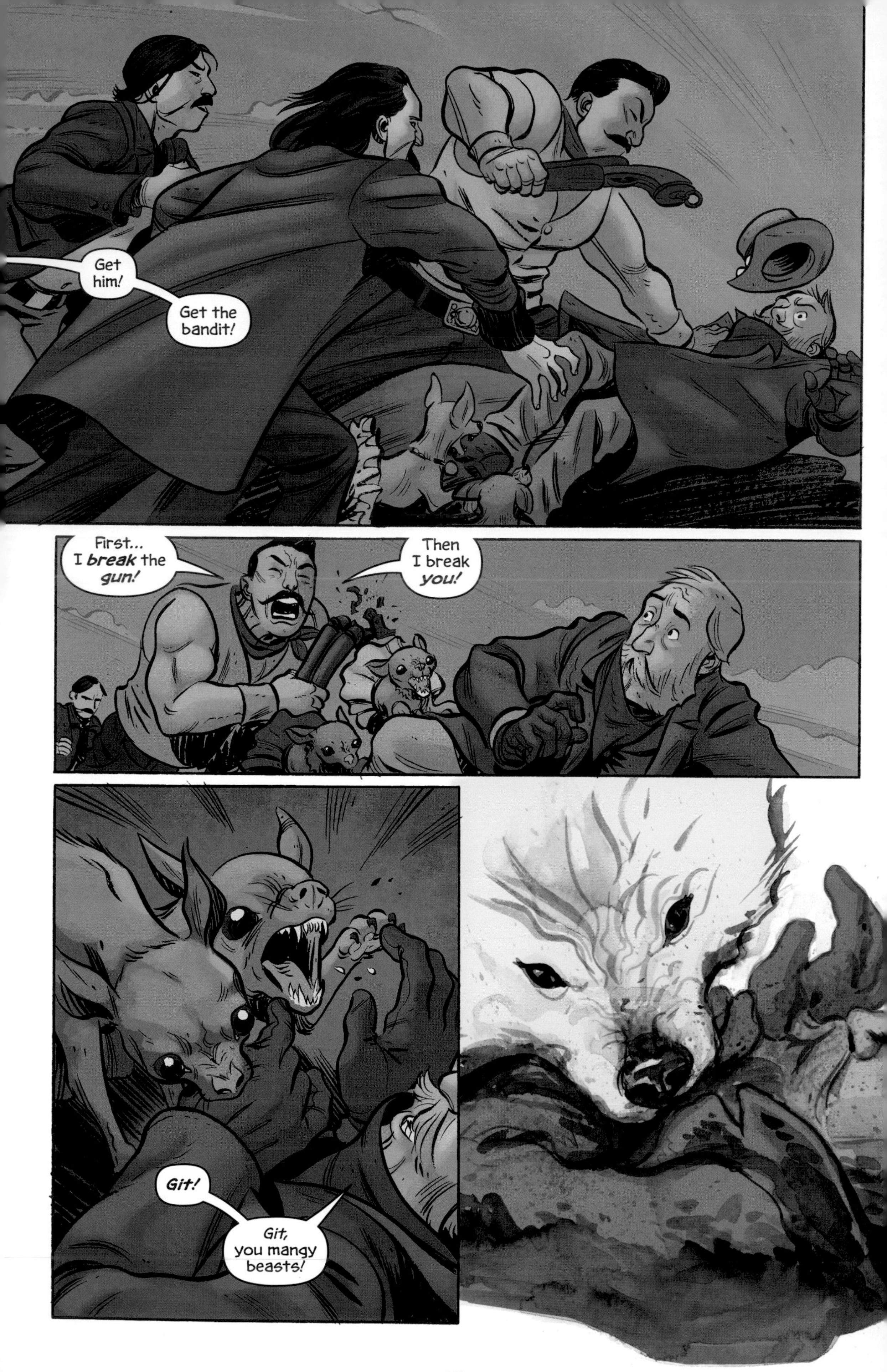
Get him!
Get the bandit!
First... I **break** the **gun**!
Then I break **you**!
Git!
Git, you mangy beasts!

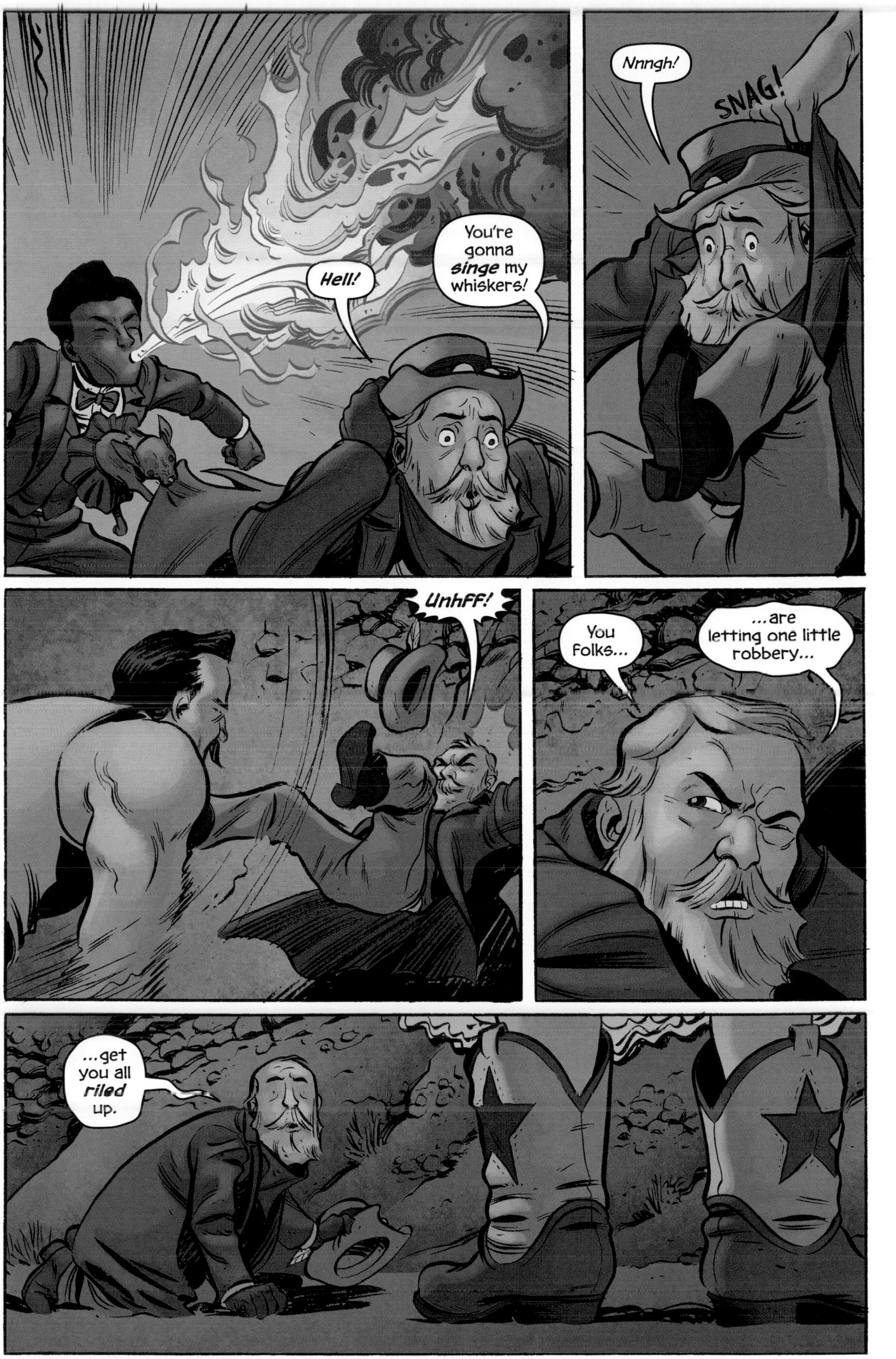

Hell!
You're gonna *singe* my whiskers!
Nnngh!
SNAG!
Unhff!
You folks...
...are letting one little robbery...
...get you all *riled* up.

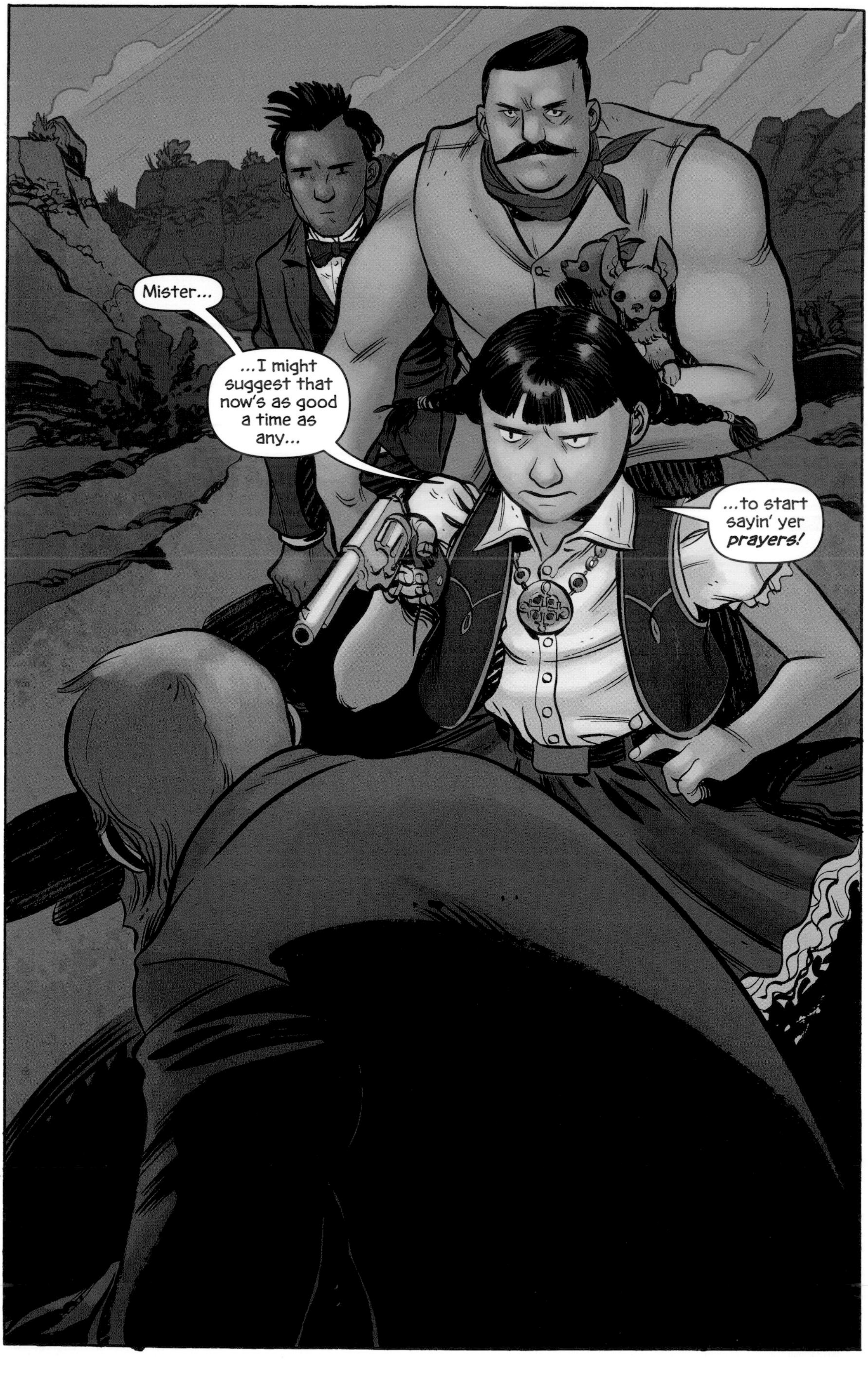
Mister...
...I might suggest that now's as good a time as any...
...to start sayin' yer *prayers!*

CHAPTER
THREE

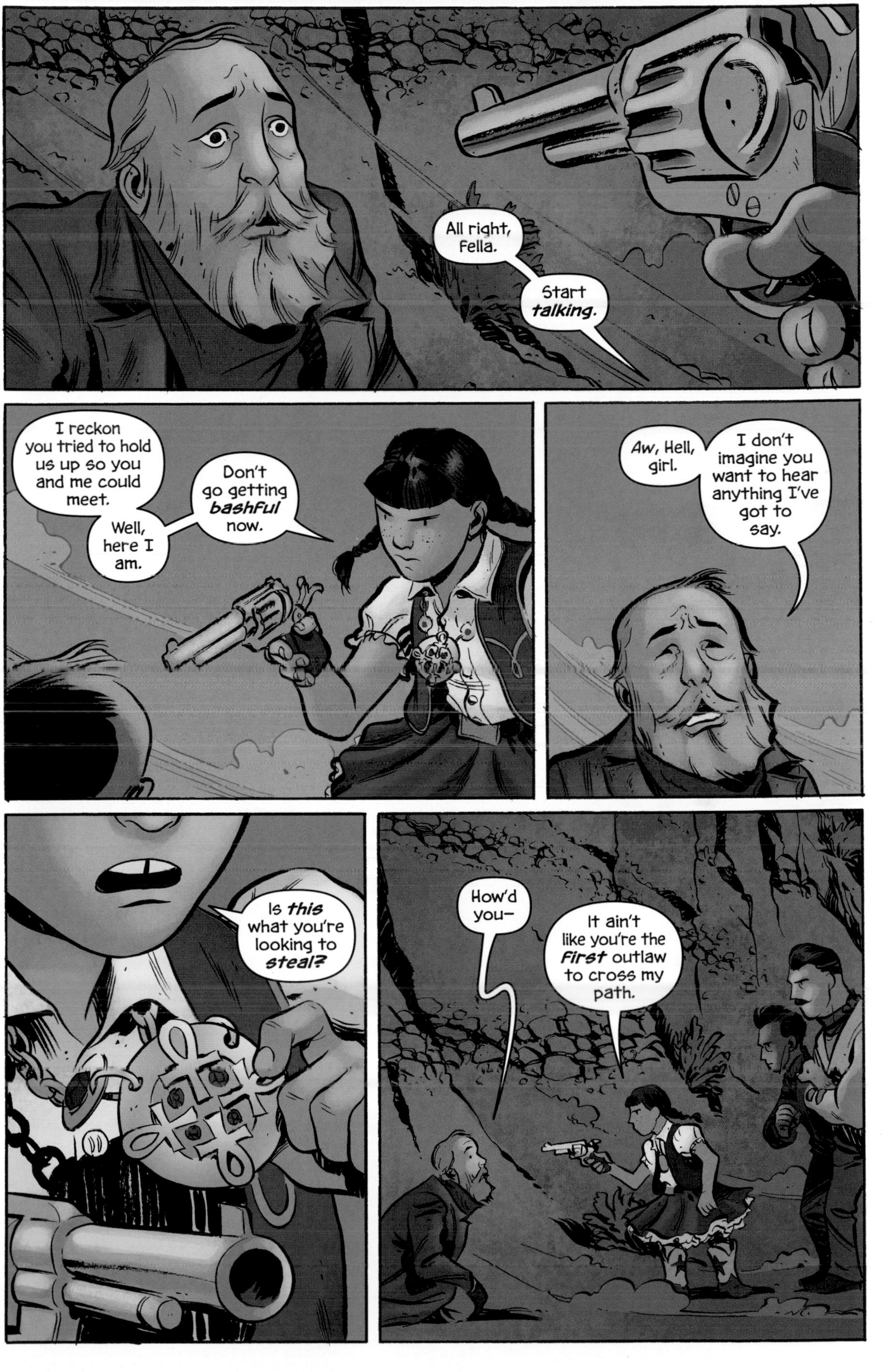
All right, Fella.
Start *talking*.
I reckon you tried to hold us up so you and me could meet.
Well, here I am.
Don't go getting *bashful* now.
Aw, Hell, girl.
I don't imagine you want to hear anything I've got to say.
Is *this* what you're looking to *steal?*
How'd you–
It ain't like you're the *first* outlaw to cross my path.

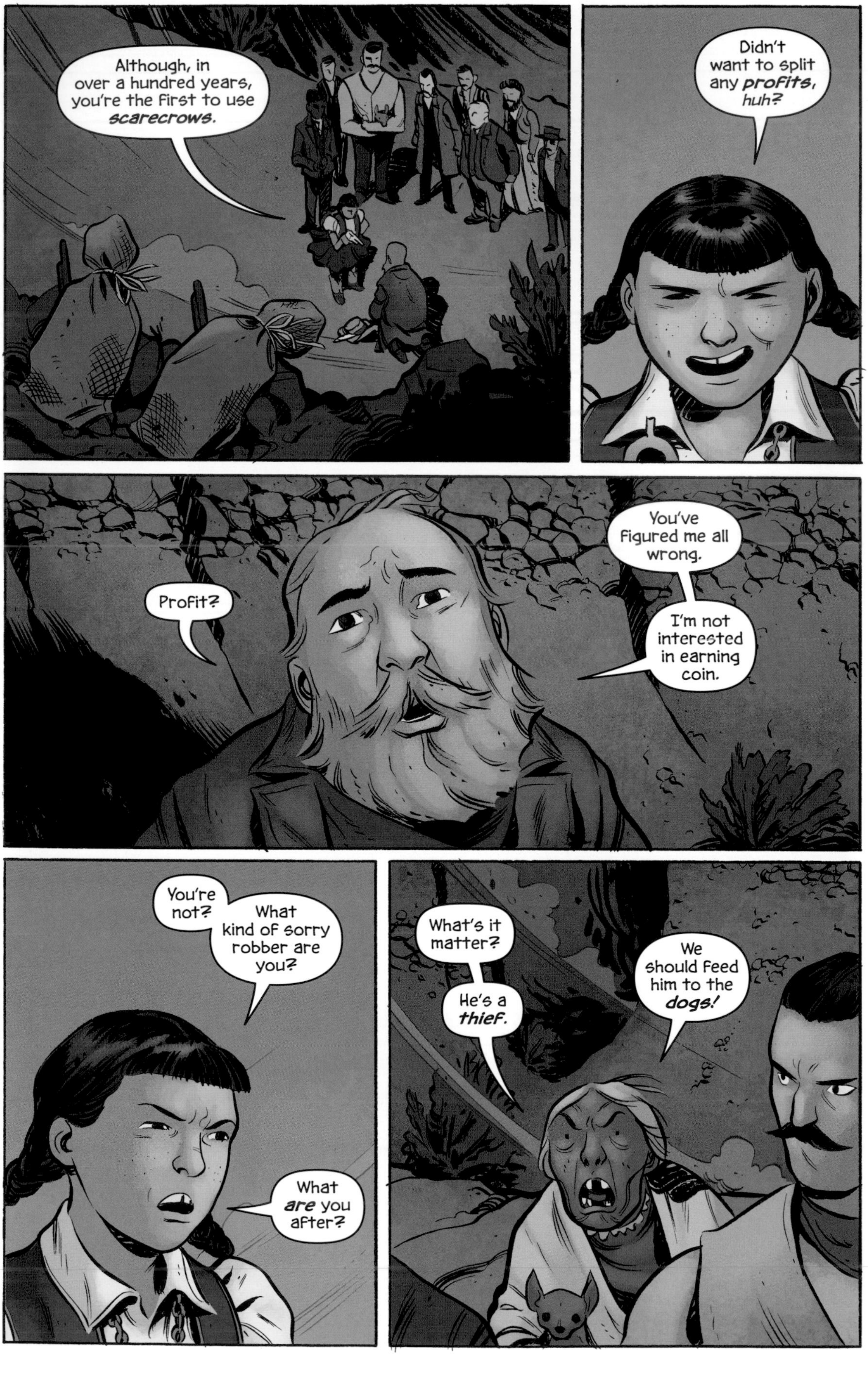
Although, in over a hundred years, you're the first to use *scarecrows*.
Didn't want to split any *profits*, huh?
Profit?
You've figured me all wrong.
I'm not interested in earning coin.
You're not?
What kind of sorry robber are you?
What *are* you after?
What's it matter?
He's a *thief*.
We should feed him to the *dogs!*

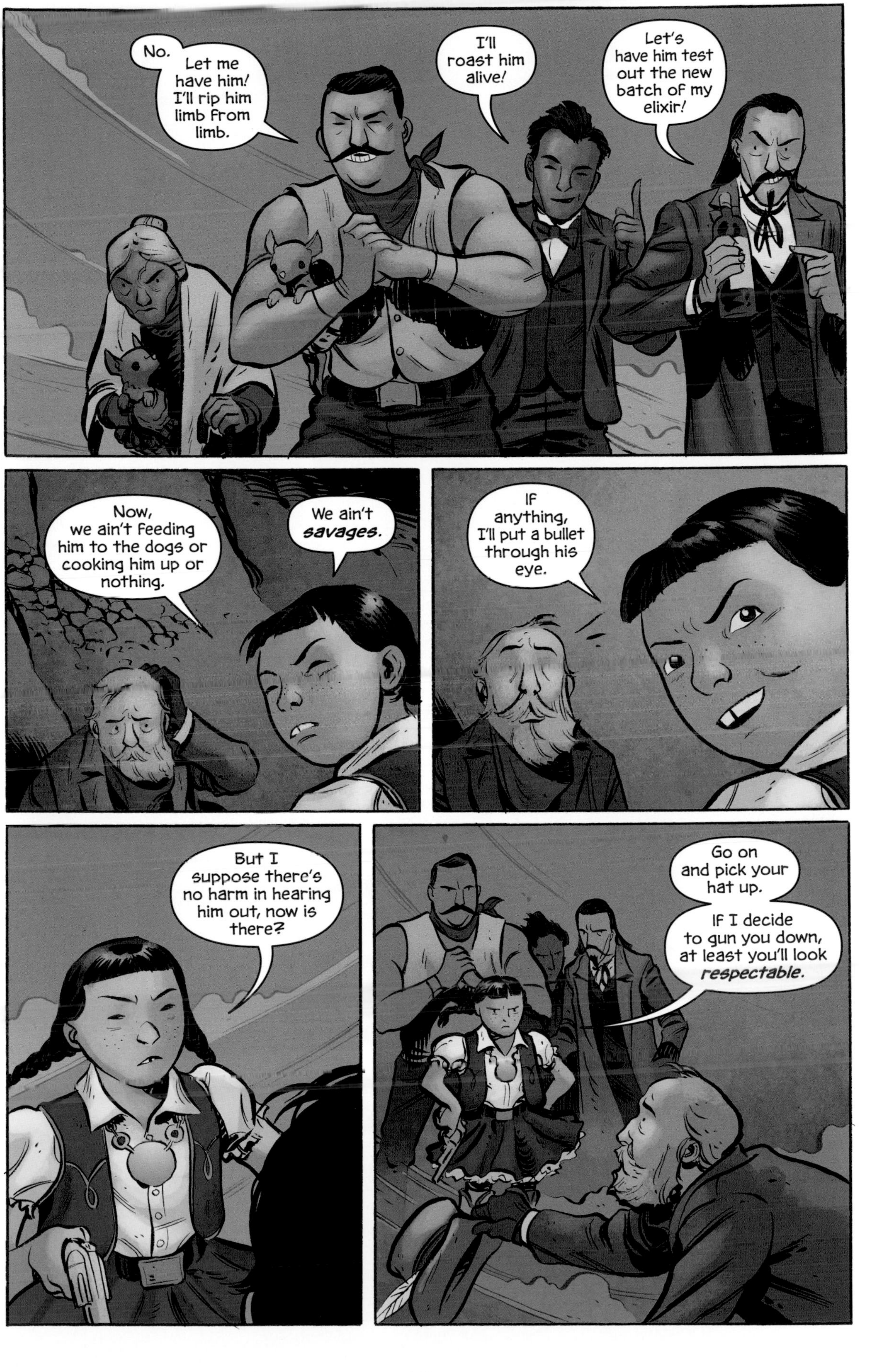
No.
Let me have him! I'll rip him limb from limb.
I'll roast him alive!
Let's have him test out the new batch of my elixir!
Now, we ain't feeding him to the dogs or cooking him up or nothing.
We ain't *savages.*
If anything, I'll put a bullet through his eye.
But I suppose there's no harm in hearing him out, now is there?
Go on and pick your hat up.
If I decide to gun you down, at least you'll look *respectable.*

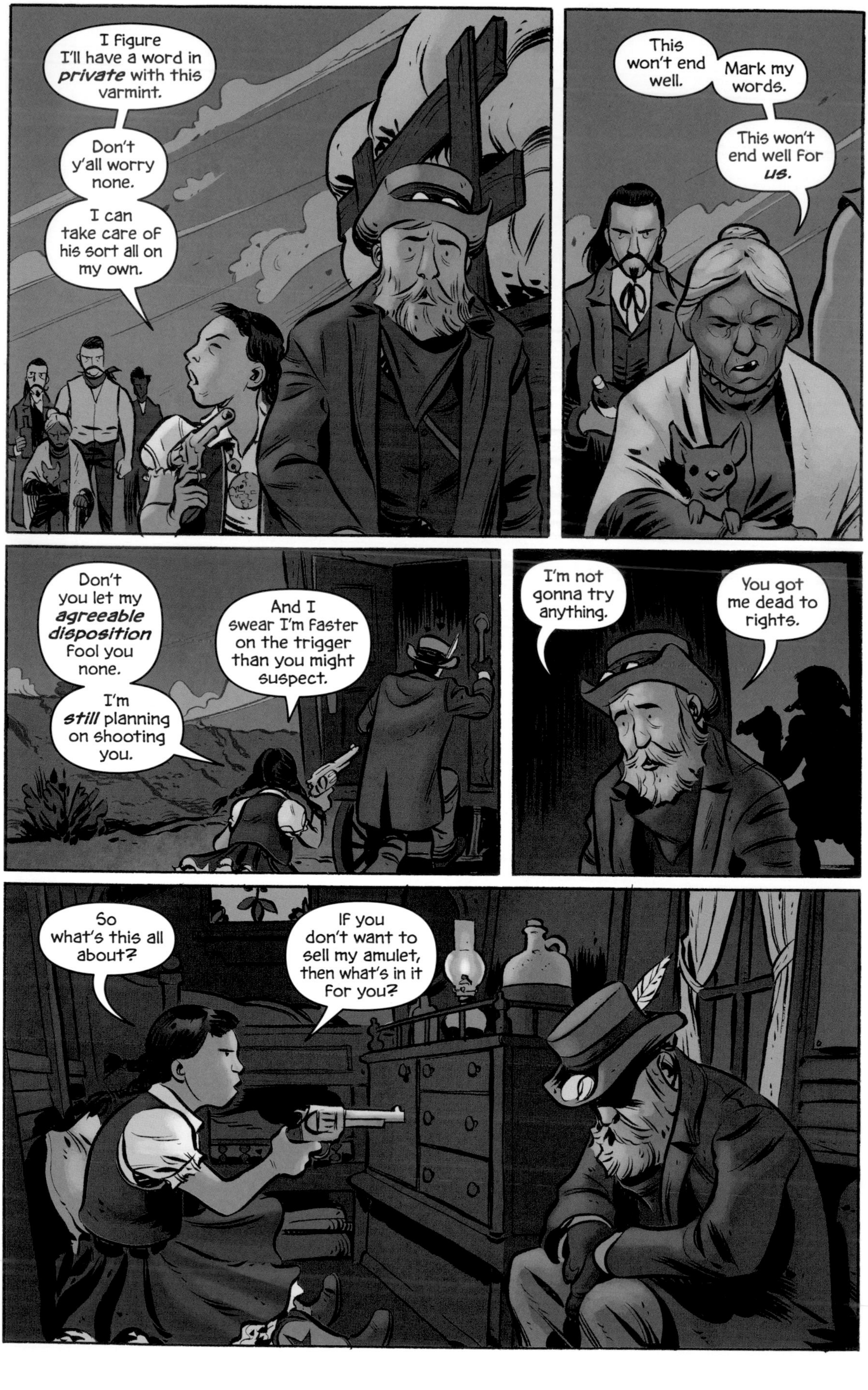
I figure I'll have a word in *private* with this varmint.
Don't y'all worry none.
I can take care of his sort all on my own.
This won't end well.
Mark my words.
This won't end well for *us*.
Don't you let my *agreeable disposition* fool you none.
I'm *still* planning on shooting you.
And I swear I'm faster on the trigger than you might suspect.
I'm not gonna try anything.
You got me dead to rights.
So what's this all about?
If you don't want to sell my amulet, then what's in it for you?

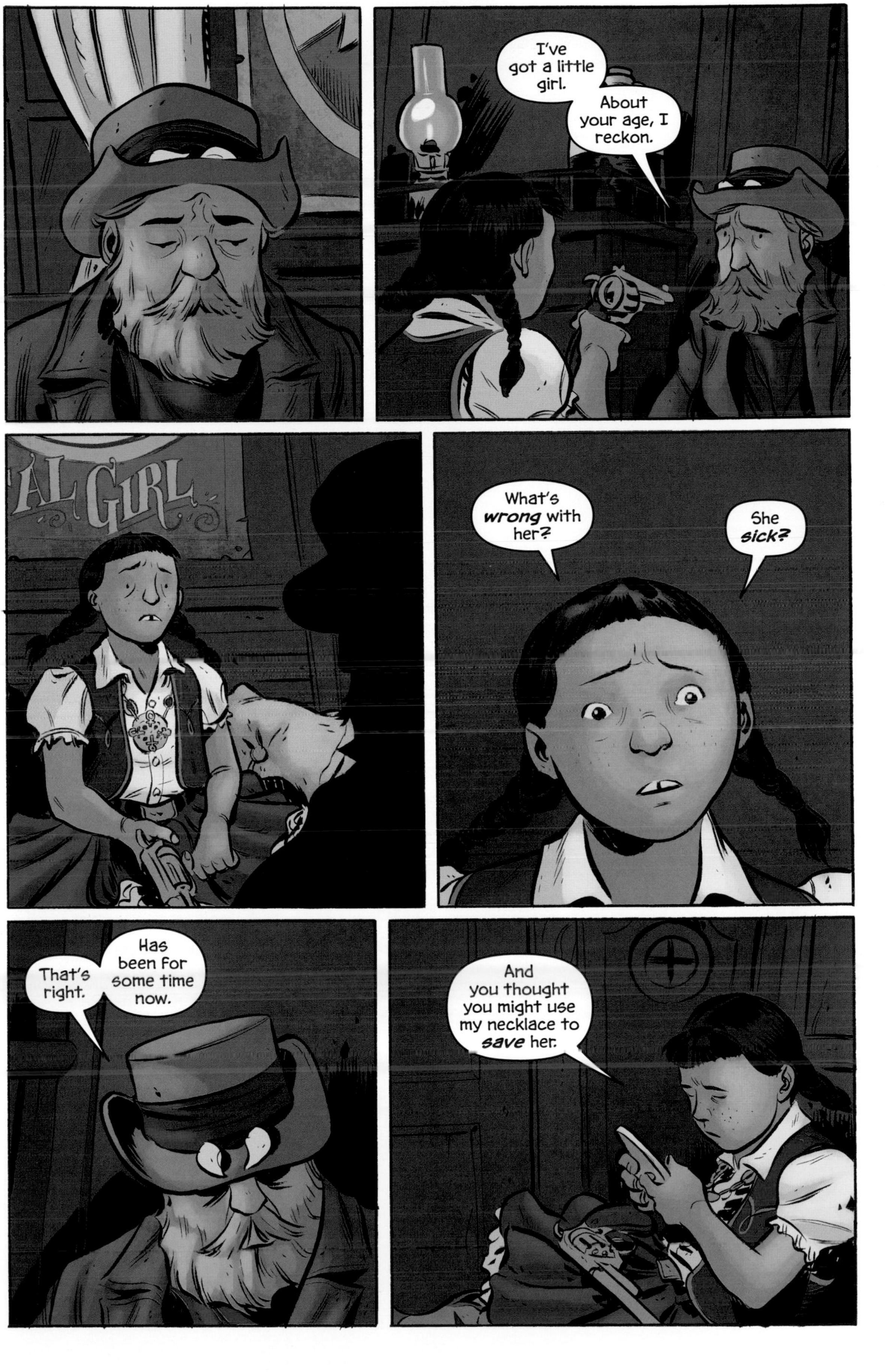
I've got a little girl.
About your age, I reckon.
AL GIRL
What's *wrong* with her?
She *sick?*
That's right.
Has been for some time now.
And you thought you might use my necklace to *save* her.

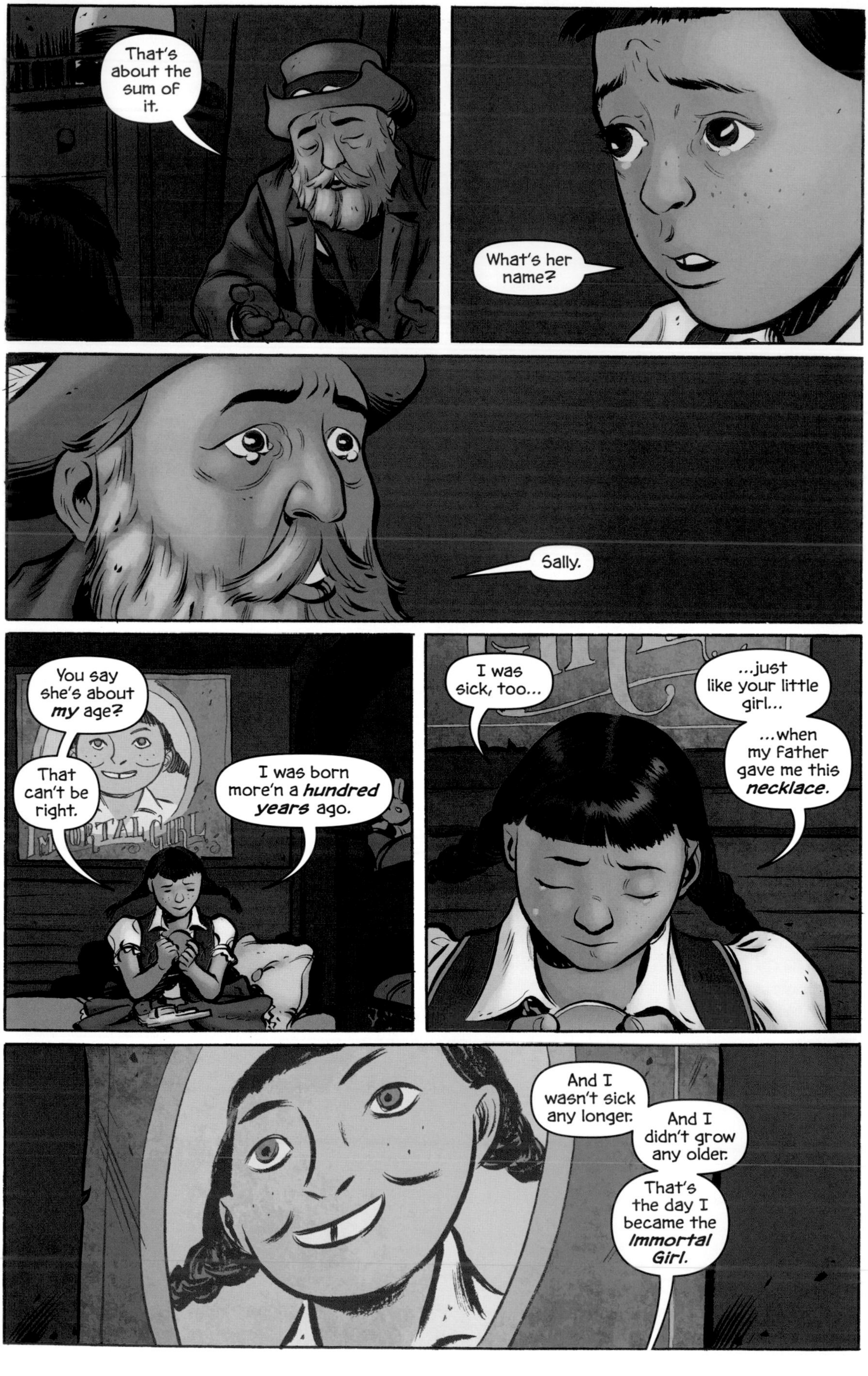
That's about the sum of it.
What's her name?
Sally.
You say she's about *my* age?
That can't be right.
IMMORTAL GIRL
I was born more'n a *hundred years* ago.
I was sick, too...
...just like your little girl...
...when my father gave me this *necklace*.
And I wasn't sick any longer.
And I didn't grow any older.
That's the day I became the *Immortal Girl*.

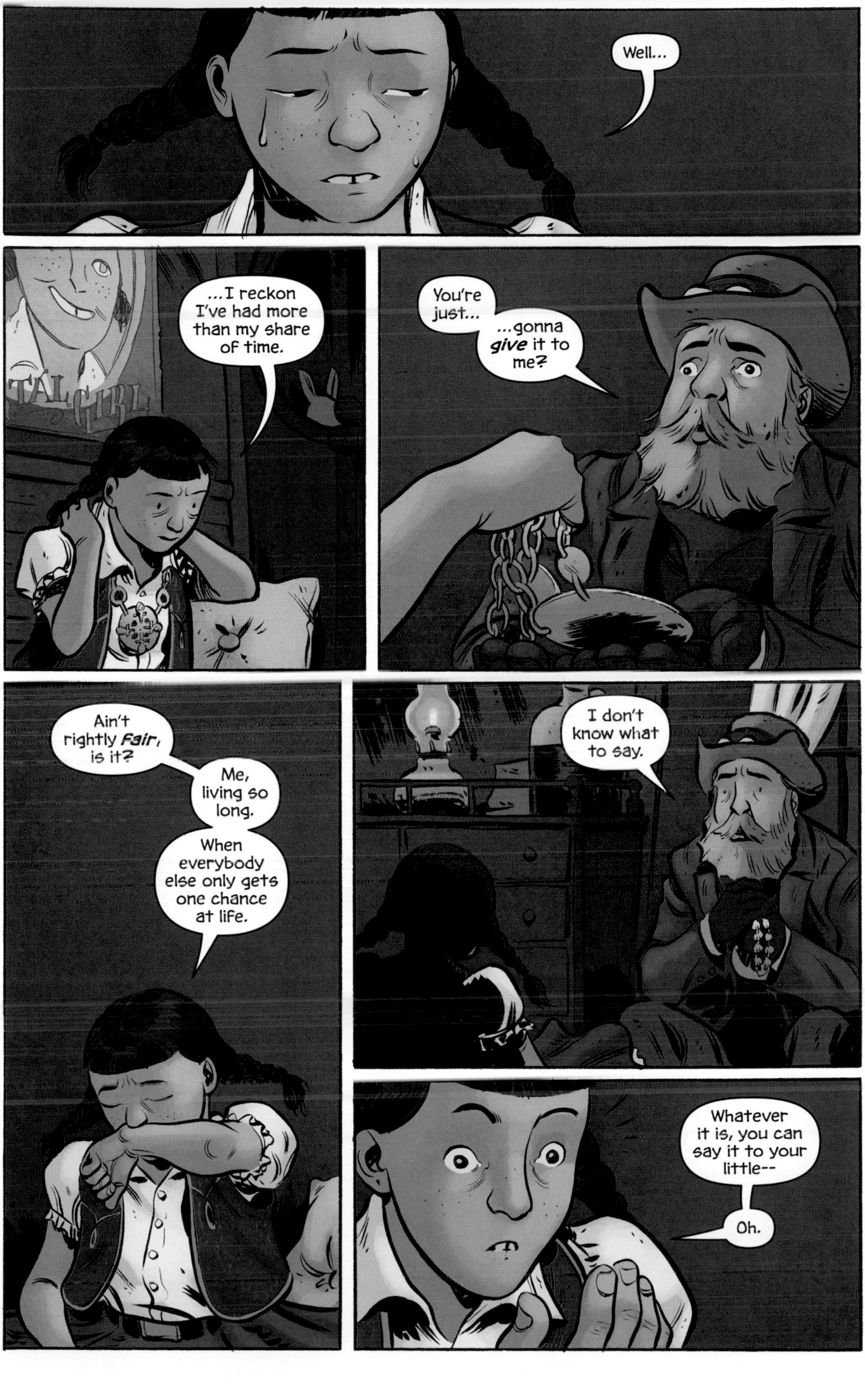
Well...
...I reckon I've had more than my share of time.
You're just...
...gonna *give* it to me?
Ain't rightly *fair*, is it?
Me, living so long.
When everybody else only gets one chance at life.
I don't know what to say.
Whatever it is, you can say it to your little--
Oh.

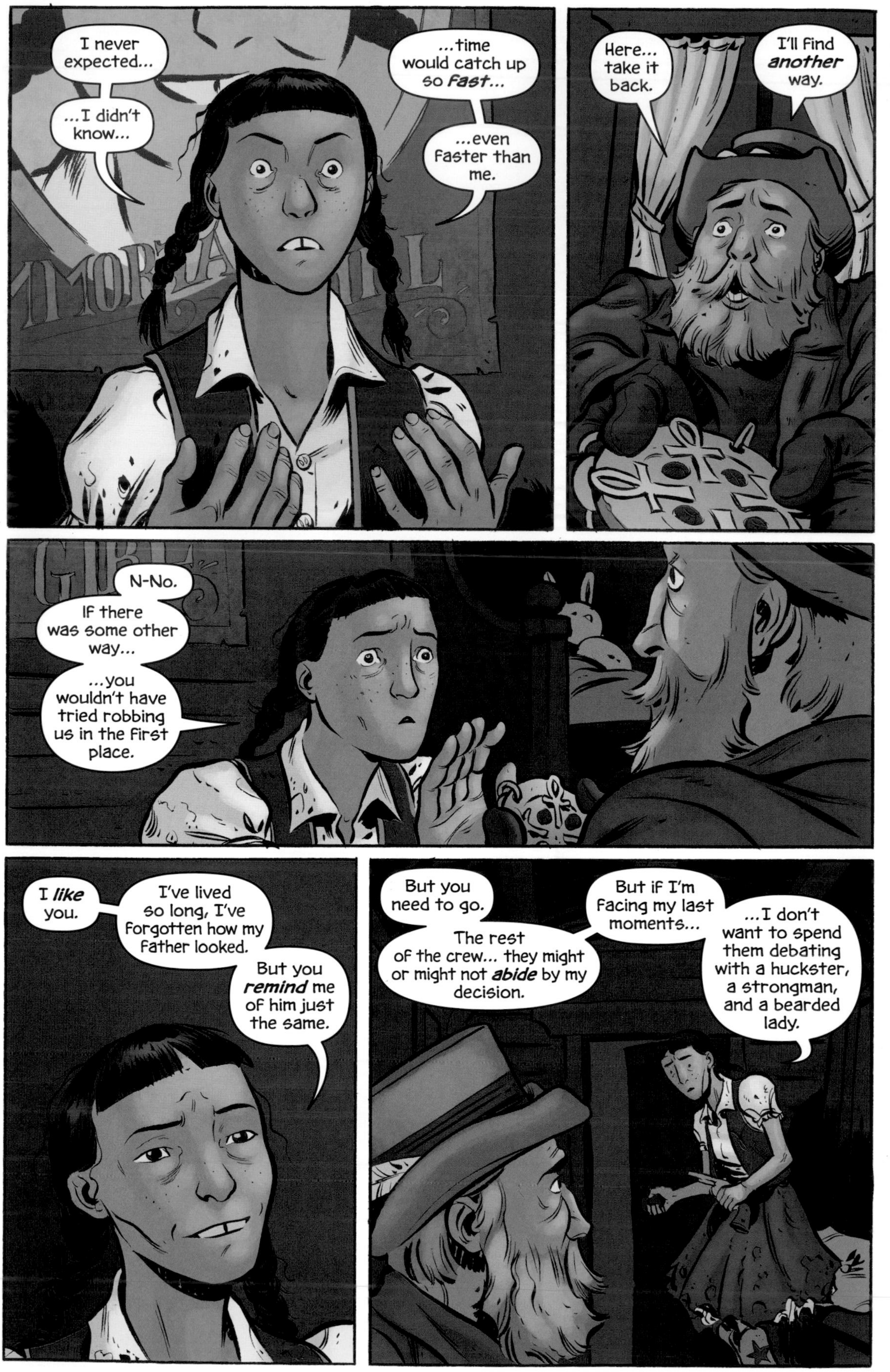
I never expected...
...I didn't know...
...time would catch up so *fast*...
...even faster than me.
MMORTAL
Here... take it back.
I'll find *another* way.
N-No.
If there was some other way...
...you wouldn't have tried robbing us in the first place.
I *like* you.
I've lived so long, I've forgotten how my father looked.
But you *remind* me of him just the same.
But you need to go.
The rest of the crew... they might or might not *abide* by my decision.
But if I'm facing my last moments...
...I don't want to spend them debating with a huckster, a strongman, and a bearded lady.

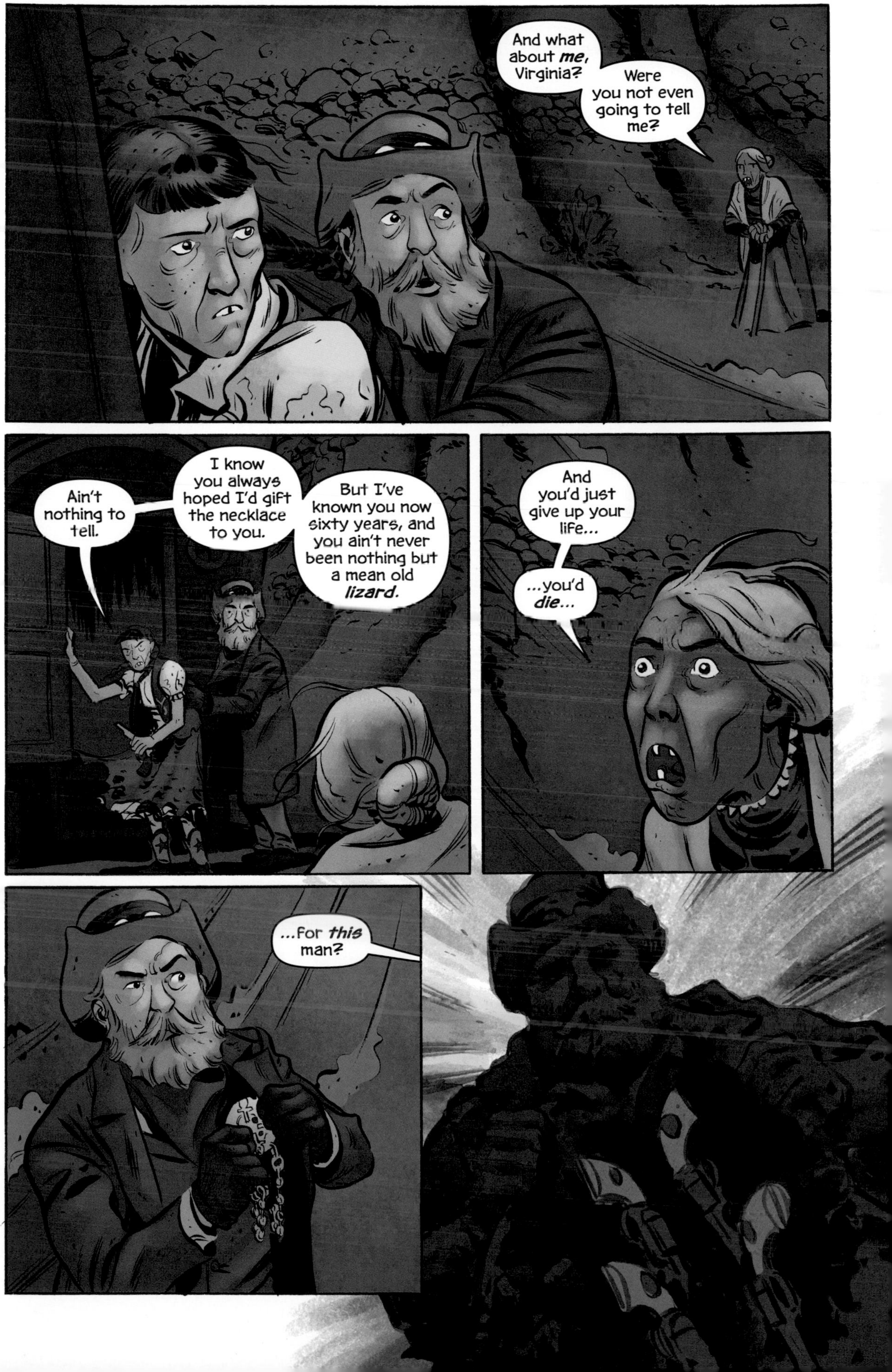
And what about *me*, Virginia?
Were you not even going to tell me?
Ain't nothing to tell.
I know you always hoped I'd gift the necklace to you.
But I've known you now sixty years, and you ain't never been nothing but a mean old *lizard*.
And you'd just give up your life...
...you'd *die*...
...For *this* man?

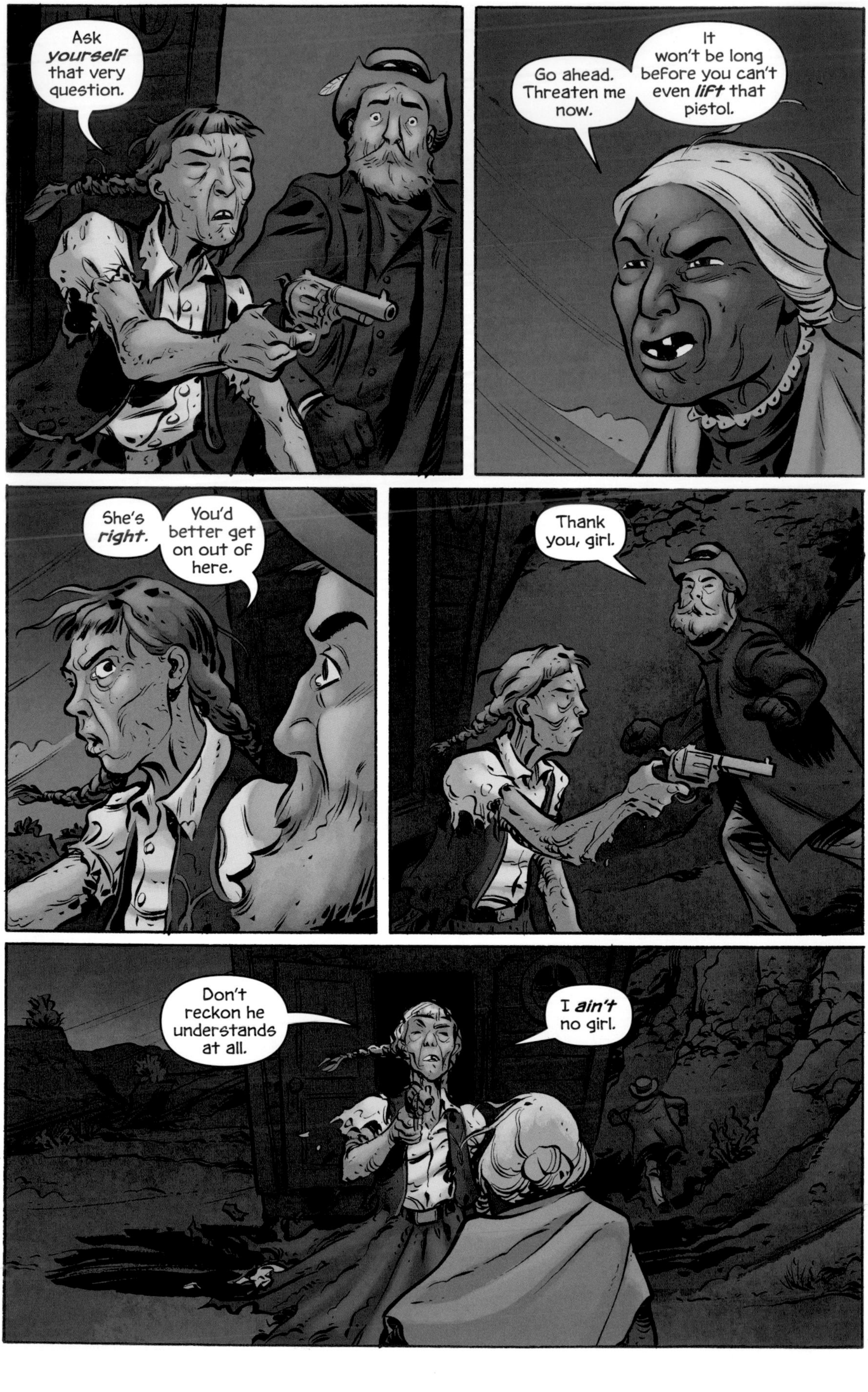
Ask *yourself* that very question.
Go ahead. Threaten me now.
It won't be long before you can't even *lift* that pistol.
She's *right*.
You'd better get on out of here.
Thank you, girl.
Don't reckon he understands at all.
I *ain't* no girl.

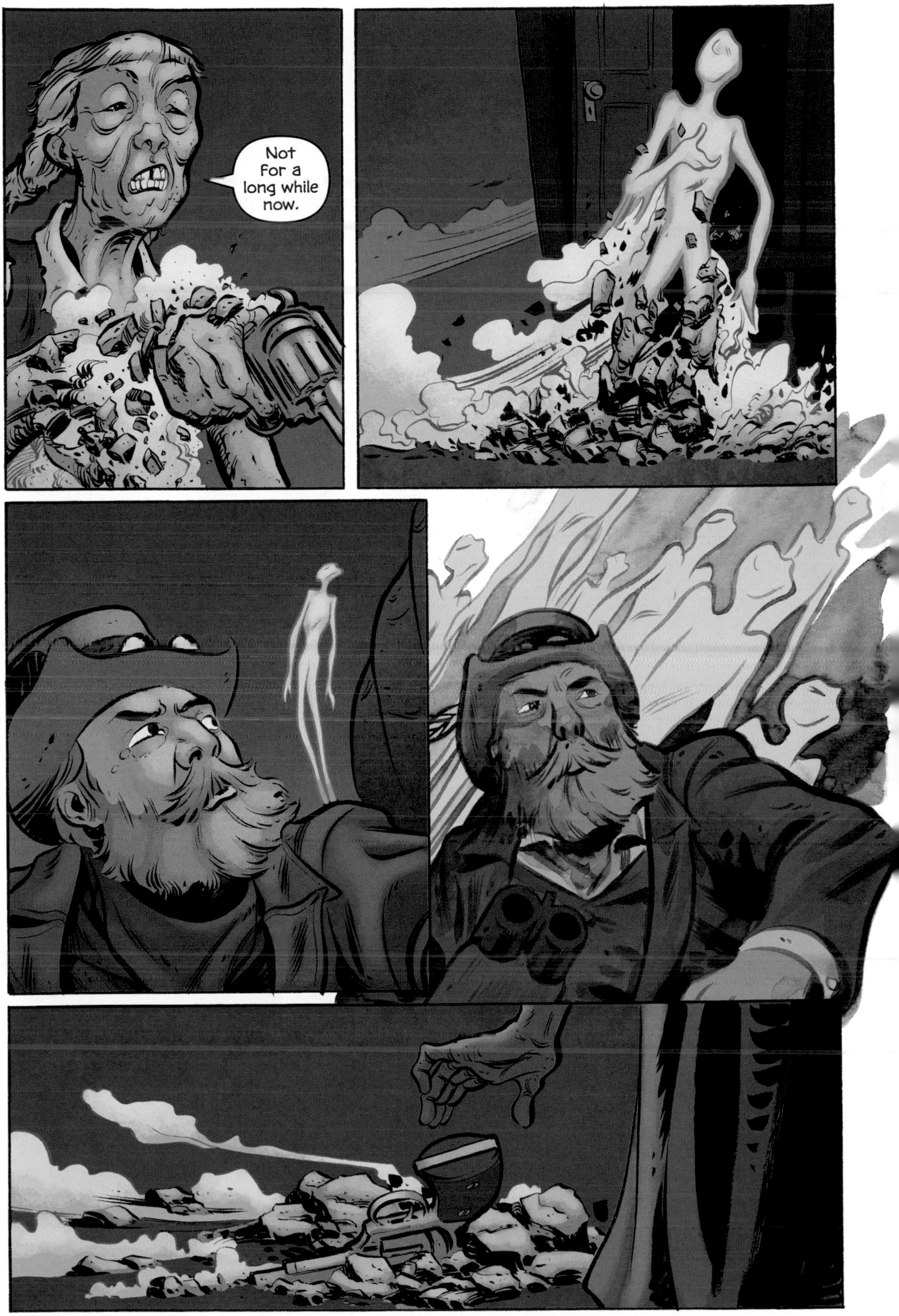
Not for a long while now.

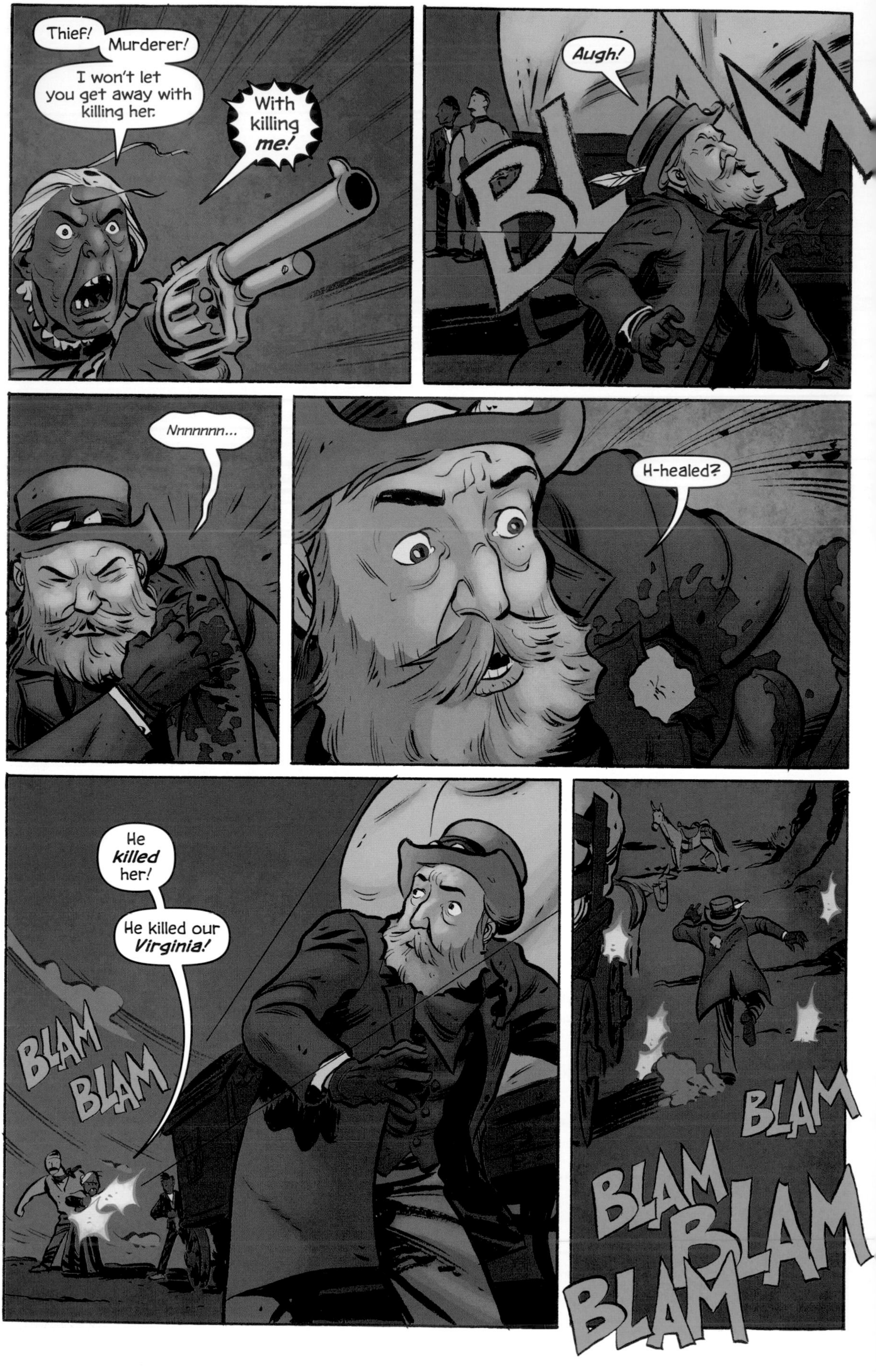
Thief!
Murderer!
I won't let you get away with killing her.
With killing *me!*
Augh!
BLAM
Nnnnnnn...
H-healed?
He *killed* her!
He killed our *Virginia!*
BLAM
BLAM
BLAM
BLAM
BLAM
BLAM
BLAM

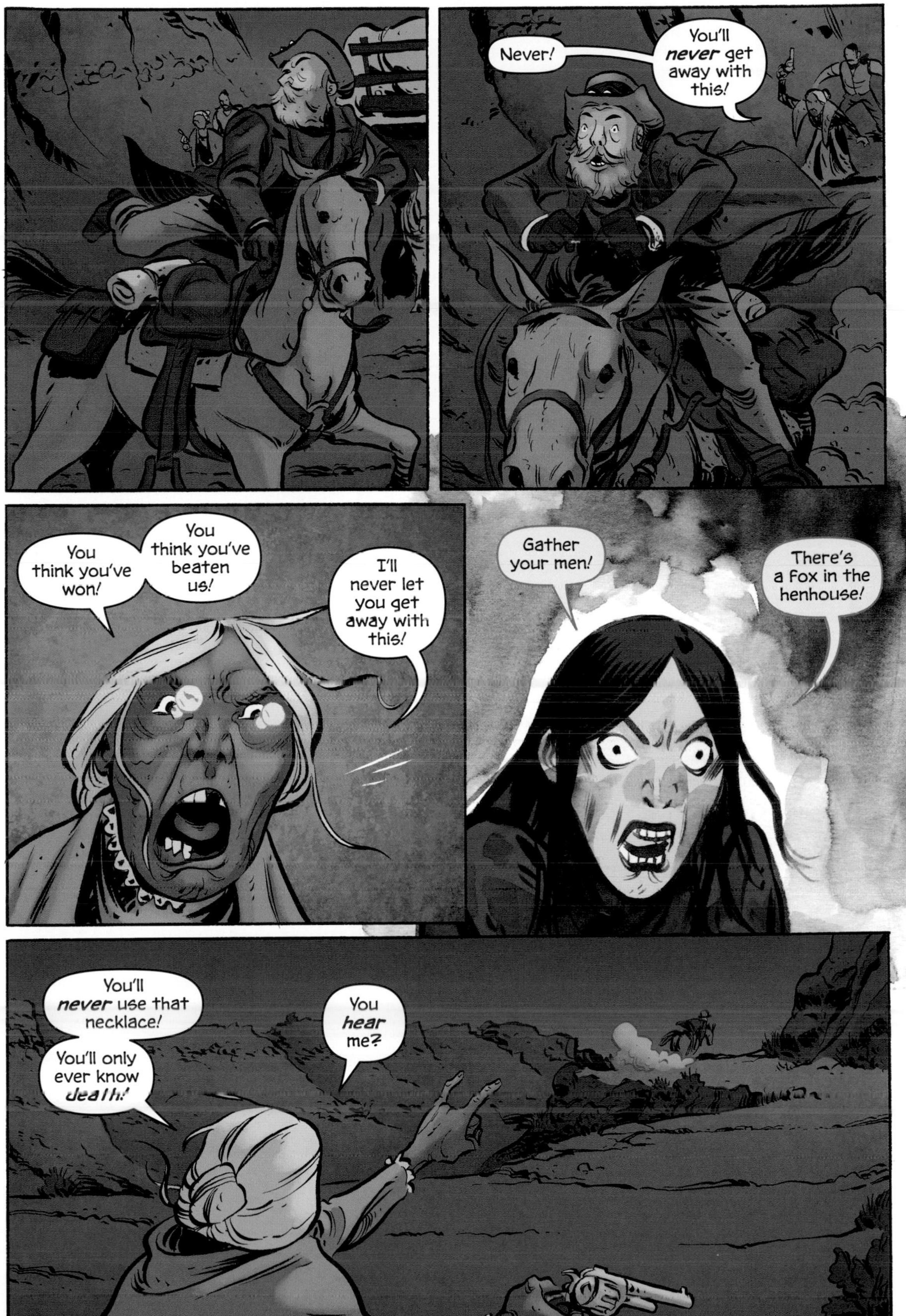
Never!
You'll **never** get away with this!
You think you've won!
You think you've beaten us!
I'll never let you get away with this!
Gather your men!
There's a Fox in the henhouse!
You'll **never** use that necklace!
You'll only ever know **death!**
You **hear** me?

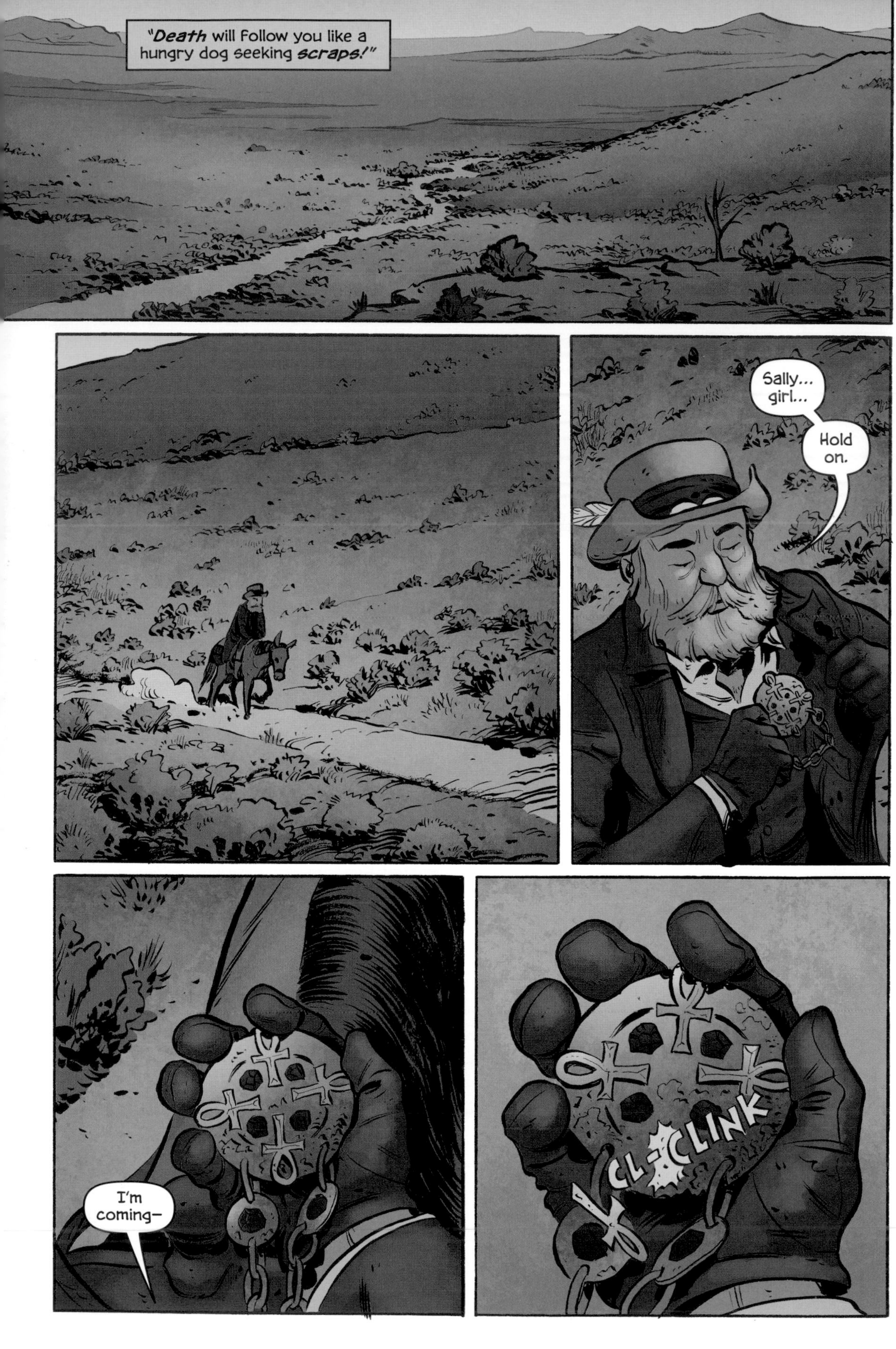
"Death will follow you like a hungry dog seeking scraps!"
Sally... girl...
Hold on.
I'm coming–
CL-CLINK

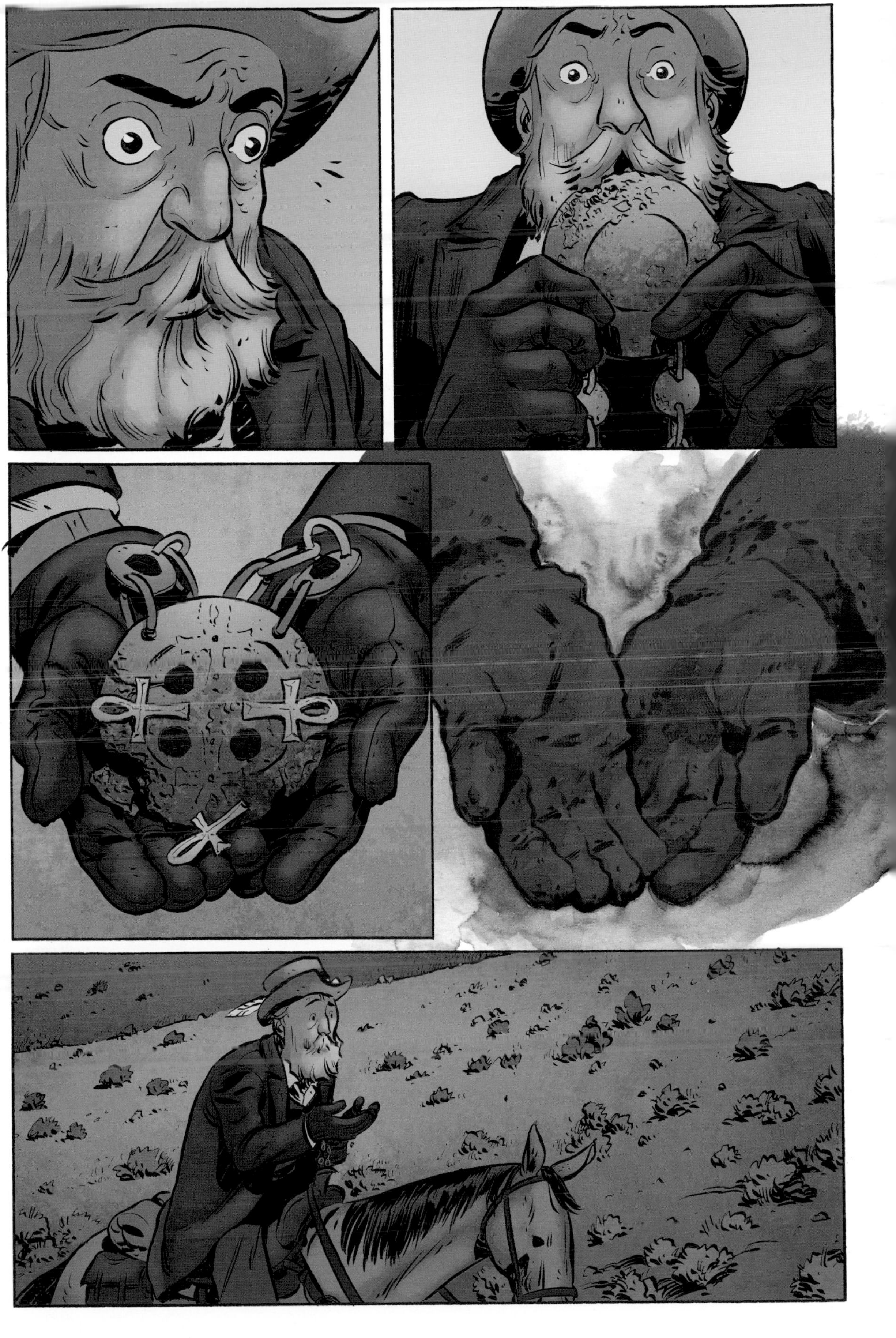

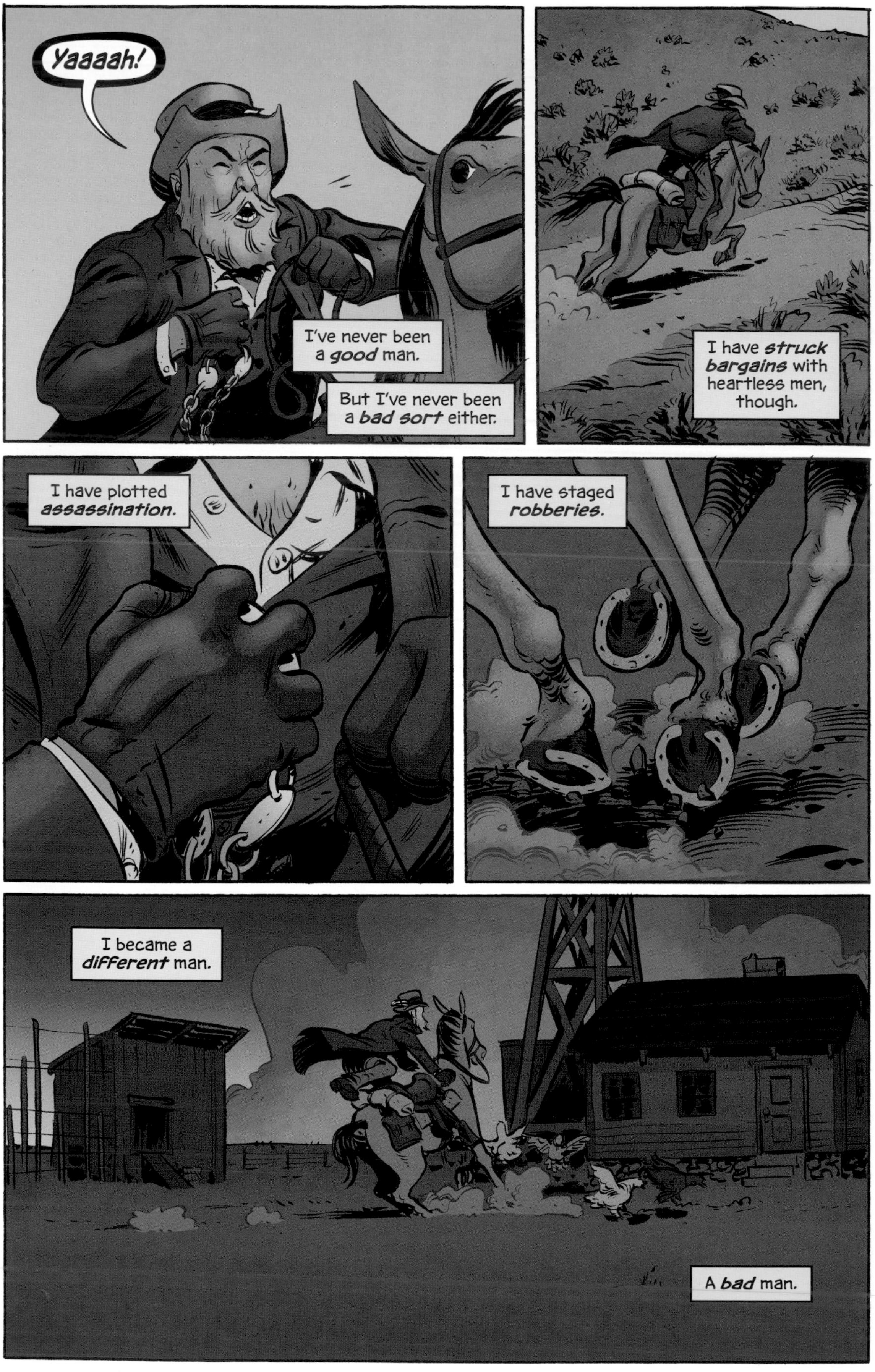
Yaaaah!
I've never been a good man.
But I've never been a bad sort either.
I have struck bargains with heartless men, though.
I have plotted assassination.
I have staged robberies.
I became a different man.
A bad man.

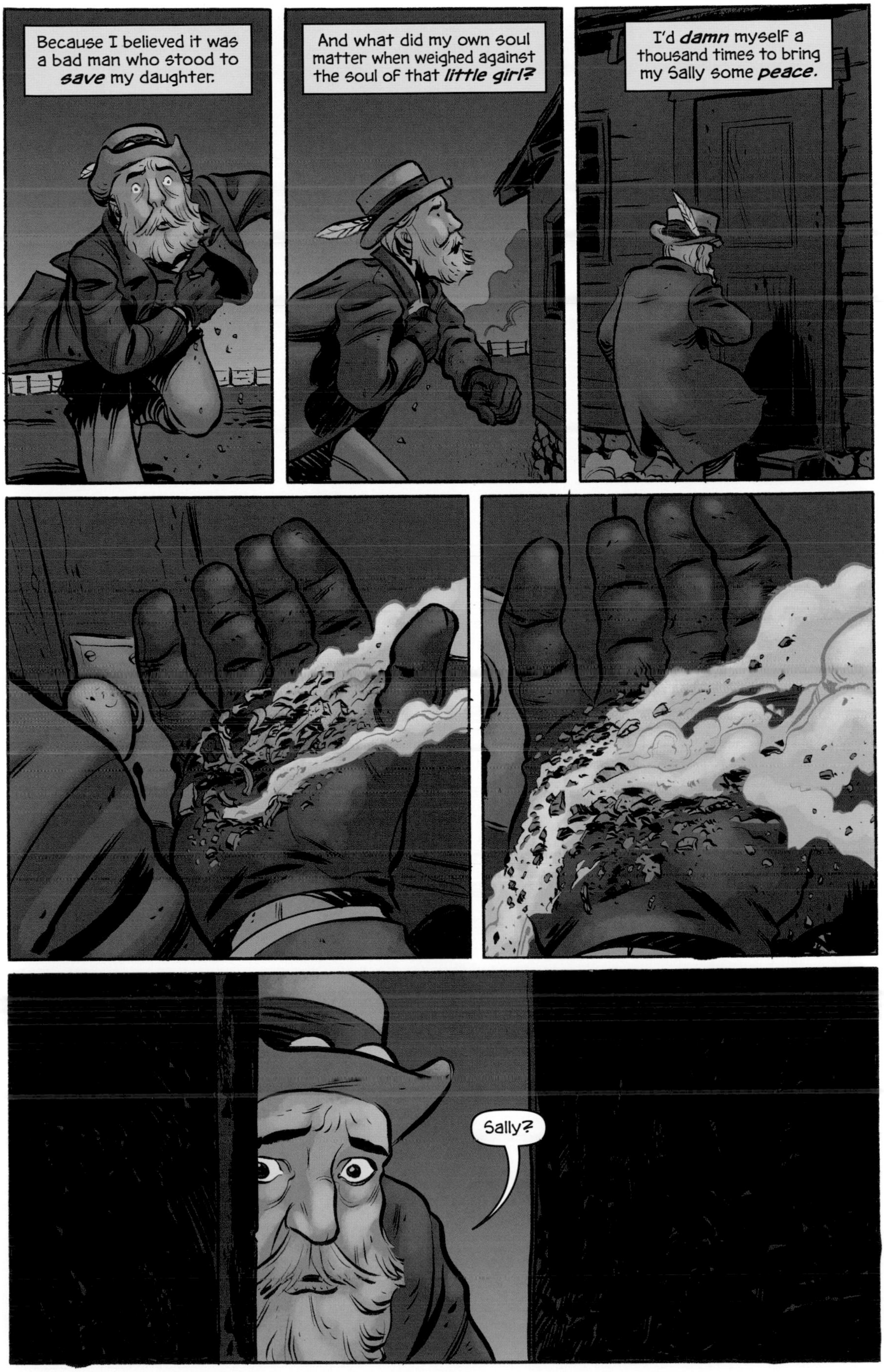
Because I believed it was a bad man who stood to *save* my daughter.
And what did my own soul matter when weighed against the soul of that *little girl?*
I'd *damn* myself a thousand times to bring my Sally some *peace.*
Sally?

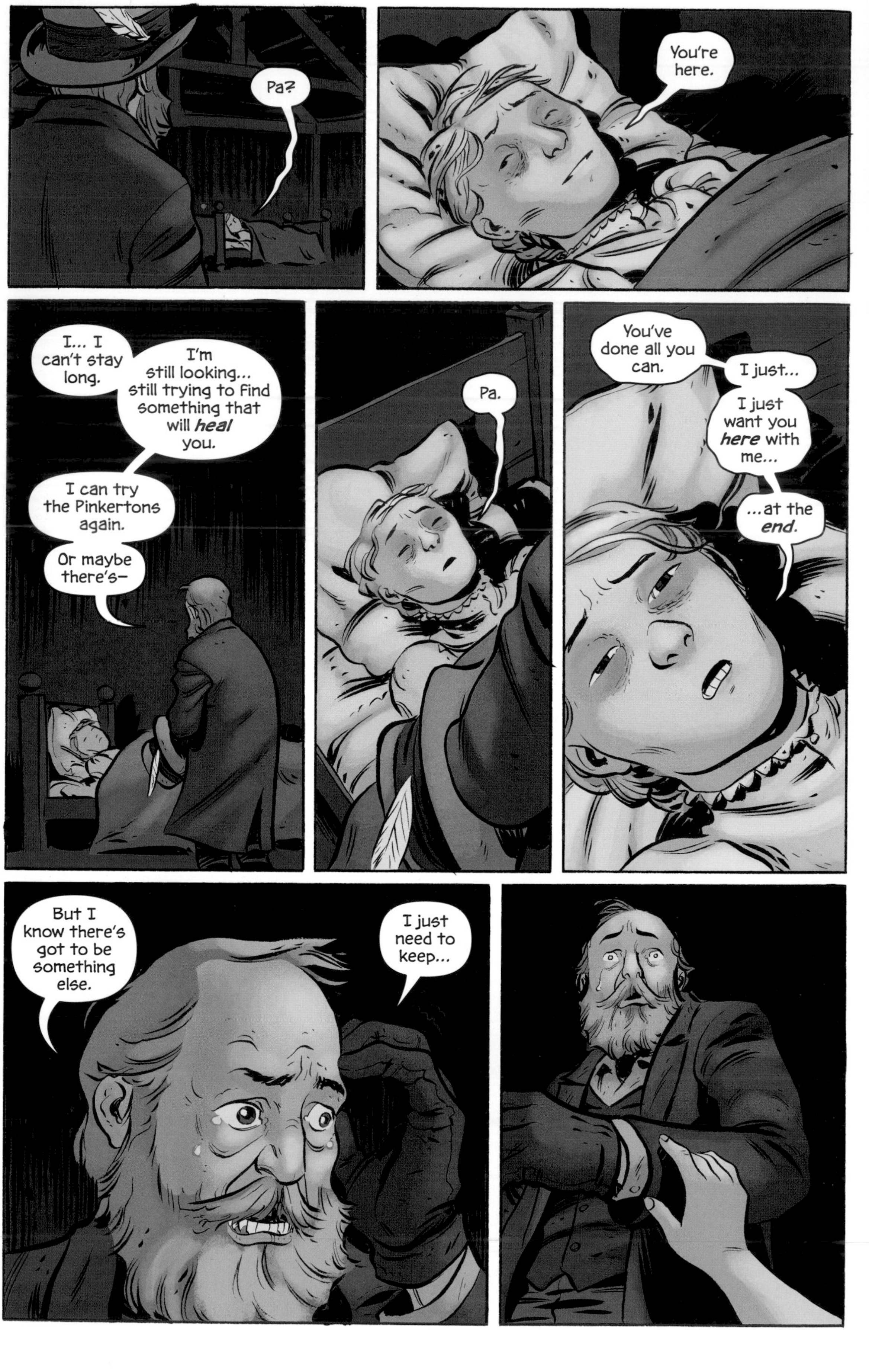

Pa?
You're here.
I... I can't stay long.
I'm still looking... still trying to find something that will *heal* you.
I can try the Pinkertons again.
Or maybe there's—
Pa.
You've done all you can.
I just...
I just want you *here* with me...
...at the *end*.
But I know there's got to be something else.
I just need to keep...

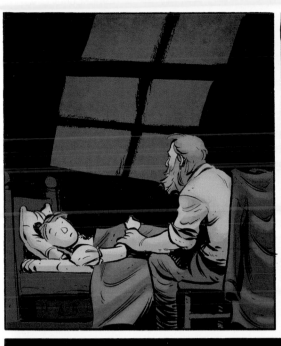

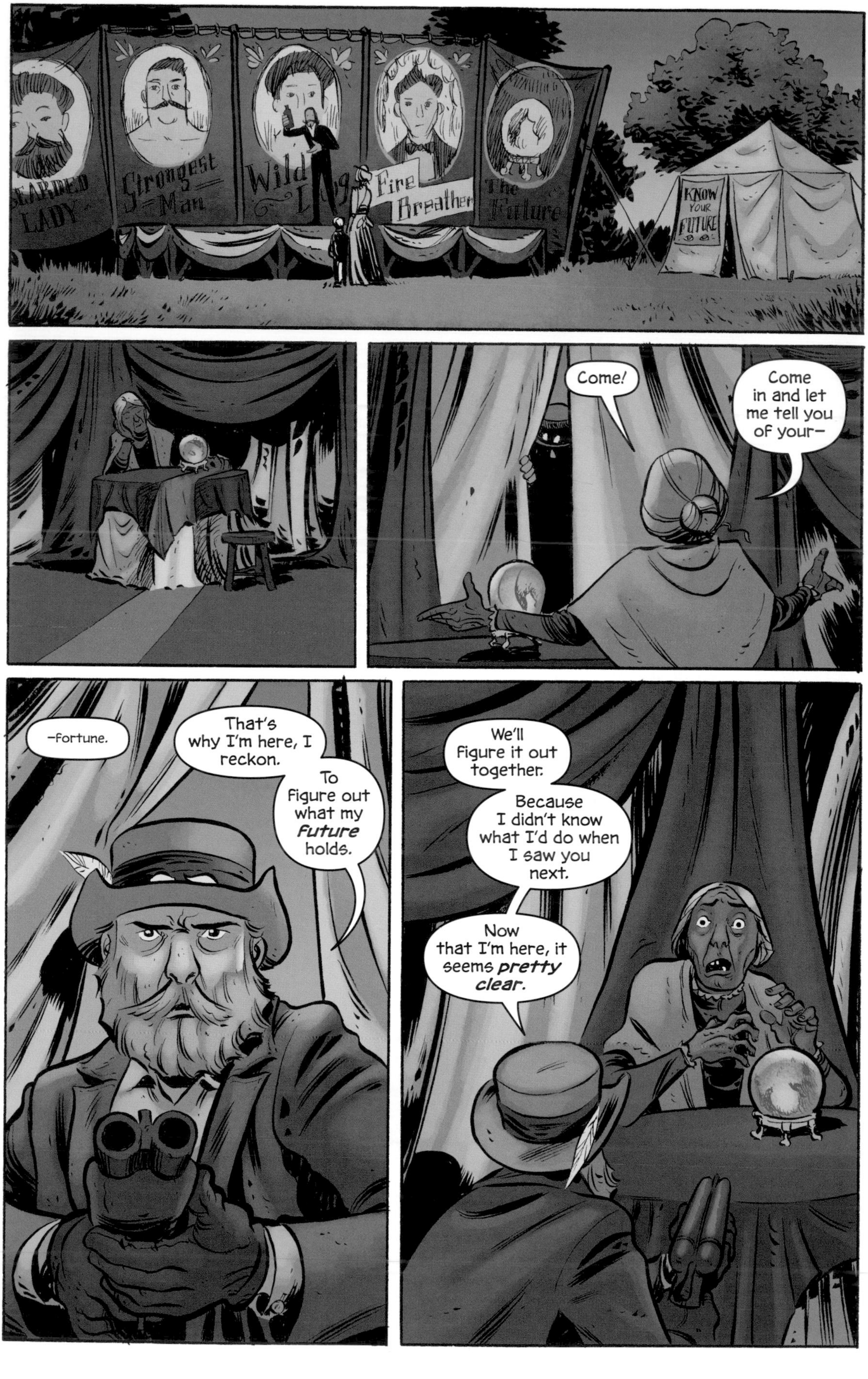
BEARDED LADY
Strongest Man
Wild
Fire Breather
The Future
KNOW YOUR FUTURE
Come!
Come in and let me tell you of your—
—fortune.
That's why I'm here, I reckon.
To figure out what my *future* holds.
We'll figure it out together.
Because I didn't know what I'd do when I saw you next.
Now that I'm here, it seems *pretty clear*.

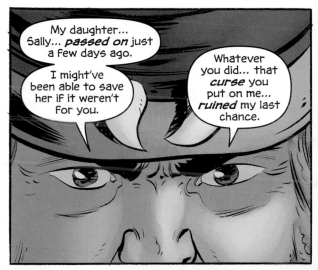

My daughter... Sally... *passed on* just a few days ago.

I might've been able to save her if it weren't for you.

Whatever you did... that *curse* you put on me... *ruined* my last chance.

So, I reckon I came here to *kill* you for what you did.

But... looking at you now... seeing how *feeble* and *scared* you are...

...I realize that Sally wouldn't *want* me to kill you.

She wouldn't want me to *sully* her memory with *your* blood.

You keep that in mind.

Whatever time you got left, it's *thanks* to a little girl you let die.

KNOW YOUR ITURE

Maybe that old woman heard what I was saying.

Maybe not.

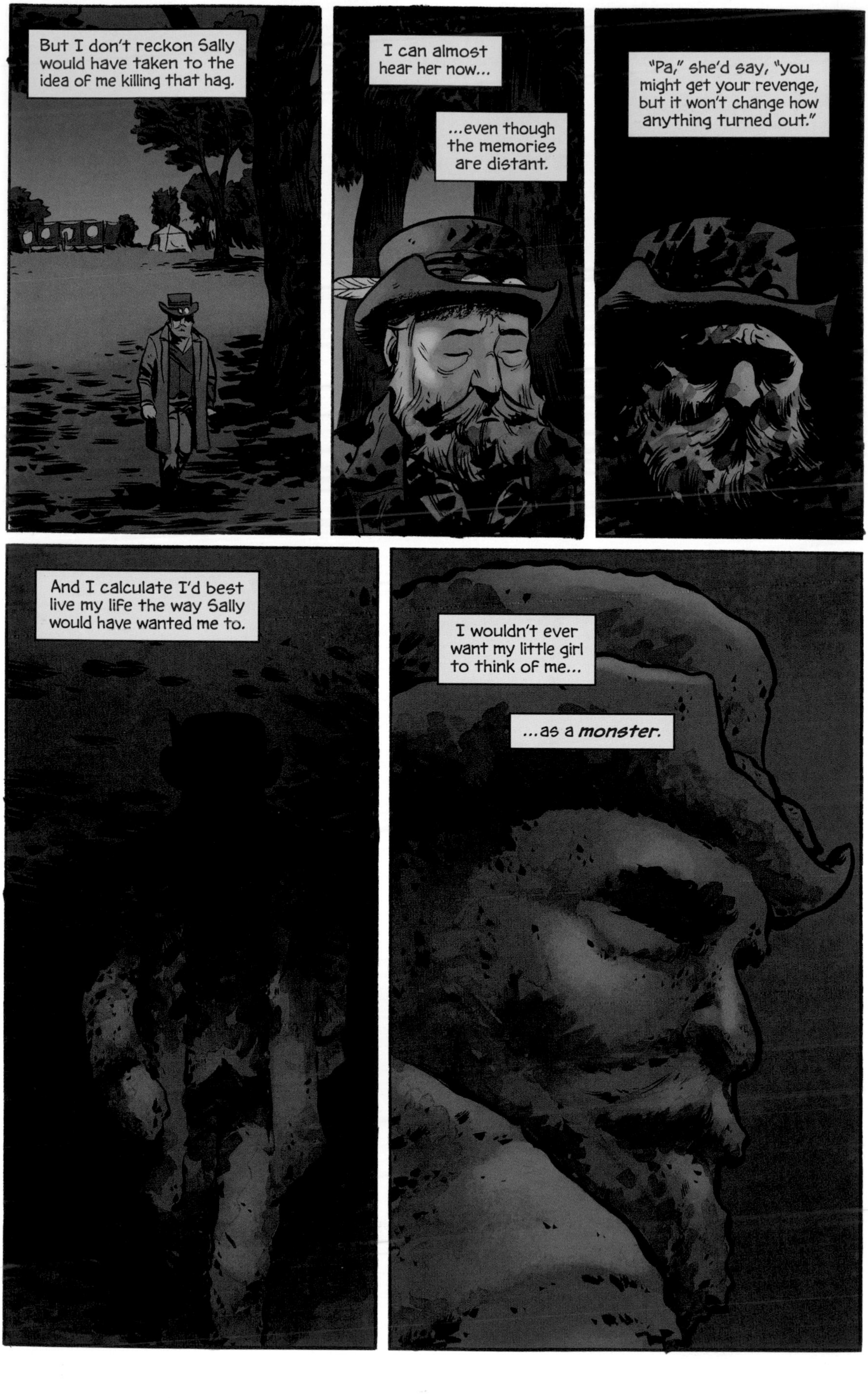
But I don't reckon Sally would have taken to the idea of me killing that hag.
I can almost hear her now...
...even though the memories are distant.
"Pa," she'd say, "you might get your revenge, but it won't change how anything turned out."
And I calculate I'd best live my life the way Sally would have wanted me to.
I wouldn't ever want my little girl to think of me...
...as a *monster*.

LIL' SIXTH GUN

BY CAT FARRIS

CATTIFER.COM · @CATTIFER

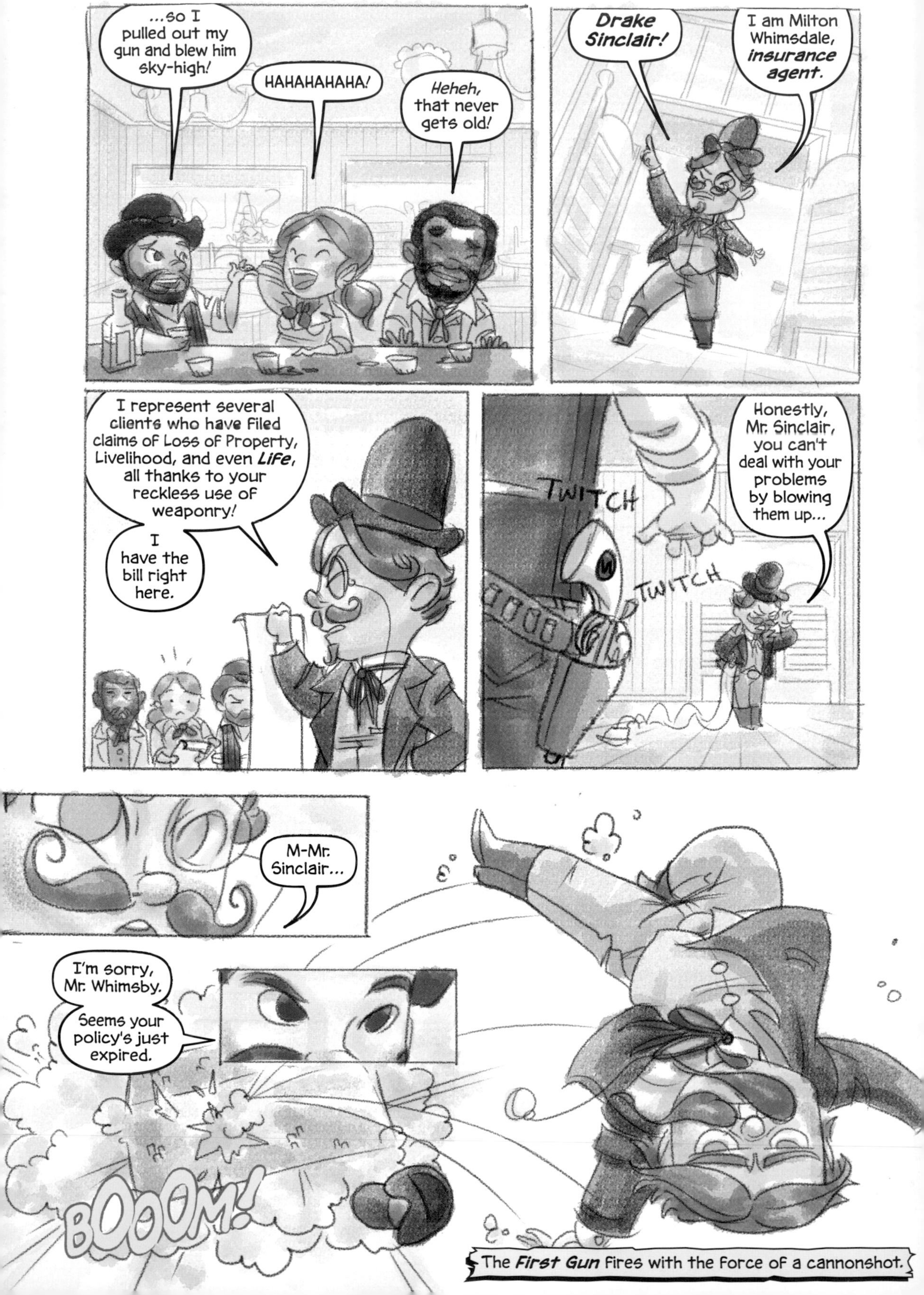
...so I pulled out my gun and blew him sky-high!
HAHAHAHAHA!
Heheh, that never gets old!
Drake Sinclair!
I am Milton Whimsdale, insurance agent.
I represent several clients who have filed claims of Loss of Property, Livelihood, and even Life, all thanks to your reckless use of weaponry!
I have the bill right here.
TWITCH
TWITCH
Honestly, Mr. Sinclair, you can't deal with your problems by blowing them up...
M-Mr. Sinclair...
I'm sorry, Mr. Whimsby.
Seems your policy's just expired.
BOOOM!
The First Gun fires with the force of a cannonshot.

LIL' SIXTH GUN

BY CAT FARRIS
CATTIFER.COM · @CATTIFER

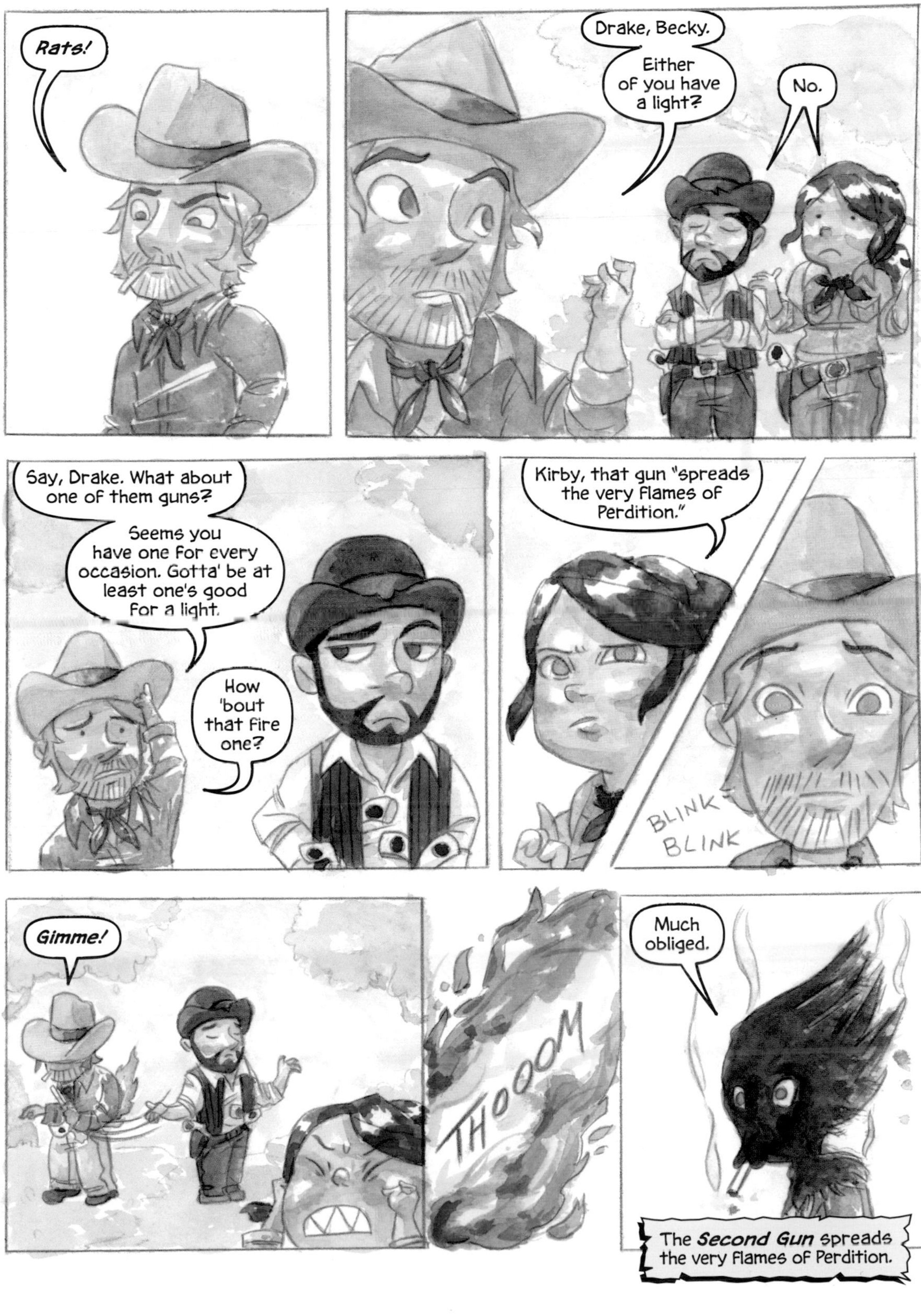
Rats!
Drake, Becky.
Either of you have a light?
No.
Say, Drake. What about one of them guns?
Seems you have one for every occasion. Gotta' be at least one's good for a light.
How 'bout that fire one?
Kirby, that gun "spreads the very flames of Perdition."
BLINK BLINK
Gimme!
THOOOM
Much obliged.
The *Second Gun* spreads the very flames of Perdition.

LIL' SIXTH GUN

By Cat Farris
cattifer.com · @cattifer

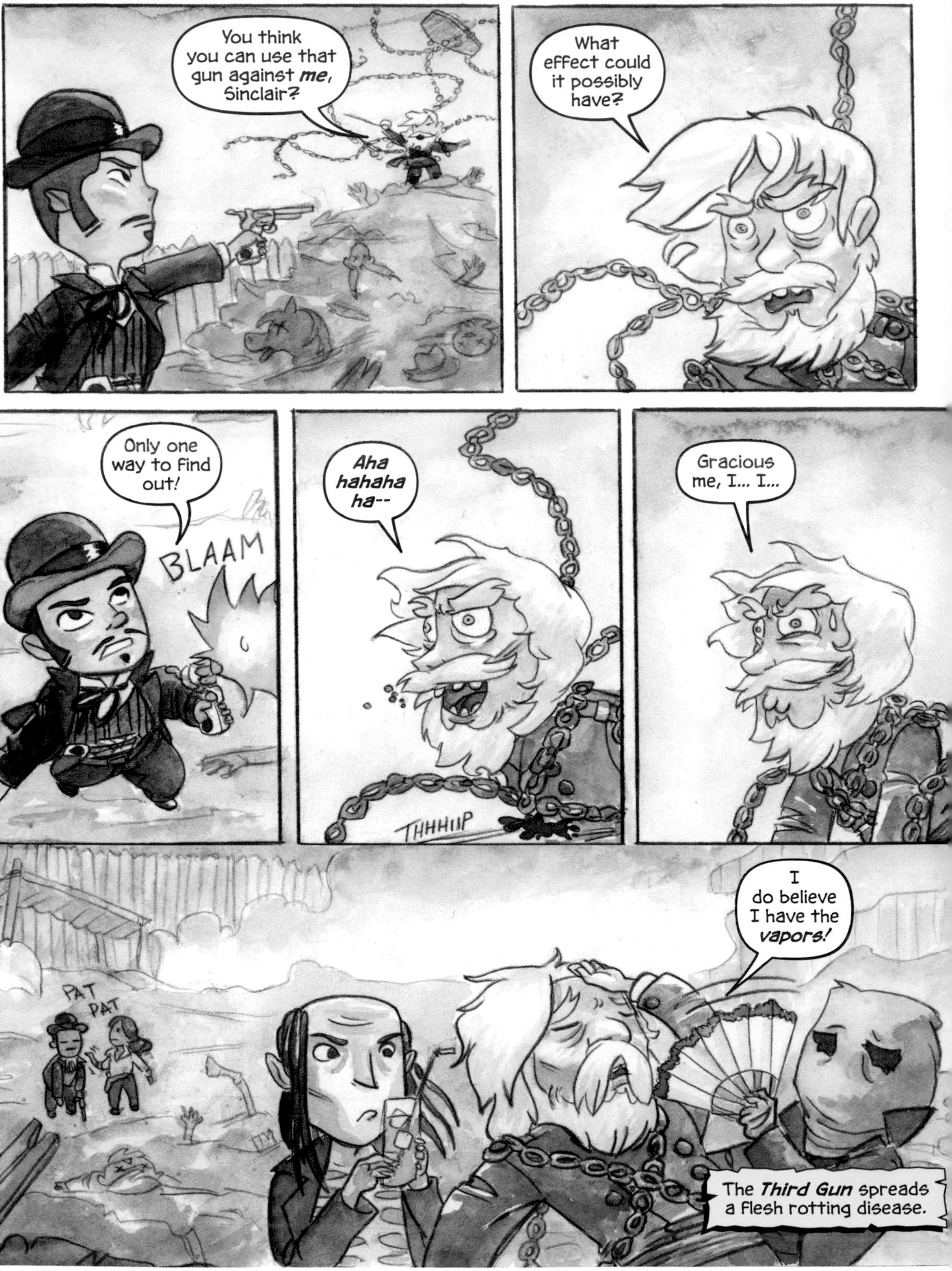
You think you can use that gun against *me*, Sinclair?
What effect could it possibly have?
Only one way to find out!
BLAAM
Aha hahaha ha--
THHHUP
Gracious me, I... I...
PAT PAT
I do believe I have the *vapors!*
The *Third Gun* spreads a flesh rotting disease.

LIL' SIXTH GUN

By Cat Farris
cattifer.com · @cattifer

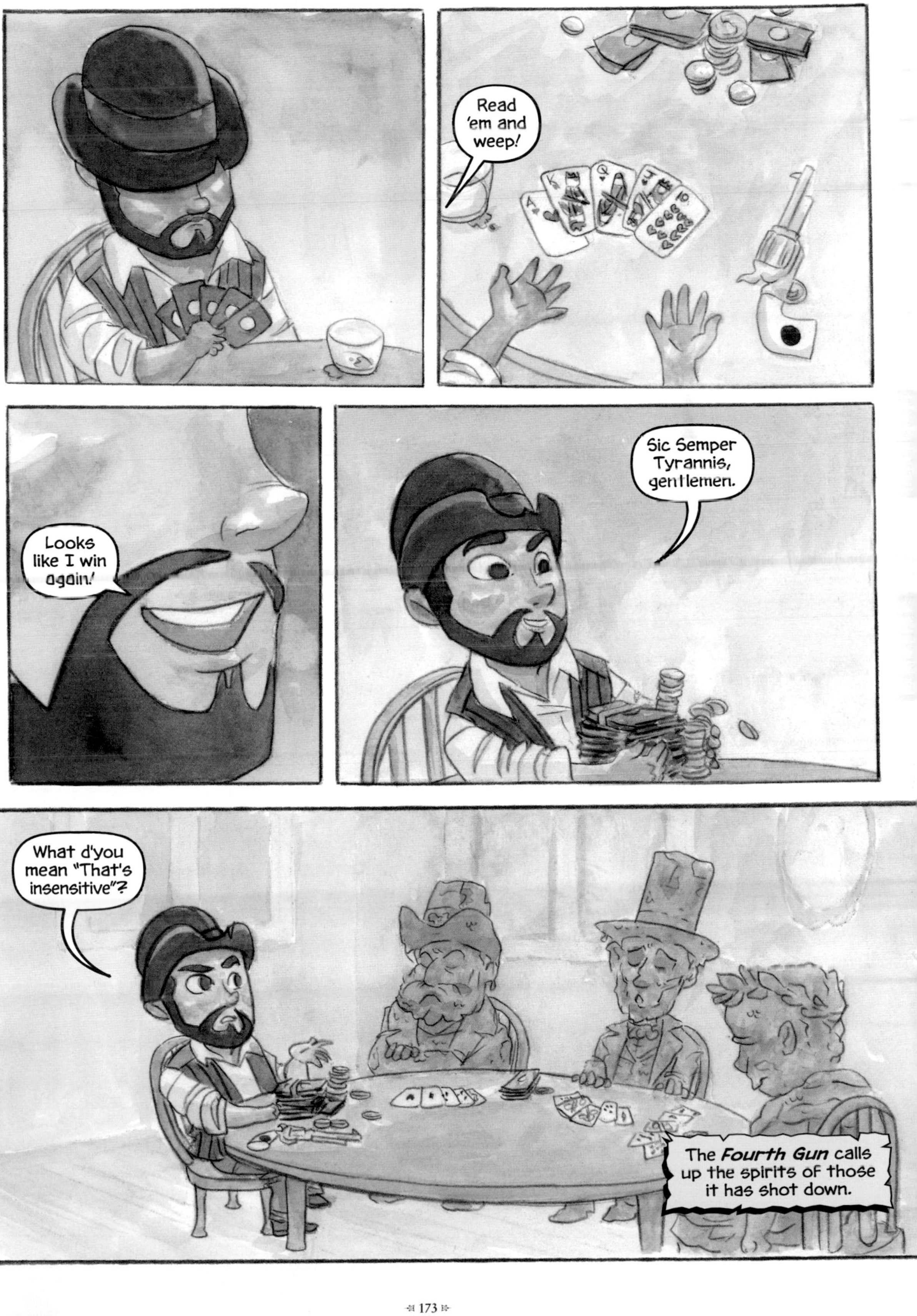
Read 'em and weep!
Looks like I win again!
Sic Semper Tyrannis, gentlemen.
What d'you mean "That's insensitive"?
The *Fourth Gun* calls up the spirits of those it has shot down.

LIL' SIXTH GUN

BY CAT FARRIS
CATTIFER.COM · @CATTIFER

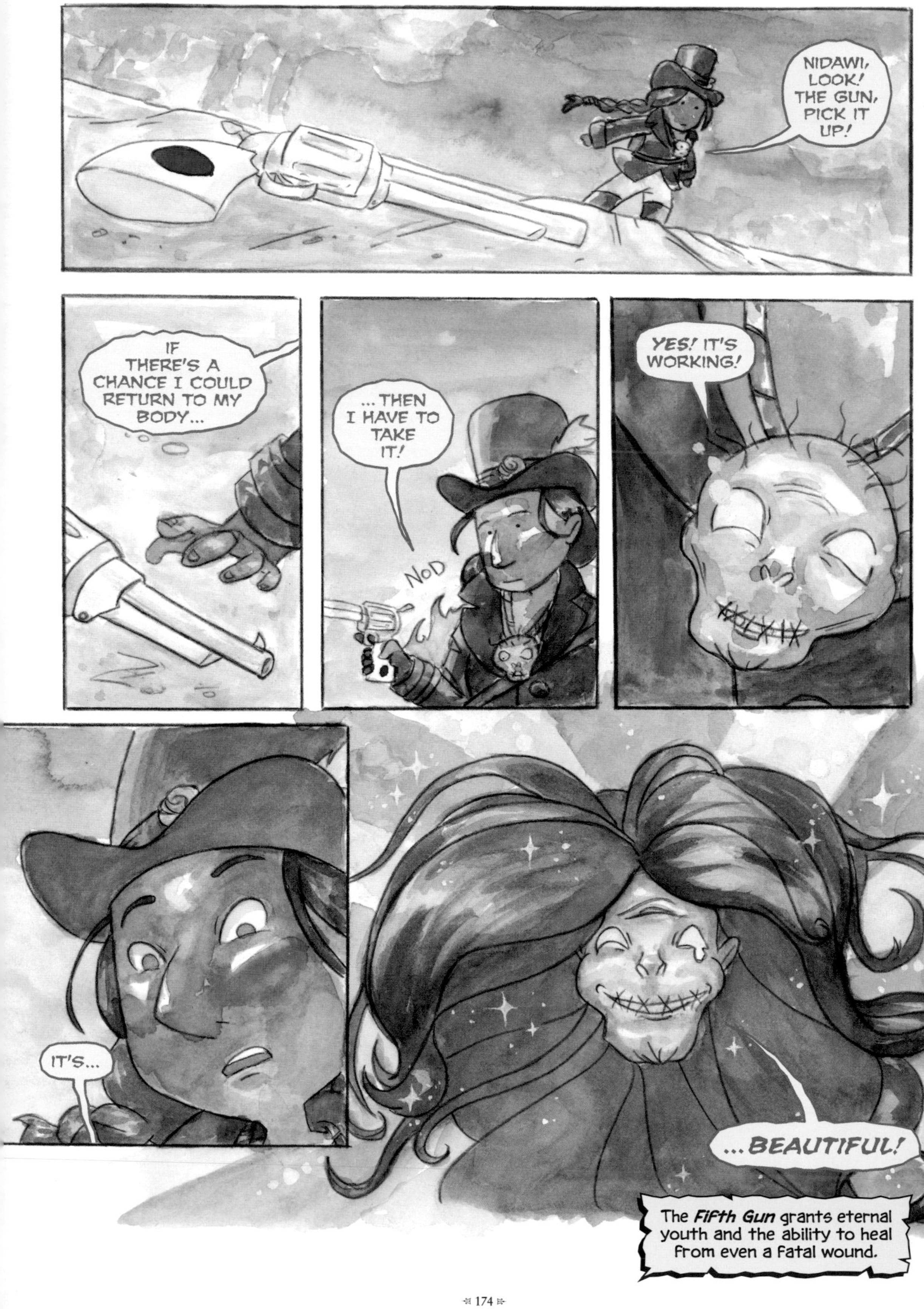
NIDAWI, LOOK! THE GUN, PICK IT UP!
IF THERE'S A CHANCE I COULD RETURN TO MY BODY...
...THEN I HAVE TO TAKE IT!
NOD
YES! IT'S WORKING!
IT'S...
...BEAUTIFUL!
The Fifth Gun grants eternal youth and the ability to heal from even a fatal wound.

By Cat Farris
cattifer.com · @cattifer

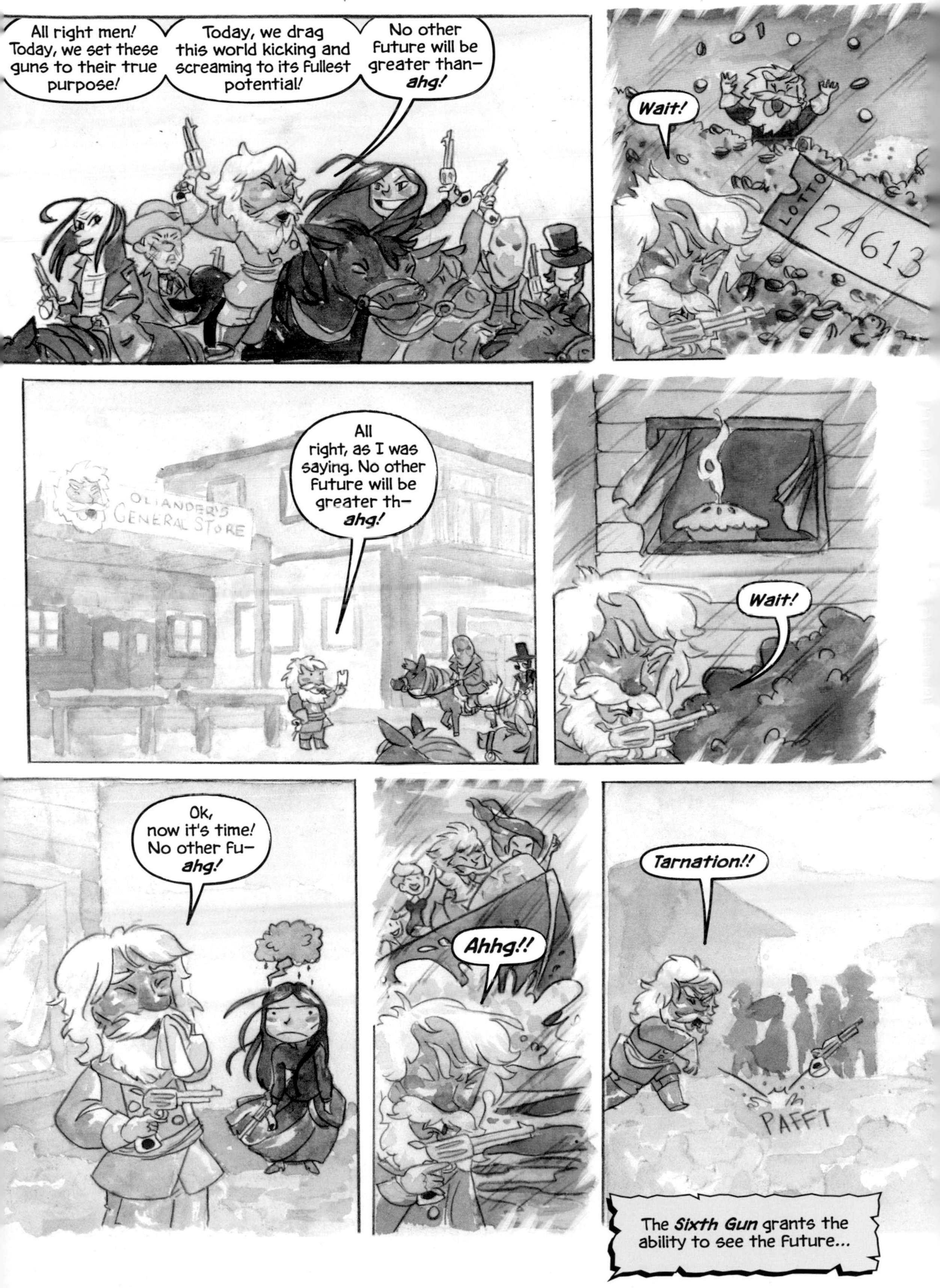
All right men! Today, we set these guns to their true purpose!
Today, we drag this world kicking and screaming to its fullest potential!
No other future will be greater than— ahg!
Wait!
LOTTO 24613
All right, as I was saying. No other future will be greater th— ahg!
OLIANDER'S GENERAL STORE
Wait!
Ok, now it's time! No other fu— ahg!
Ahhg!!
Tarnation!!
PAFFT
The Sixth Gun grants the ability to see the future...

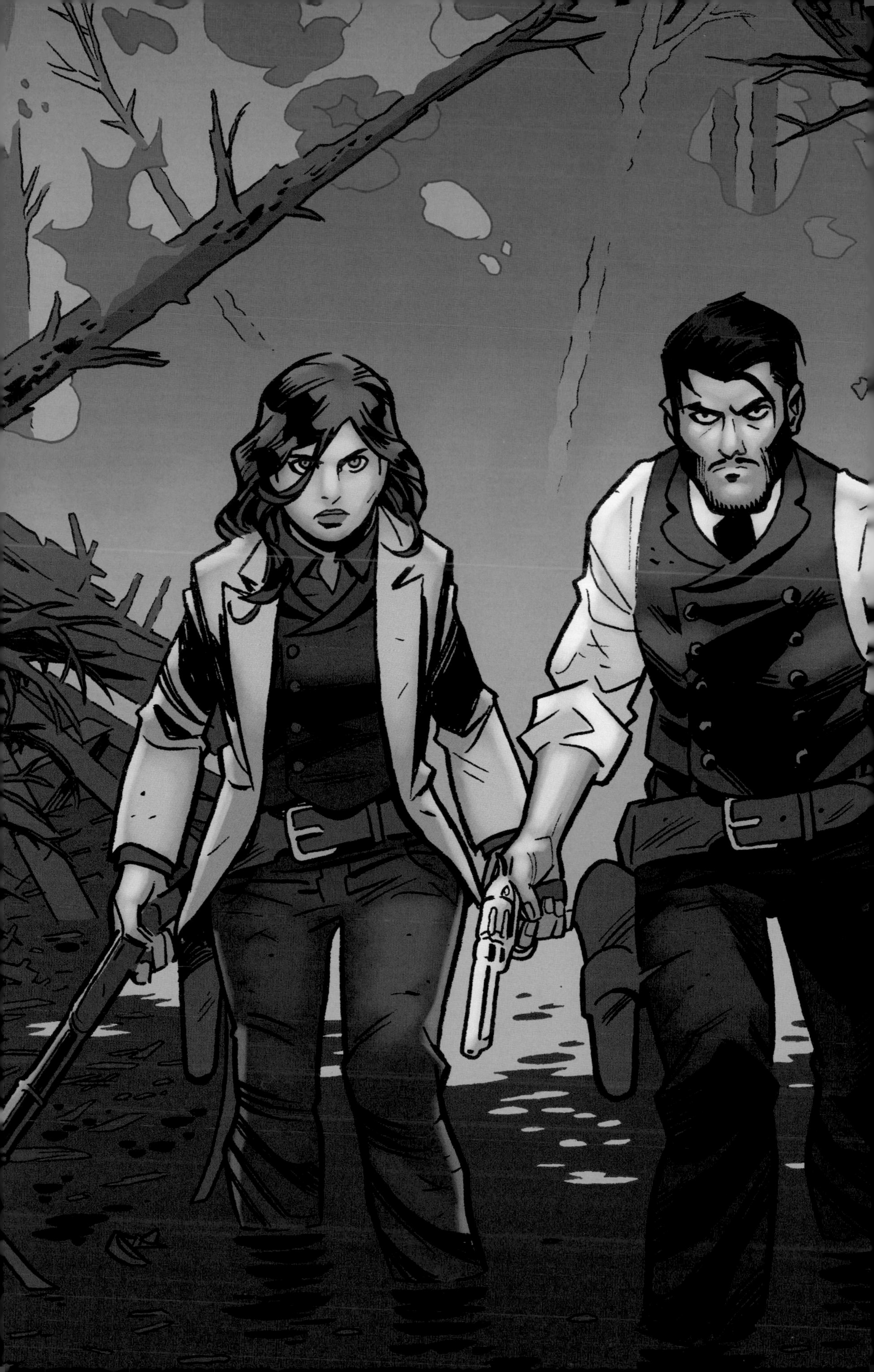

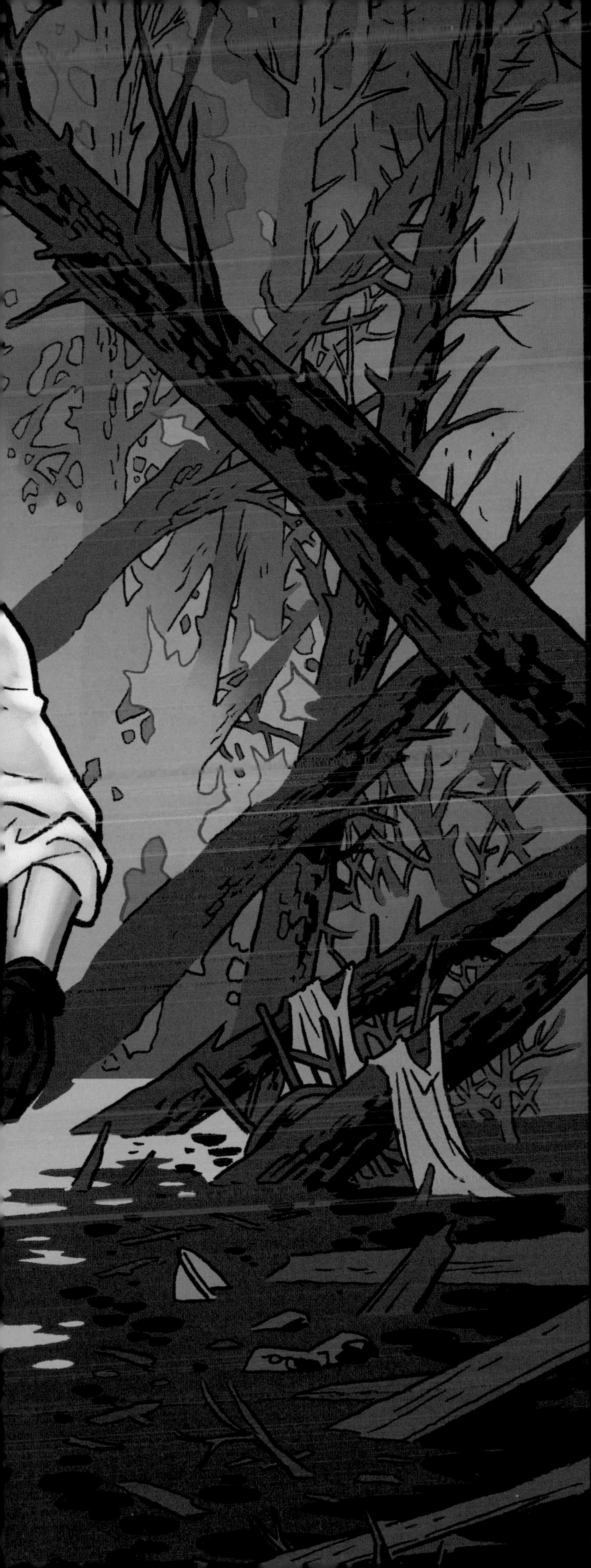

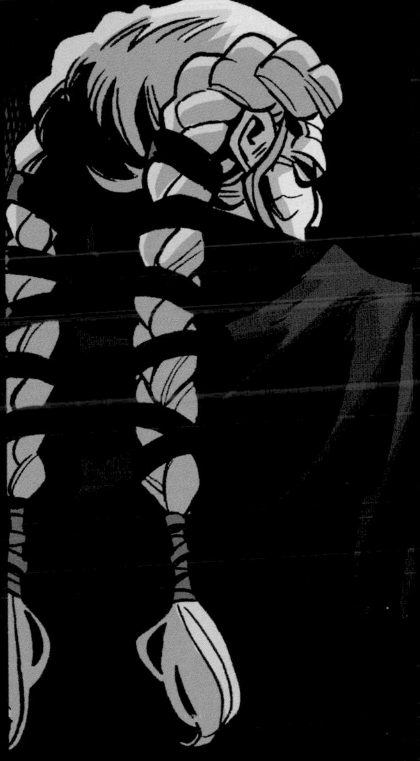

THE ADVENTURE CONTINUES!

Follow the continuing adventures of Drake Sinclair, Becky Montcrief, and Billjohn O'Henry in the ongoing tale of epic fantasy in the Old West. The Six—a set of otherworldly pistols—are fated to rewrite all of reality. The most powerful of these weapons has fallen into the hands of an innocent girl, turning her into the most deadly gun to ever roam the Earth. But the forces of darkness want to claim the Six for vile purposes. Driven through boom towns and badlands, swamps and the spirit world itself, a band of heroes embark on adventure the likes of which the Old West has never seen!

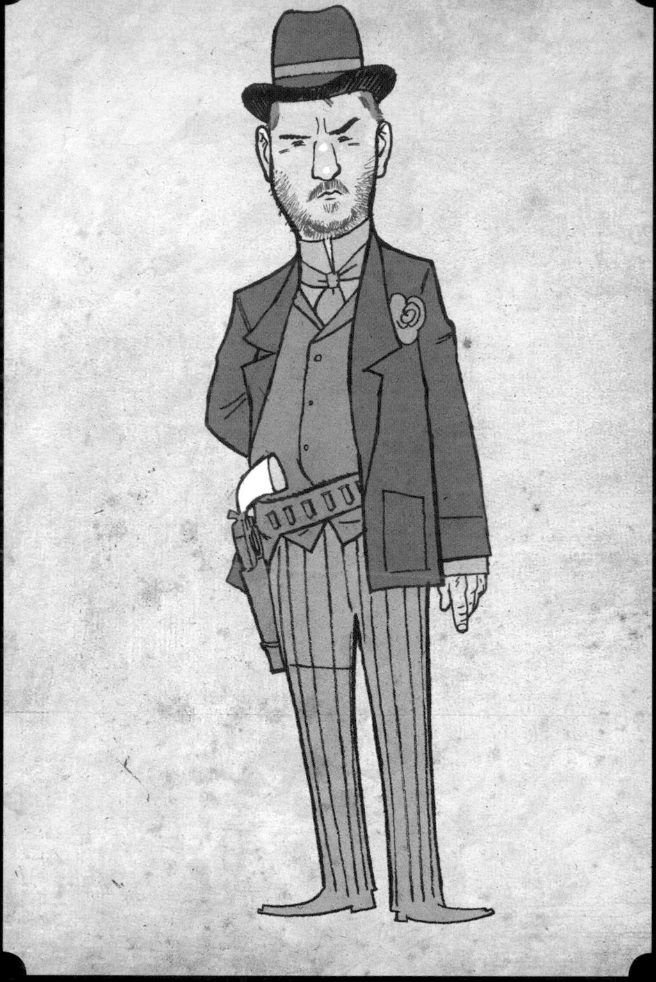

Brian Hurtt got his start in comics pencilling the second arc of Greg Rucka's *Queen & Country*. This was followed by art duties on several projects including *Queen & Country: Declassified*, *Three Strikes*, and Steve Gerber's critically acclaimed series *Hard Time*.

In 2006, Brian teamed with Cullen Bunn to create the Prohibition-era monster-noir sensation *The Damned*. The two found that their unique tastes and storytelling sensibilities were well-suited to one another and were eager to continue that relationship.

The Sixth Gun is their sophomore endeavor together and the next in what looks to be many years of creative collaboration.

Brian lives and works in St. Louis, Missouri.

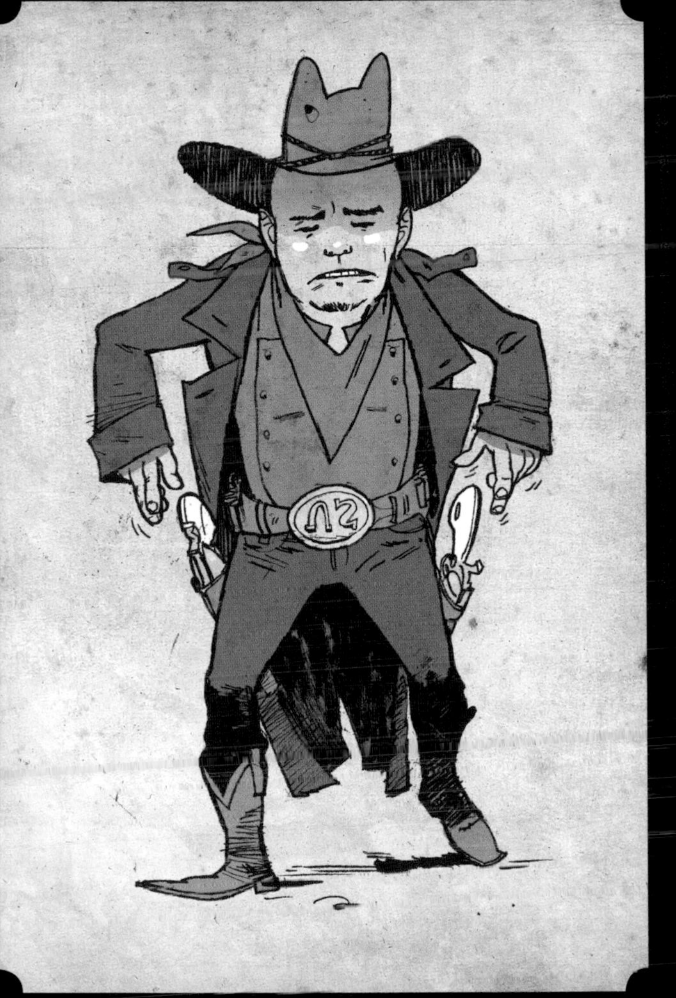

Cullen Bunn is the writer of comic books such *The Damned*, *The Sixth Gun*, *Helheim*, *The Tooth* and *Terrible Lizard* for Oni Press. He has also written titles including *Wolverine*, *Fearless Defenders*, *Venom*, *Deadpool Killustrated*, and *Magneto* for Marvel Comics.

In addition, he is the author of the middle reader horror novel, *Crooked Hills*, and the collection of short fiction, *Creeping Stones and Other Stories*.

His prose work has appeared in numerous magazines and anthologies. Somewhere along the way, he founded Undaunted Press and edited the critically acclaimed horror zine *Whispers From the Shattered Forum*.

Cullen claims to have worked as an Alien Autopsy Specialist, Rodeo Clown, Pro Wrestling Manager, and Sasquatch Wrangler. He has fought for his life against mountain lions and performed on stage as the World's Youngest Hypnotist. Buy him a drink sometime, and he'll tell you all about it.

cullenbunn.com / @cullenbunn

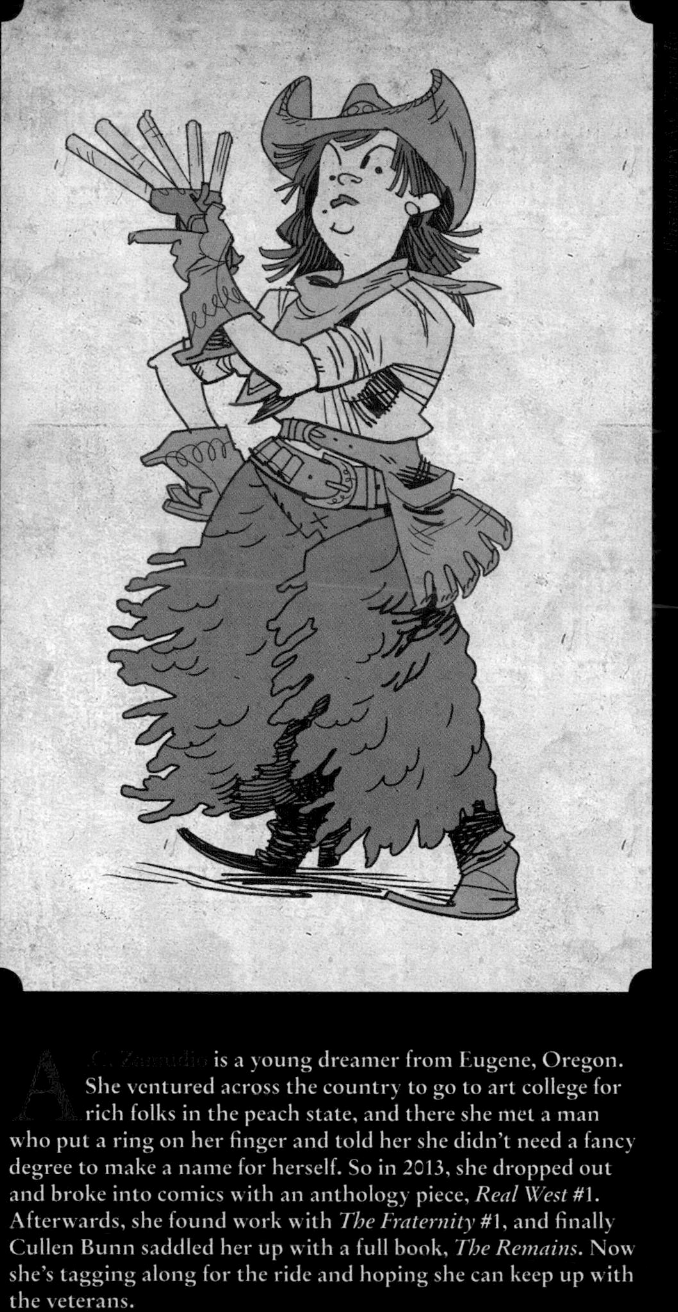

A.C. Zamudio is a young dreamer from Eugene, Oregon. She ventured across the country to go to art college for rich folks in the peach state, and there she met a man who put a ring on her finger and told her she didn't need a fancy degree to make a name for herself. So in 2013, she dropped out and broke into comics with an anthology piece, *Real West* #1. Afterwards, she found work with *The Fraternity* #1, and finally Cullen Bunn saddled her up with a full book, *The Remains*. Now she's tagging along for the ride and hoping she can keep up with the veterans.

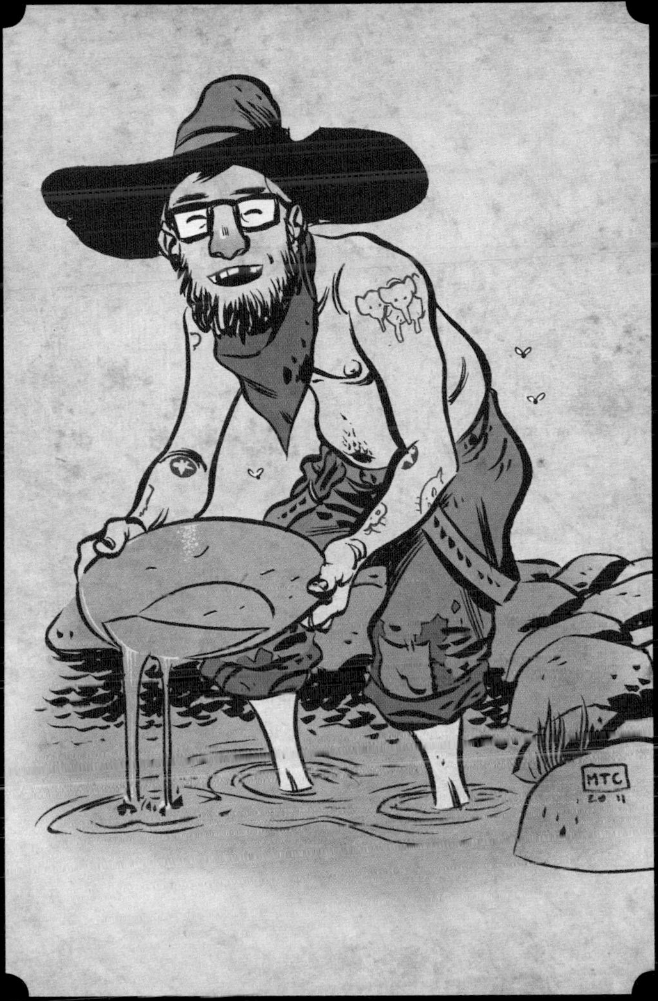
MTC
2011

Illustration by Tyler Crook

Mr. Tyler Crook is an American artist living in the 21st century. For twelve years he toiled in an unlit cubicle making art for sports video games. This left him bearded and almost completely translucent. Then in 2011 he struck gold, comic book gold, with the release of *Petrograd* an original graphic novel written by Philip Gelatt and published by Oni Press. He is survived by his wife and many pets... but he's not dead... yet. In fact, he is very busy working on titles like *Witchfinder*, *Badblood*, *B.P.R.D. Hell on Earth* and *Harrow County*. And oh yeah, he won a Russ Manning award in 2012 which is kind of an Eisner Award... but not really.

He lives in Oregon with his amazing wife and weird pets.

briburtt.com / @briburtt

Ryan Hill lives in Portland and worked in the comic industry for over a decade but has been coloring the last few years on titles like *Rick and Morty*, *Terrible Lizard*, *Judge Dredd: Mega City Two*, *Stumptown*, *Dark Matter*, and *Age of Reptiles*. He really feels his work is about to turn a major corner since he just learned Postmates can deliver Taco Bell straight to his house until 3:00 am. His future, like his work, is now debatably brighter.

@josephryanhill

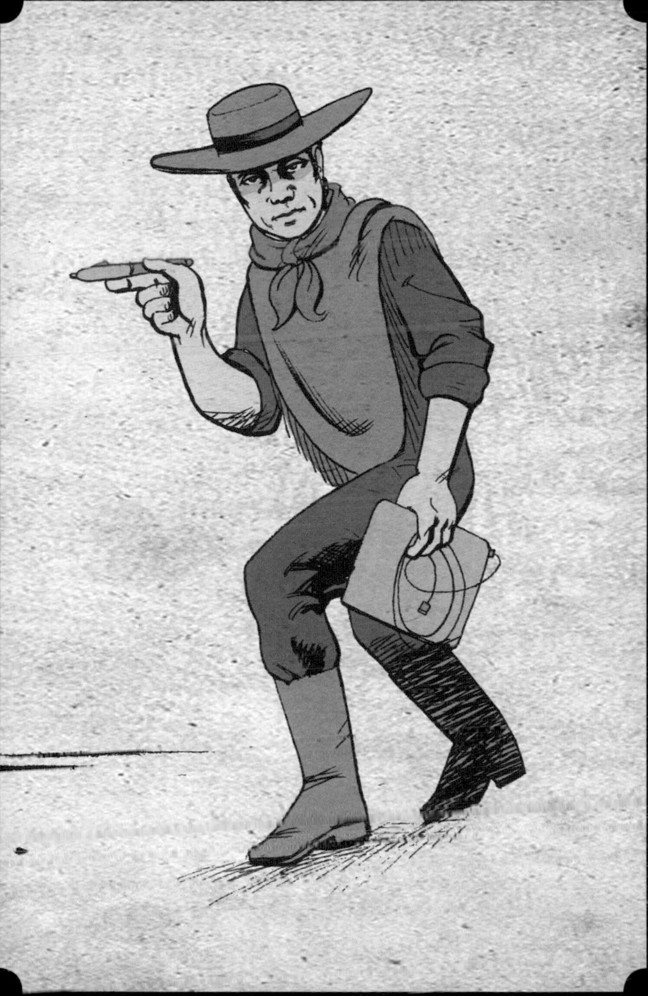

Bill Crabtree's career as a colorist began in 2003 with the launch of Image Comic's *Invincible* and *Firebreather*. He was nominated for a Harvey Award for his work on *Invincible*, and he went on to color the first 50 issues of what would become a flagship Image Comics title. He continues to color *Firebreather*, which was recently made into a feature film on Cartoon Network, *Godland*, and *Jack Staff*.

Perhaps the highlight of his comics career, his role as colorist on *The Sixth Gun* began with issue 6, and has since been described as "like Christmas morning, but with guns."

@crabtree_bill

Also Available From Oni Press...

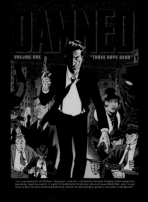

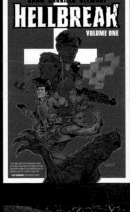

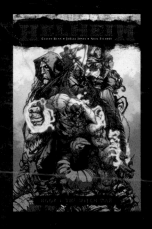

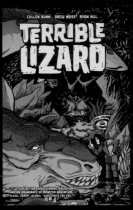

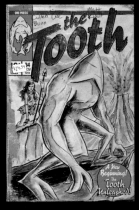

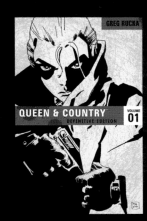

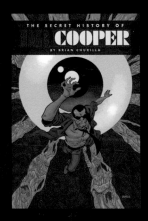

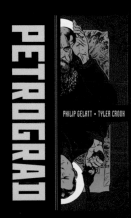

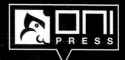